Red Scare
affords a brilliant analysis of a nearly
disastrous two years which should go a long
way toward helping us to avert some of
the tragic consequences of hysteria and fear.

Robert K. Murray is currently Professor of
American History and Head of the Department
at the Pennsylvania State University.

University of Minnesota Press

Red Scare
A Study of National Hysteria, 1919-1920

Robert K. Murray

McGraw-Hill Book Company
New York Toronto London

Library of Congress Catalog Card Number: 55-7034

First McGraw-Hill Paperback Edition, 1964

2 3 4 5 6 7 8 9 0 MPC 75 74 73 72 71 70 69 68 67 66

TO EVE

Bolshevism . . . a baby born by the great world war already is the talk of the whole globe. . . .

If the baby causes such a stir, what will the man do?

International Revolutionist
Vol. 1, No. 1, February 1919

Preface

THIS book is the story of a phenomenon. I use the word "phenomenon" because the Great Red Scare following World War I was precisely that. Few occurrences in modern American history have been surrounded with so much mystery. Few have involved so much exaggeration and fear. None was so fraught with rank intolerance and mob violence. And for sheer excitement and drama it certainly has no peer.

I hold no brief that this phenomenon was therefore the most important occurrence of modern times. Nor do I contend that its existence basically diverted the stream of American experience from its traditional channels. The event was actually more symptomatic than causal in its relationship to its environment and, while it left its mark upon the society of which it was a part, its significance was more peripheral than basic.

Nonetheless, to modern American history the Great Red Scare remains important — important because it provides us with a concrete example of what happens to a democratic nation and its people when faith and reason are supplanted with fear. Moreover, it demonstrates clearly how easily the seeds of excessive hate and intolerance, which for the most part have remained dormant in modern American society, can suddenly develop into dangerous malignancies that spread with lightning rapidity through the whole social system. And, in view of current events, the Red Scare also can offer many valuable lessons to those of us who, like the people of that earlier postwar era, are presently bewildered and feel insecure in a restless world of rapidly changing moods and conditions.

Of course, the major outline of the Red Scare is well known to all American historians and I do not claim that I have uncovered anything essentially new which will upset or greatly modify existing knowledge of the incident. The many single events of the Red Scare period have received exhaustive treatment in one form or another, and almost every college history textbook contains at least a brief description of the occurrence. However, nowhere in print is there a full-length analysis of the Red Scare and this fact supplied the chief impetus for the pages which follow. If this book has any justification for existing at all, it rests largely on this basis.

Any historian who writes about a state of mind, which the Red Scare mainly was, usually finds the path strewn with many obstacles and pitfalls. At best, the handling of such an amorphous subject is not easy; but when the original sources with which the historian must work are willfully biased, colored by emotion, or inaccurate, the task becomes doubly difficult. Much of the contemporary material on the Red Scare was exactly that and I found myself having to sift and weigh each piece of evidence before it could be set in its proper place. Worse still, I had to be wary not only of my material, but also of my own emotions, for try as I might, I could not divorce myself successfully from an environment wherein thinking on the Communist menace is presently still colored by many of the same forces which colored it then.

As a result, I make no pretense of having completely achieved historical detachment. Although I have attempted to be as objective as possible, I realize that under the circumstances the result must be less than perfect. Hence, for all which appears on the pages of this book I assume full responsibility, with the foreknowledge that while the facts may be incontrovertible, the interpretation of those facts is not. In this respect let the reader be warned that my approach to history is mainly moral, and if my words sometimes seem sharp and offend, I hope he will remember that I am also indicting myself.

In pursuing the story of the Red Scare, I seriously endeavored to consult all the essential material which is currently available. To maintain constant contact with the public mood of the period and evaluate the growth of hysteria, I employed more than ninety periodicals and newspapers ranging in opinion from the *Wall Street Journal* to the *Communist*. In addition, I also exploited fully the radical literature collection in the Library of Congress as well as a great amount of pamphlet material sponsored by such diverse organizations as the American Legion and the Third International. The published writings, memoirs, or collected manuscripts of the important figures in the Red Scare story were used as well as the important existing biographies. I also utilized to advantage a host of monographic studies relating to the many incidents and phases of the Red Scare. Perhaps of greatest importance to this book, however, were the various federal and state publications covering the years 1919–21. These sources played a major role not only in my search for facts, but also in the development of my conclusions and summaries. The many reports of the hearings held by congressional committees as well as the annual reports of the heads of the bureaus and departments of government proved to be invaluable. The most useful of these materials are listed at the end of this volume in a Note on Sources.

Fortunately, I was not alone or without moral and financial support while collecting and evaluating this mass of material. To Professor Foster Rhea Dulles of Ohio State University must go the credit for my original interest in this subject and, through his historical zeal and knowledge of writing techniques, I gained much of the inspiration and direction necessary for the completion of the task. My heartfelt thanks are also extended to three of my colleagues, Professors Joseph G. Rayback, Joseph H. Dahmus, and Philip S. Klein of the Pennsylvania State University, for their encouragement when I was depressed, their help when I was in need, and their criticism when I was in error. I wish to express my indebtedness to that multitude of library workers at the Congressional Library, Ohio State University Library, and the Pennsylvania State University Library who patiently submitted to my seemingly endless requests for books, periodicals, pamphlets, manuscript collections, and newspapers. A special debt of gratitude is owed to the Penn State Council on Research, whose several monetary grants aided me materially at crucial points in my research.

A special debt is also due all those who granted permission for reprinting or reproducing some of the material contained herein. Particularly do I wish to thank the NEA Service for its permission to use the poem "Bol-she-veek!"; the editors of the *Mississippi Valley Historical Review* for their permission to use Chapter 9 which was published in essentially the same form in Volume XXXVIII, No. 3 (December 1951) of their magazine; and the Press Publishing Company, St. Louis *Post-Dispatch*, Washington *Star*, New Orleans *Times-Picayune*, New York *Herald Tribune*, Philadelphia *Inquirer*, Lost Angeles *Times*, and Hearst Newspapers, Inc., for their permission to reproduce the selected cartoons.

In conclusion, I can only express my regret at the complete inadequacy of words to convey to the person named in the dedication my very sincerest and deepest appreciation.

R.K.M.

State College, Pennsylvania
September 1, 1954

Table of Contents

Red Scare

A STUDY IN NATIONAL HYSTERIA, 1919–1920

I ★ ★ ★ ★ ★ ★ ★ ★ ★ ★

The Contemporary Scene

THE Great Crusade was over. The "war to end war" had been won and a happy, victorious nation was again at peace.

To the millions of Americans standing expectantly on the threshold of that first postwar year of 1919 the return of peace represented the successful conclusion to a great and noble venture. Now a promising future stretched before them as far as the eye could see and, basking in the glorious relief and satisfaction of a difficult task well done, they were anxious to get on with it.

In particular, the end of the war meant for most Americans the immediate opportunity of returning to a more familiar pattern of life in which one could pursue without interference his deferred personal ambitions. Some citizens were anxious to renew careers which the war had interrupted; others wished to begin an adult life postponed by Army service; still others hoped to take advantage of the opportunities the war had opened to them, or maintain the economic and social gains they had fought for earlier and had won.

Indeed, the American nation as a whole hurried from the war hoping to resume an "old" pattern of life. There was no clear agreement on what that was exactly or how to find it; nevertheless the average American in 1919 was sure he wanted it. Nostalgia had glorified peacetime living until it appeared much more attractive than it really had been. Inevitably, almost two years of war with its uncomfortable restrictions, its tensions, and its killing had sharpened a longing for peacetime "normalcy." But this was an illusory "normalcy" that the nation wanted since it was actually searching for a life completely devoid of either political or social responsibility. It seemed that what the average American really longed for was an existence wherein nothing of importance would appear on the front page of his newspaper and it would only be necessary to glance briefly at the headlines before plunging on into the sports section.

That way of life, had it ever existed, was irrevocably gone. No amount of dancing in the streets, or unloosing tons of confetti down the canyons of Manhattan, or effigial burnings of the Kaiser could restore such a pattern. New forces, new events, and new responsibilities, whether accepted or not, had already shattered the possibility of escaping into the future through the past.

As a result, the nation in 1919 soon found itself frustrated, not because its hopes were awry, but because it sought to fulfill them by moving backward. It erroneously assumed that its job had ended with the signing of the Armistice and that progress both domestically and internationally would thereafter take care of itself. The American people in 1919 simply refused to face reality and, rejecting the challenges of a promising future, gradually sank into despair and irresponsibility.

Some observers have suggested that the United States in 1919 was tired — tired of Great Crusades, of reform, even of progress. It was. But certainly the fatigue was not physical. The country still had sufficient energy to expend on new automobiles, new fashions, new fads. Instead, it was a spiritual fatigue, involving a lack of moral stamina, of faith in the principles of democracy, of wisdom, and of effective leadership, which finally brought the nation to the brink of nervous exhaustion.

In such circumstances, America stood naked before the future. Psychologically and morally she was ill equipped to meet the simple basic challenge of democratic action let alone solve successfully the many complex postwar problems which confronted her. Hence, the year 1919, rather than being remembered for its great hopes and its promise, remains on the pages of American history as one of the most futile and tragic.

The basic key to an understanding of the prevailing mood of 1919 is to be found not only in the misguided philosophy of a people rushing pell-mell into peace, but in the counteraction between that attitude and the course of historical events.

As the months ahead presented the nation first of all with the many economic problems left as a legacy of war, it found itself completely unprepared to deal with them adequately and the solutions it adopted were at best only makeshift. Indeed, there seemed to be no desire to establish any unity of purpose whatsoever except to dispense with all such problems as quickly as possible and get down to the pleasant business of everyday living.

Here, certainly, was a paradox of magnificent proportions. The business of everyday living should have automatically involved the intelligent solution of these problems because the very foundation of a stable "normalcy" was contingent upon their successful resolution. Instead, the public and its leaders insisted on looking elsewhere for their stability and refused to meet the problems as they arose. Consequently, they did not find the only real normalcy worth seeking.

That this mistake would bring unfortunate results became apparent immediately upon the close of the war. When the Armistice was signed on November 11, 1918, there were approximately 9,000,000 persons engaged in war industries and 4,000,000 men in the armed forces. Yet, no sooner was the news received that the war was over than dollar-a-year men rose from their desks in Washington, locked their offices, and resumed their lucrative peacetime jobs. On the day after the Armistice, telephone wires were hot with calls canceling war contracts, and these cancellation orders usually included allowance for no more than a month's further operation at the current production rate.[1] As a result many industries, particularly the war industries, were caught short and were faced with the necessity of making a rapid conversion.

It is obvious that few in authority had given any real thought to this problem of reconverting America's vast industrial system to peacetime production. True, the end of the war had come rather abruptly. Nevertheless, there was no excuse for official Washington's negligence in permitting the nation to be so completely unprepared. As it was, many war industries simply had to dissolve thereby creating much waste, dislocation of matériel, and economic as well as labor unrest.

Even so, industry buckled down to the problem and, despite the lack of an over-all, systematic plan, effected a substantial reconversion in a remarkably short time. Industrial production fell off a maximum of 10 per cent by the middle of 1919, but the loss was quickly recovered in the latter half of the year as the production index rose above even the 1918 wartime high.[2] However, these statistics do not record the psychological torment and confusion experienced by those who were so suddenly left jobless and who were forced to readjust their own and their families' lives.

Demobilization offers a further case in point. Again there was no effective direction exercised from Washington and the reduction of the military establishment proceeded almost by chance. The demand to bring the boys home was so strong and Washington succumbed so easily that 600,000 men were released almost immediately; by November 1919 almost the whole force of 4,000,000 had been demobilized.

To the average doughboy, longing for home and family, this was undoubtedly an unmixed blessing. Yet for postwar society as a whole it represented a blunder. At best, it is no mean problem to reassimilate millions of men, skilled in war, into a peacetime economy and the faster it is attempted the more difficult the problem becomes. Many of these dischargees of 1919, caught up in a labor market already strained by the casualties of reconversion, soon became disillusioned about the advantages of peace. Newspapers were still running cartoons portraying the returning hero-soldier as the savior of civilization with the caption "Anything You Want," at the very time when the answer was quite plain — a job.

Fortunately the peak of this difficulty was reached by the late spring of 1919, and thereafter, with an upward trend in industrial production, unemployment declined.[3] But not before some damage was done. Cut loose by the Army to shift for himself and disheartened by the hard economic facts of peacetime life, the ex-soldier was prone to search for scapegoats in order to rationalize his predicament. Sometimes he allowed his bitterness to break out in such a virulent form that he became a liability to a society searching for serenity, not an asset.

Meanwhile, the general public, itself pinned between the twin problems of reconversion and demobilization, was helplessly submerged in a wave of spiraling prices. By late 1919 the purchasing power of the 1913 dollar had shrunk from 100 to 45. Food costs had increased 84 per cent, clothing 114.5 per cent, and furniture 125 per cent. For the average American family in 1919 the cost of living was 99 per cent higher than it had been five years before.[4]

This surging inflation was the immediate cause of much postwar instability and unrest. Again, there was no governmental attempt or inclination to deal realistically with this problem and, except for the wealthy few who could withstand the pressure, disastrous results ensued. Salaried employees, whose incomes had increased during the war period either not at all or at the most only 5 to 10 per cent, struggled under the load of trying to balance a stable income against the rising cost of living. Actually, the professional classes, salaried clerks, civic officials, police, and others in a similar category were worse off economically than at any time since the Civil War. Such a condition naturally caused great dissatisfaction, but their lack of organization and their middle-class pride precluded any effective protest on their part.

Quite different was the position of organized labor. During the Progressive Era, organized labor had made striking gains. The benign attitude of the prewar administrations, culminating in Woodrow Wilson's New Freedom program, had been evidenced by such legislation as the Clayton Act, the Seamen's Law, and the Adamson Act, and labor had made the most of the friendly atmos-

7

phere. American Federation of Labor membership had skyrocketed from about 500,000 in 1900 to 4,169,000 in 1919.

During the war, this block of organized workmen had maintained an effective truce with management in the interest of wartime production even though wages had fallen somewhat behind prices. However, as the war drew to a close and the cost of living increased markedly, organized labor went on the offensive. Unions immediately demanded higher wages from employers and pulled their members from factories and shops in order to obtain them.

But, actually, the problem of inflation served merely as the superficial cause for much of the resultant labor unrest. The issue of unionism and collective bargaining was much more basic. Many employers were willing to grant moderate wage increases but they absolutely drew the line at employees' use of the collective bargaining principle to secure them. That principle was an anathema to the American businessman because he saw in it the ultimate capitulation of organized capital.

In fact, in 1919 the industrialist was spoiling for a fight. Since the advent of the muckrakers at the turn of the century, it had become rather fashionable to attack organized capital and the holders of great wealth. Much of the progressive movement's original steam had been generated because of capital's predominant position in American life and progressives had successfully put the sins of the businessman on parade for all to see. The general public had emotionally, rather than intelligently, joined the movement and soon adopted the premise that all big businessmen were robber barons. Naturally the industrialist had bitterly resented this, not only because some of the progressive charges were unfounded, but mainly because progressive activity had meant a loss of prestige and power for him.

With the coming of the war all that had changed. In the wartime drama the businessman's importance and his hold over the public mind had increased tremendously since, to a large extent, it was upon his factories and his financial ingenuity that the fate of the nation had rested. President Wilson had clearly foreseen this turn of events and had expressed the fear that it foreshadowed the end of progressivism. Just before our intervention in 1917, he had remarked to Secretary of the Navy Josephus Daniels: "Every reform we have won will be lost if we go into this war. We have been making a fight on special privilege. . . . War means autocracy. The people we have unhorsed will inevitably come into control of the country for we shall be dependent upon the steel, ore and financial magnates. They will run the nation." [5]

Woodrow Wilson's analysis proved completely correct. The industrialist, like the rest of the nation, wanted a return to normalcy. But his normalcy was a special kind. It was the normalcy of the pre-Spanish-American War era. Normalcy to him meant freedom from government regulation, from labor unions, from public responsibility — the freedom of *laissez faire*. He certainly had no love for the pre-World War I period with its progressive reforms and its New Freedoms, and he had eyed apprehensively the growing power of labor. Therefore, with the cessation of hostilities, he was more than happy to engage labor in battle. Capitalizing on postwar confusion and reaction, he fought with every means at his disposal to undermine organized labor's position and stamp out economic liberalism wherever it existed.

Great industrial unrest resulted. Major strikes, which had been relatively few, now became prevalent. During the year virtually every kind of organized laborer found himself on the picket line at one time or another, striking for higher wages, shorter hours, and the right of collective bargaining. Altogether in 1919 there were 3600 strikes involving more than 4,000,000 workers — and in only a handful did the strikers win. [6]

The prevailing drive for normalcy which had such a pronounced effect on the 1919 economic scene also caused serious repercussions in the political field. In the preceding November, the American people had elected over the pleas of a worried Democratic president a Republican majority to both houses of Congress. After the cessation of hostilities, this Republican-dominated Congress not only refused to consider the temporary retention of regulatory wartime agencies and bureaus, at least until a new peacetime stability could be sustained, but even exhibited a desire to strike down the many reforms which had proven so beneficial to the nation in the prewar years. In addition, during the course of the year the nation's railroads, which had been operated by the government during the war for efficiency's sake, were unreservedly restored to their former owners, and similar steps were taken to surrender to private management the vessels built by the United States Shipping Board at tremendous cost to the taxpayer. Meanwhile, this same Congress arbitrarily deprived organized labor of much of the governmental support which it had come to enjoy in the preceding years.

Of even greater significance was the blunt refusal of the Senate to accept the League of Nations. Here modern American politics hit an all-time low in mistaken self-interest. Although public opinion, at least at first, rather favored the League, the mulish stubbornness of the President, the personal venom of certain senators, and general political partisanship ultimately wrought its defeat. And the United States emerged from the incident stripped of its dignity, bereft of its principles, and standing alone. Thus, even in the foreign field America had turned her back on a promising future and there was no place to look except upon the failures and frustrations of the past.

Of course, the Senate's action exactly epitomized the change in the nation's thinking and orientation which accompanied the return to peace. The American people, who but a few years before had so enthusiastically embraced the reform spirit of progressivism and then had projected themselves with great zeal into the lofty idealism of war, were weary of any further experimentation either domestically or internationally. In short, Americans were already a little sick of the whole European "mess" and were much more interested in remaining on familiar ground than in embarking on a journey into an unknown future. The irony is that they embarked on the journey anyway, against their will and despite any action they might have taken. But they did so unknowingly. Meanwhile, they were far less concerned with making the world safe for democracy than with making America safe for themselves.[7]

President Wilson had sensed the impending catastrophe implicit in America's refusal to join the League and had attempted valiantly to forestall it. Thoroughly enraged and at the same time disheartened by the opposition which the League met, he started on a western speaking tour in September 1919, seeking to bolster lagging popular support. But the immense task he had undertaken proved too much for his physical powers, and in the course of the tour he suffered a nervous breakdown that led to a paralytic stroke; thereafter he was confined to the White House, a sick and bitter man.[8]

For the rest of Wilson's term, to March 1921, the nation remained virtually leaderless. This fact gave added succor to all those who were seeking by various means to stymie the President's domestic and foreign programs, and offered an excellent opportunity for smaller men, with less vision and little principle, to command the attention of a drifting public. These individuals were the chief apostles of that false security which it seemed the whole nation was seeking and, burning with personal ambition and trafficking in human weakness and emotion, they more than the ailing President fashioned the mood of the 1919 political scene.

In connection with the writing of his spectacular multivolumed history of the fall of Rome, Edward Gibbon once remarked that the most distressing task for any historian is to chronicle the death of a great nation. What is even more distressing is to describe the convulsions of a great nation which, while alive, is in the process of losing its soul.

In 1919 America's soul was in danger. It was in danger not merely because of the nation's refusal to accept its moral responsibilities, or solve intelligently its economic problems, or shun the pitfalls of unbridled self-interest. Primarily it was in danger because the nation was deserting its most honored principles of freedom — principles which had made it great and which had given it birth.

Nowhere was this fact more obvious than in the social scene of 1919. The war was largely to blame. During the conflict the demand for absolute loyalty had permeated every nook and cranny of the social structure. Independent agencies, such as the National Security League and the American Defense Society, together with the government-sponsored American Protective League, had converted thousands of otherwise reasonable and sane Americans into super-patriots and self-styled spy-chasers by spreading rabid propaganda which maximized the dangers of wartime sabotage and sedition. Supposedly these agencies represented the nation's first line of defense against wartime subversive activity. But by the close of the war they actually had become the repository of elements which were much more interested in strengthening a sympathy for economic and political conservatism than in underwriting a healthy patriotism. Under the guidance of their leaders, these organizations often used "Americanism" merely to blacken the reputation and character of persons and groups whose opinions they hated and feared.[9]

In this connection, the activity of the government's Committee on Public Information was especially significant. Under the chairmanship of George Creel, it had preached patriotism to the American public by means of the written word, spoken word, motion picture, signboard, and poster, and had so directed its propaganda that "every printed bullet might reach its mark."[10] The public press had followed in the pattern set by the committee and the net result had been an indoctrination of hate, prejudice, and 100 per cent Americanism on a colossal scale. As Frank Cobb, editor of the New York *World*, later claimed: "Government conscripted public opinion as they conscripted men and money and materials. Having conscripted it, they dealt with it as they dealt with other raw recruits. They mobilized it. They put it in charge of drill sergeants. They goose-stepped it. They taught it to stand at attention and salute."[11]

Under such circumstances the free play of opinion and the opportunity for independent action had practically ceased to exist. The home front, unable personally to lay hands on the hated Huns, had made scapegoats of the "draft-dodger," the "slacker," and anyone else who did not conform. Teachers in certain areas had been forced from their jobs for making allegedly unpatriotic statements to their classes about the causes of the war. In some states, the teaching of the German language had been outlawed from the public schools because of its possible subversive influence. Wagnerian selections had all but disappeared from the repertoire of the nation's musicians. In self-defense, towns and individuals with German names had appealed to the courts for relief and Schmidts became Smiths while Berlins became Bellevilles. For a time there had been congressional talk of passing a "no strike" law in order to compel greater labor cooperation than already existed, and in the nation at large men had been beaten and tarred and feathered for failure to buy war bonds or support Red Cross drives. Conscientious objectors such as the Mennonites, Dunkards, and Quakers had been subjected to even worse indignities, while political objectors to the war had been particularly persecuted and scorned.[12]

Meanwhile both the state and federal governments had sought to enforce loyal conduct by passing a mass of sedition and espionage legislation. Most of these wartime laws were still in effect in 1919 and served as a constant reminder that animosity to nonconformity was still very much the vogue. Of these laws, the three passed by the federal Congress were particularly significant to the 1919 scene.

The first was the Espionage Act of 1917 which, while primarily directed at treason, was so constructed and interpreted that it covered much lesser disloyal activity. This law made it a crime, punishable by a $10,000 fine and twenty years in jail, for a person to ". . . convey false reports or false statements with intent to interfere with the operation or success of the military or naval forces of the United States or to promote the success of its enemies . . . or attempt to cause insubordination, disloyalty, mutiny, or

13

refusal of duty, in the military or naval forces of the United States, or . . . willfully obstruct recruiting or enlistment service. . . ." [13]

② [The second piece of legislation was the Sedition Act of 1918, which dealt more directly with the problem of sedition per se] The law prohibited a person, under pain of $10,000 and twenty years' imprisonment, to ". . . utter, print, write, or publish any disloyal, profane, scurrilous, or abusive language about the form of government of the United States, or the Constitution of the United States, or the uniform of the Army or Navy of the United States, or any language intended to . . . encourage resistance to the United States, or to promote the cause of its enemies. . . ." [14]

③ [The third in this series was of a slightly different character since it was designed to curb the activities of nonconforming aliens who were thought to be a particular threat to the nation. Passed in October 1918,] this law decreed that all aliens who were anarchists or believed in the violent overthrow of the American government or advocated the assassination of public officials were henceforth to be excluded from admission into the United States. The law further provided that ". . . any alien who, at any time after entering the United States, is found to have been at the time of entry, or to have become thereafter, a member of any one of the classes of aliens [above mentioned] . . . shall upon warrant of the Secretary of Labor, be taken into custody and deported. . . ." [15]

In spite of the nation's desire for a rapid return to peace, it was obvious the American public of 1919 was still thinking with the mind of a people at war. Many prosecutions, already begun on the basis of the acts mentioned above, were just coming before the courts and served to remind the nation of the existence of disloyalty. Returning soldiers, evidencing an intense love of country, added to the excitement by howling for the immediate and summary punishment of all such nonconformity. To the 1919 public the German was still a barbarian capable of committing any atrocity, while those who had sympathized with him or who had even slightly opposed the war were equally depraved. Indeed, anyone who spoke with an accent or carried a foreign name, German or otherwise, remained particularly suspect as American super-patriots continued to see spies lurking behind every bush and tree. Still in existence were the National Security League, the American Defense Society, and other such patriotic organizations which in order to live now sought to create new menaces. In short, insofar as the 1919 social mood was concerned the nation was still at war.

It was in the midst of this confusing, intolerant, and irresponsible atmosphere that the Great Red Scare occurred. The taproots of this phenomenon lay embedded in the various events growing out of the Bolshevik Revolution of November 1917. Denying most of the principles that older governments had been founded to secure and advancing the idea of world-wide proletarian revolution, the Bolshevik experiment was destined from the very beginning to represent one of the most crucial problems facing the world both during and after the war.

Losing little time in indicating their lack of interest in capitalist wars, the Bolsheviki concluded a separate peace with Germany in March 1918 and took Russia out of the conflict. Falsely believing that this proved the movement was actually German controlled, the Allies, with the United States participating, intervened in Russia to reactivate the eastern front against Germany and thereby eliminate the source of Bolshevik power. In spite of such action, the Bolshevik power remained and indeed became more aggressive. In March 1919 the Third International was formed to serve as a spearhead for a global proletarian revolution, and it seemed to be having some success. In early 1919 Germany was racked with revolution, the situation in Poland and Italy was uneasy, and Hungary actually established a soviet regime.

From the beginning the American public was shocked by the Bolsheviki's disregard for the traditional and considered their separate peace with Germany a great betrayal. The nation then watched apprehensively as the Red Scourge moved westward into Europe. Patriotic societies, meanwhile, consistently denounced the Bolshevik as a counterpart of the dreaded Hun, and the press circulated much exaggerated information about the Bolshevik reign in Russia. Naturally, economic conservatives eagerly seized upon bolshevism's dangers in order to further their own campaign of stifling political and economic liberalism. The net result was the implantation of the Bolshevik in the American mind as the epitome of all that was evil.

On the other hand, great sympathy was immediately forthcoming from many American radicals for the Russian revolution and some openly advocated a similar upheaval in this country. In September 1919 two domestic Communist parties were formed, and while the movement remained very small, its noise more than compensated for its size. These American Communists held parades and meetings, distributed leaflets and other incendiary literature, and issued revolutionary manifestoes and calls for action.

In an intolerant postwar year in which people were still conditioned to the danger of spies and sabotage, these domestic Bolsheviki seemed particularly dangerous. As labor unrest increased and the nation was treated to such abnormal events as general strikes, riots, and the planting of bombs, the assumption that the country was under serious attack by the Reds found a wide acceptance. In the long run, each social and industrial disturbance was received as prima-facie evidence of the successful spread of radicalism. Even the temporary instability arising from demobilization and reconversion, and the many justified protests concerning high prices, were traced to the Reds.

As a result, exaggerated conclusions were reached concerning the size and influence of the movement. Indeed, never before had the nation been so overwhelmed with fear. It is understandable. Because of its waning faith, its political and moral irresponsibility, and its momentary abandonment of high ideals, the nation had been susceptible as never before. Harassed by the rantings and ravings of a small group of radicals, buffeted by the dire warnings of business and employer organizations, and assaulted daily by the scare propaganda of the patriotic societies and the general press, the national mind ultimately succumbed to hysteria. As one English journalist described the prevailing scene: "No one who was in the United States as I chanced to be, in the autumn of 1919, will forget the feverish condition of the public mind at that time. It was hag-ridden by the spectre of Bolshevism. It was like a sleeper in a nightmare, enveloped by a thousand phantoms of destruction. Property was in an agony of fear, and the horrid name 'Radical' covered the most innocent departure from conventional thought with a suspicion of desperate purpose. 'America,' as one wit of the time said, 'is the land of liberty — liberty to keep in step.'" [16]

[Thus, continued wartime intolerance, postwar industrial unrest, the lack of statesmanlike leadership, and the ill-fated quest for a false normalcy paid pernicious dividends. Fortunately, the Great Red Scare soon subsided, but not before the forces of reaction implicit in the 1919 economic, political, and social environment achieved their goal. Civil liberties were left prostrate, the labor movement was badly mauled, the position of capital was greatly enhanced, and complete antipathy toward reform was enthroned. In this respect, the Red Scare served as the major vehicle on which the American nation rode from a victorious war into a bankrupt peace.]

American Radicals

WHILE the contemporary scene with its prevailing atmosphere of political reaction, economic confusion, and general lack of moral compulsion is vital in understanding the environmental factors which helped produce the Red Scare, the story of the Scare itself properly begins with the American radical. He was, after all, the central figure in the unfolding drama, for it was around his philosophies and his actions that much of the Scare revolved.

It has often been claimed that the immediate cause for the Scare was the intense public suspicion and fear aroused by the domestic radicals' sudden and enthusiastic espousal of the Bolshevik philosophy. This is true as far as it goes, but it is only a part of the story. By 1919 American radicals had already engendered much suspicion and fear for other reasons, particularly for their violent and uncompromising opposition to the war. Hence, the acceptance of bolshevism by many domestic radicals in 1919 was really supplementary in its effect — it simply intensified a hostile attitude which had been in operation for some time.

For this reason the activities of American radicals before their surrender to bolshevism in 1919 assume a definite significance.

During the pre-1919 period, there was no real unity in the domestic radical movement. Although all domestic radicals were opposed to the existing capitalistic system, they espoused such a variety of differing philosophies that no one organization could possibly contain them. Some were Marxists in belief, emphasizing either the revolutionary or the evolutionary phase of that doctrine; some were anarchists, of either the pacifistic or the terroristic school; and some were syndicalists, who desired direct economic action through the use of the industrial union.

Advocates of these varying philosophies organized themselves into a multitude of small groups during the prewar period. By 1919, however, there were two organizations which had succeeded in unifying the radical movement to some extent and with these the nation was most familiar. The one was the Socialist party; the other was the Industrial Workers of the World.

Of the two, the Socialist party was the more important. It had been formed in 1901 as the result of an amalgamation between the conservative faction of the old Socialist Labor party and the Social Democratic party of Victor Berger and Eugene Debs. While not embracing all Socialists under its banner (the Socialist Labor party continued on its doctrinaire way, although by 1916 it ceased to exist as a factor in the domestic radical movement), it soon harbored the vast majority and was less dogmatic in theory and more practical in action than its smaller competitors. It was opposed to force and violence and placed primary emphasis on legal political pressure to secure its desired goals. It believed in cooperation with bourgeois government, was opportunistic in its application of Marxist theory to domestic conditions, and often leagued itself with the conservative trade union movement.

During the prewar period, the party met with a measure of success. Containing fewer than 10,000 members when it was launched, it increased its membership to slightly more than 100,000 by 1912 and in that same year garnered 897,000 votes for its presidential candidate, Eugene Debs. By the outbreak of the war in 1914 it had thirty members in the legislatures of twelve states and more than 1000 members in various municipal offices.[1]

The war stopped the forward motion of the party. From the very beginning it opposed the war as a crime against humanity and sought to prevent American participation if at all possible. For a time the position of the Socialists and that of the many non-Socialist antipreparedness groups coalesced. However, when American intervention occurred, antipreparedness groups generally renounced their earlier position and supported the war effort. Not so with the Socialists.

In April 1917 the Socialists met in an emergency convention in St. Louis where, despite the opposition of a small pro-war group, they overwhelmingly accepted a declaration which denounced American intervention and pledged "continuous, active, and public opposition to the war through demonstrations, mass petitions, and all other means within our power." Throwing its hundred-odd daily, weekly, and monthly publications into the fray, the party thereafter condemned the war as "the greatest victory the American plutocracy had won over the American democracy." Socialist speakers took to the hustings and described it as not a war for freedom but merely a device "to secure the profits of the ruling class of this country." [2]

The general public, which heretofore had tolerated the Socialists, now unleashed a wave of hatred for these nonconformists. Newspapers and periodicals heaped calumny upon their heads, and patriotic societies ranted against their sedition. The Socialists' opposition to the war was universally regarded as irrefutable proof that they were either spies or pro-German and wanted the enemy to win. In view of their opposition to the war even before the United States intervened, these charges were utterly ridiculous. But under the influence of wartime emotionalism the public was not thinking clearly and the net result was vigorous repression. Throughout the country Socialist headquarters were raided by mobs and sacked by soldiers, while individual Socialists were treated shamefully.

The Socialists experienced difficulty not only with the general public but also with the government and the courts. From time to time, federal and state authorities made official raids on Socialist headquarters. The postal department denied mailing privileges to many Socialist publications. The courts applied the Espionage

Law so stringently in Socialist cases that only a few were decided in favor of the defendants. Scott Nearing, indicted jointly with the American Socialist Society for publishing an antiwar pamphlet entitled *The Great Madness*, was one of the few who escaped. But even here there were extenuating circumstances, for the trial occurred after the war was over and, although Nearing was acquitted, the Socialist Society was convicted as charged.[3]

Of the many Socialist trials, there are three which bear special mention because of their later Red Scare connections. The first involved Victor L. Berger, one of the founders of the Socialist party. Berger's background is of particular interest for a study of the Socialist movement. Born in Austria in 1860, he migrated to this country in 1878. For a time he held various laboring jobs, but in 1881 he entered the teaching profession and taught German in the public school system of Milwaukee. However, because of his consummate interest in radical affairs in the Milwaukee area, he soon resigned this position in order to participate more actively in the radical movement and he founded the Socialist daily *Wisconsin Vorwärts* shortly before becoming editor of the famous *Milwaukee Leader*.

Berger was one of the chief figures at the 1901 Unity Convention which resulted in the formation of the Socialist party, and since that time he had served as an influential member of its Executive Board. Later, he became interested in local Milwaukee and Wisconsin state politics and in 1910 was elected by the Fifth Wisconsin District as the first Socialist to serve in the United States House of Representatives. Re-elected in 1912 and again in 1914, he was regarded as an honorable, although somewhat eccentric, member of the House.

Certainly Berger was no revolutionist. He had behind him a long record of opposition to force of any kind. He firmly believed that socialism should be achieved only through peaceful and orderly means and at the founding of the party he had championed adherence to this principle. In the ensuing years, he had opposed all anarchists, syndicalists, and direct-actionists within the party who desired an aggressive policy and, as a result, the more radical Socialists considered him one of the most "bourgeois" members of the organization.[4]

Nevertheless, Berger, like all good Socialists, had opposed the war from the beginning. The general public and the courts interpreted this position to mean that he wanted Germany to win. Such was simply not the case, for in June 1917 he said, "Personally, I was against the war before war was declared. . . . But now since we are in the war, I want to win this war — for democracy. . . . Let us hope we will win the war quickly."[5] Unfortunately, however, Berger was not always so guarded in his opinion. On another occasion he wrote, "The war of the United States against Germany can not be justified," and somewhat later, "the blood of American boys [is] being coined into swollen profits for American plutocrats."[6]

Because of statements such as the latter, Berger was indicted for violation of the Espionage Act in February 1918 but was not tried until ten months later. In the interim, he occupied his time by running for the United States Senate from Wisconsin, being barely defeated by Irvine L. Lenroot in the spring of 1918. Later, in the fall of that same year, he ran for his old seat in the House of Representatives and won the November election on a peace platform.[7]

Two months later, in January 1919, Representative-elect Victor Berger was found guilty of conspiracy to violate the Espionage Act and was sentenced by Judge Kenesaw Mountain Landis to twenty years in Fort Leavenworth. An appeal was immediately filed by Berger's lawyers charging Judge Landis with partiality in handling the trial testimony, and Judge Samuel Alschuler of the Circuit Court of Appeals ordered Berger's release on $25,000 bail pending a review of his case.[8]

Meanwhile, if the Berger case was important because of the personality involved, the Schenck case was no less important because of the legal interpretation used. Charles T. Schenck was a general secretary for the Socialist party and in this capacity had printed for distribution about 15,000 leaflets which discouraged enlistments in the armed forces. One side of the leaflet quoted the first section of the Thirteenth Amendment to the Constitution with the exhortation "Do not submit to intimidation," while the reverse side denied the validity of conscription and urged draftees to "Assert Your Rights." Tried and convicted for violation of the Espionage Law, Schenck appealed his case to the Supreme Court and in March 1919 Justice Oliver W. Holmes, Jr., delivered the unanimous opinion of that body. Declaring that "the question in every case is whether the words used . . . create a clear and present danger," Holmes maintained that in this instance they had and thereby affirmed the judgment of the lower courts.[9]

This clear and present danger principle was used thereafter as the authoritative judicial yardstick by which all subsequent expressions of nonconformity were measured. It supposedly provided the courts with an acid test for determining which actions were permissible and which were not, and served as the basis upon which all subsequent civil liberty cases were decided.

[In actual practice, however, securing agreement on what actually constituted a clear and present danger was not easy, and justices were left to apply the principle as best they could according to their own dictates and beliefs. For this reason, the clear and present danger principle was especially significant in the intolerant postwar period — it enabled the legal limits, as well as the actual limits, of civil liberty to be set not by the courts but by public opinion. Momentarily, at least, this principle served as an excellent rationalizing device by which the courts could tailor their decisions to fit the existing public mood.]

While not nearly so significant as either the Berger or the Schenck case in its later Red Scare implications, the third in this series of Socialist trials was much more spectacular and far more indicative of public resentment toward the Socialist movement by 1919. This case involved the "grand old man" of the Socialist party, Eugene V. Debs.

Debs was born, one of ten children, to Alsatian immigrant parents in Terre Haute, Indiana, in 1855. As a boy, he attended the

Terre Haute public schools until the age of fifteen when he went to work in one of the local railroad shops. He later became a locomotive fireman and in 1875 was instrumental in organizing the local lodge of the Fireman's Brotherhood. By 1885 he was both a national officer in the brotherhood and a respected member of the Indiana State Legislature.

However, Debs had a burning desire to further the workingman's interests and, ultimately convinced that the real solution to the worker's problem lay in industrial unionism rather than craft unionism, he devoted full time after 1893 to organizing such a group. The result was the American Railway Union of which he became president.

His rise to national fame came the next year, in 1894, when he threw the ARU's support behind the embattled Pullman Car Company strikers and refused to abide by a sweeping injunction issued by the federal courts. As a result he was arrested and convicted of contempt; after spending six months in jail, he emerged not only a national figure but also a hero of the working class.

Although he supported Bryan for the presidency in 1896, Debs already had been sufficiently exposed to radical ideas so that he had begun to despair of achieving any real progress for the workingman through the major political parties, and in 1897 he followed what was left of the ARU into the Social Democratic party. Along with Berger, he represented this group at the Unity Convention of 1901 and joined with other Socialist elements to form the Socialist party. Since that time he had been the party's perennial candidate for the presidency and his appeal at the polls during the prewar years reflected both the increasing stature of the man himself and the growth of the Socialist movement. In 1904, he received 402,000 votes; in 1908, 421,000; and in 1912, 897,000.

While Debs without question was the titular head of the Socialist party, he was not its intellectual leader. Indeed he bothered little about dialectical matters and remained merely an impassioned advocate of the movement. As a speaker, however, he was superb. Tall, lean, supple, and with countenance aflame, he could spellbind audiences as he leaned far over the edge of the platform, stabbing with his finger and all the while hurling invectives at the capitalistic system. Unlike Berger he continually referred to class warfare in his speeches and flirted from time to time with the idea of direct action. Yet, like Berger, he really was no revolutionist. He believed in reform through legal political pressure, often showed that he was basically opposed to violence and force, and, unlike many radicals, was a devout Christian. 'Gene Debs was one of the few radicals who could mention God's name on a public platform and get away with it.[10]

There was no more bitter opponent of the war than Eugene Debs. His vitriolic tongue lashed the American government for its intervention and he openly defied the Espionage and Sedition laws even when he knew Justice Department agents were within hearing. Such was the situation, when, in June 1918, at the Ohio State Socialist Convention at Canton, Ohio, he took the opportunity to launch one of his most scathing attacks. Reminding his audience about the "unjust" convictions of such prominent Socialists as Charles E. Ruthenberg, Alfred Wagenknecht, Kate Richards O'Hare, and Rose Pastor Stokes, he bitterly denounced the government's action, decried the wild persecution involved, and exhorted Socialists to continue their nonsupport of the war. "Do not worry over the charge of treason to your masters," he shouted, "This year we are going to sweep into power and in this nation we are going to destroy capitalistic institutions."[11]

Although Debs had been saying essentially the same, if not worse, things for years, four days after the Canton speech he was indicted and arrested for violation of the Espionage Act. During his trial Debs did not flinch, and even while making his final plea before the jury declared, "I have been accused of obstructing the war. I admit it. Gentlemen, I abhor war. I would oppose it if I stood alone."[12] As a result, on September 12, he was convicted and two days later was sentenced to ten years in prison. His case was immediately appealed, but to no avail. On March 10, 1919, Justice Holmes delivered the unanimous opinion of the Supreme Court by upholding the original conviction on the basis of the clear and present danger principle.[13]

Because of the fame of the person involved, this case had stirred widespread interest and the judgment met with almost universal approval. The *Christian Science Monitor* maintained, "There can be no question as to the guilt of Eugene Debs." The Atlanta *Constitution* entoned, "Poor, old, sour Debs! . . . a victim of his own acidity of soul." Said the Cleveland *Plain Dealer*, "Debs' voice is now stilled as it should have been long ago." [14]

But Debs's voice was not stilled. Two days after the Supreme Court decision, he called Lenin and Trotsky the "foremost statesmen of the age" and in the same breath denounced the Supreme Court justices as "begowned, bewhiskered, bepowdered old fossils." Two weeks later, when the mayor of Toledo refused Socialists admission to Memorial Hall to hear Debs deliver a farewell address before going to prison, 5000 of his followers stormed the building, broke doors and windows, and shouted "To hell with the mayor." In the long run, even the thick walls of a federal prison failed to contain his voice, for his cell in the Atlanta penitentiary became the virtual headquarters of the Socialist party. Despite repeated appeals for his release, Atlanta convict #9653 remained the most famous wartime martyr of American socialism.[15]

The other major radical organization in operation during the prewar and wartime periods was the Industrial Workers of the World, or so-called Wobblies. Because of their extremely aggressive policy and their willingness to combine words with deeds, the IWW's suffered an even greater concentration of public wrath and created more fear than did the Socialists.

The organization was founded in Chicago in 1905 mainly through the efforts of William S. Haywood, a radical labor leader from the West. "Big Bill," as he was popularly called, was born in 1869 near Salt Lake City, Utah, and almost from that moment on led a rough-and-tumble life. At the age of three, Bill's father died and left him to the care of a mother who was much more interested in replacing the father than in rearing the son. Before the age of ten he suffered the loss of an eye and by fifteen he was working as a miner doing a "man's work for a boy's pay."

Successively, he then became a cowboy, a homesteader, and a general roustabout before returning to the mines, this time to be very active in the affairs of the Western Federation of Miners, ultimately becoming its national secretary-treasurer. By 1905 he had gained at least local notoriety by leading the federation on some of the most bitter strikes the West had yet seen.

More than six feet tall and of powerful build, Haywood was the personification of the tough radical labor leader. He was assertive, rough-mannered, and a forceful, if somewhat crude, speaker. Yet, he also had his gentle side and could be an amiable companion. Although he was known to have crushed two men's heads together during a labor strike, he was once described by one of his friends as being so gentle he "could not kill a fly."

In many respects the IWW exhibited some of the same qualities as its founder. Drawing together all the dissident elements within the American labor movement, it represented a hodgepodge of anarchists, general strike advocates, direct-action Socialists, and syndicalists. In reality it was a protest against the conservative craft unionism of the AFL and a defense in behalf of industrial unionism. Espousing a Sorelian anarcho-syndicalist philosophy with Marxist trimmings, the organization evidenced little sympathy for political action and placed primary emphasis upon direct economic pressure to overthrow the capitalistic system.[16]

Yet, despite its disregard for political activity and its professed belief in violence, for a time the IWW drew heavily upon the support of various leaders of the Socialist party. Indeed, at its founding convention in 1905, Eugene Debs was present and praised the movement highly. He even expressed some sympathy for its principle of the general strike. However, more conservative members of the party, such as Victor Berger, looked askance at this radical upstart and as early as 1906 began a successful move to force the party hierarchy to forswear any support. Even so, as late as 1919, the membership roles of the various Socialist organizations and those of the IWW were still inextricably interwoven, and some Socialist funds continued to make their way into Wobbly hands.[17]

Declaring its major object to be the seizure of the machinery of production by the working class and the complete abolition of the wage system, the IWW surged forth to draw American labor into its "One Big Union." But with such phrases as "Take what you need where you find it; it is yours" and "Arise!! Slaves of the World!!! No God!! No Master!!!" the Wobblies did more to repel than beguile. The Wobbly hymns of "Dump the Bosses Off Your Back," "What We Want," and "Hallelujah! I'm a Bum!" although reflecting their own intense spirit did not inspire the average American worker and relatively few were enticed into the movement.

However, since the IWW oftentimes was the only organization that would extend a helping hand to the unorganized, unskilled laborer, it met with some sporadic success in certain areas of the country prior to the war. Its greatest appeal was to western miners, construction gangs, lumberjacks, and migratory harvest hands. Some few converts were also found among the immigrant workers of steel mills, packing plants, and textile mills. Denouncing the AFL as the "American Separation of Labor," the Wobblies led such individuals in wildcat strikes in mining fields, on lumbering projects, and in construction camps in the Northwest; in eastern textile and silk mills; and in midwestern steel and packing plants. Probably the IWW's most famous strikes were the successful Lawrence textile strike of 1912 and the unsuccessful Paterson silk strike of 1913.

The IWW remained small despite such aggressive activity. Encountering bitter opposition from the AFL, and with the rank and file of American workmen holding aloof, the IWW at its peak had no more than 60,000 members.[18] Actually, even this membership fluctuated greatly from one time to another, for the IWW was a violent fighting machine which thrived only on action and once a strike crisis was passed many of its followers disappeared. Western migratory workers were difficult to keep track of and did not remain long in the ranks. Unorganized eastern workers, who were willing to accept IWW help during a strike, soon lost interest after the struggle was over. Nevertheless, in spite of its meager size, the IWW had a significant impact on both the labor movement and public opinion. It served to warn conservative union leaders of the needs of the vast numbers of unskilled, unorganized workmen, and by its stormy action it had aroused popular fears of labor violence and radicalism.

As in the case of the Socialists, the Wobblies were bitterly opposed to the war. But unlike most Socialists, they were willing to implement verbal opposition with concrete action. Members signed up for the draft as "IWW, opposed to war," while IWW posters were distributed, saying, "Don't Be a Soldier, Be a Man" and "Slow down. The hours are long, the pay is small, so take your time and buck them all." Wobbly antiwar pamphlets were particularly vociferous, exhorting workers not to become "hired murderers" and not to make themselves "a target in order to fatten Rockefeller, Morgan, Carnegie . . . and the other industrial pirates." [19] Although not Wobblies themselves, most free-lance radicals, such as the anarchists, followed in the vein established by the IWW and supplemented its propaganda by declaring "Already the war is being conducted with the skins of the poor — Refuse to Join the Army . . . Refuse to Go to War." [20] The nation's two most famous anarchists, Emma Goldman and Alex Berkman, often sponsored official IWW propaganda in their publications, *Mother Earth* and *The Blast*.[21]

As a result of these rabid assertions and "slow down" tactics, the Wobblies were suspected of every type of crime. It was claimed that they drove spikes into logs, set buildings on fire, blew up munition factories, destroyed grain, poisoned cattle, and smashed farm machinery in order to hinder the war effort. It was further charged that in some areas of the Northwest, loyal timbermen were afraid to report for work because of the lawlessness of the Wobbly. It was even rumored that the Wobblies threw union workmen under the wheels of freight trains if they refused to cooperate in harassing the war program.[22]

Not bothering to separate fiction from truth, the American public now shrieked at the IWW. Patriotic societies called them "traitors" and "agents of Germany," and maintained that German gold was financing their program. The newspapers labeled the organization "America's canker sore" and characterized the Wobbly as "a sort of half wild animal." Theodore Roosevelt described the movement as "a homicidal march," while Senator Henry F. Ashurst of Arizona claimed the Wobblies had reduced murder to a science and called for their immediate extinction. As the war progressed, this hang-them-all-at-sunrise attitude further deepened and soon all super-patriots were believing that the only remedy was to take them "out into the desert and shoot them." [23]

In some cases this is almost what happened. Infuriated by the Wobblies' lack of patriotism, the populace countenanced almost any type of action against them. Not only were their headquarters and meeting halls raided, but some members were seized, loaded into cattle cars, and shipped hundreds of miles without food or water. Others were whipped and tarred and feathered, or were hunted down like fair game thereby giving sport to whole communities. A few, like IWW official Frank H. Little of Butte, Montana, were brutally murdered.[24]

As with the Socialists, the public was not alone in its wartime drive on the Wobbly. Both the federal and state governments struck at the menace through their various espionage and sedition laws, culminating in the federal raids of September 1917, when most of the leaders of the organization were apprehended. The biggest fish netted was "Big Bill" Haywood who, along with 165 other Wobbly defendants, was tried before Judge K. M. Landis in April 1918. Ninety-nine of the defendants, including Haywood, were found guilty of violating the Espionage Act and Judge Landis imposed sentences ranging from ten days to twenty years with fines amounting in the aggregate to $2,300,000. Bill Haywood claimed, "Pontius Pilate or Bloody Jeffreys never enjoyed themselves better than did Judge Landis when he was imposing these terrible sentences." Said Senator William S. Kenyon of Iowa, "If we had more judges like him it would be well for the country." [25]

The fact is that as a result of this and other similar action the movement was so crippled that its estimated membership fell by half. Actually, for the remainder of the war, the organization went underground. Wobblies hid their union cards and credentials, and only in the larger cities of the East and in the Pacific Northwest did they continue to maintain halls and offices. By 1919, it was definitely unwise for a person to declare openly he was a Wobbly.

Regardless of all the sound and fury, it is certainly obvious that the domestic radical movement had met with relatively little success by 1919. Up to that point American radicals had not constituted a real menace, and, when viewed rationally, even during the war period itself they did not represent any serious chink in the democratic armor. The Socialist party, which represented a majority of those in the radical movement, could command no more than 100,000 members, and its growth, while steady, was insignificant when compared with that of the traditional political parties. The same was true of the IWW, which in no way challenged either the supremacy or the continued growth of the conservative trade union movement. At no time, either before or during the war, did the basic philosophy of those two organizations appeal to the rank and file of Americans, and even the workingman, who seemingly had the most to gain, remained highly skeptical of both their methods and their practices.

On the basis of this experience, even the most zealous radical should have seen that the American nation was an extremely infertile field in which to sow the seeds of either evolutionary socialism or violent revolution. American society was much too expansive in its interests, too fluid in its composition, and far too hopeful of the future to be compressed into any doctrinaire pattern of development.

Before the war there was every indication that the public realized this even if the radicals did not. Confident in its ability to weather the harangues of a few men, the nation tolerated their existence and permitted them to talk. Moreover, before the war, the public evidenced the ability to distinguish between the various shades and degrees of radicals. They always scorned the anarchists and other direct-actionists of the Wobbly strain. But toward the evolutionary Socialists of the Berger type they practiced moderation and even accorded them some respect. Such individuals were allowed to hold responsible positions, even responsible political positions, without fear or prejudice. It was felt that there was still a legitimate place for them within the American system.

Then the war came. And because of their universal opposition to the conflict, all radicals, regardless of their various persuasions, were lumped into the same category. The public mind suddenly lost its earlier ability to discriminate. As wartime fervor flamed hot and bright, the general press, the courts, patriotic societies, government officials — the whole nation — regarded them all as traitors and sought to suppress them by force.

By this, the public indicated its surrender to a tremendous fear complex, for under the emotional strains of a wartime situation it was in the process of losing its former faith in the ability of the democratic system to sustain itself without force against such puny opposition. Hence, in 1919 when some of these domestic radicals switched to an advocacy of the detested Bolshevik system and began to work for a Russian-type revolution in the United States, the American people were not prepared to meet the assault wisely. Not only that, but conditioned by their wartime experience, they were also ill equipped to assess correctly either the size or the influence of this new radical movement.

3 ★ ★ ★ ★ ★ ★ ★ ★ ★ ★

The Fire behind the Smoke

THE emergence of bolshevism as a powerful ideological force and the impact of that philosophy upon American life constituted the most disquieting, if not the most significant, phase of the 1919 postwar scene. Whatever legitimate reasons existed for the coming Red Scare, they stemmed almost solely from this parent source. Indeed, in a turbulent postwar era, bolshevism's disruptive power seemed particularly active and its ideological appeal especially strong. To a nation seeking normalcy, this philosophy represented the direct antithesis of all that was hoped for, and seemed to presage a move backward in the quest for peace.

American contact with bolshevism began with the Russian November Revolution of 1917. At that time, Bolshevik rule under Nikolai Lenin and Leon Trotsky supplanted the Social-Democratic government of Alexander Kerensky which but a short time before had startled the world by overthrowing the old Czarist regime.

Although from the first it was feared this change might mean an end to Russian participation in the war, hopes momentarily ran high throughout the Allied world that the Bolsheviki would continue in the path established by the moderate Kerensky. Such hopes, tentative though they were, were smashed to bits by the infamous Brest-Litovsk Treaty at which time the Bolsheviki not only deserted the Allied cause but impertinently called for the immediate cessation of hostilities everywhere through universal proletarian revolution and the dissolution of all capitalistic governments.

As a result of these events, American thinking on bolshevism was conditioned first of all by the wartime situation and was inevitably colored by the intense emotionalism which surrounded the conflict. Since the Bolshevik movement was thought to be German-spawned, the Bolsheviki and their sympathizers were erroneously considered agents of the Kaiser and were so treated. Public animosity was immediately aroused because of their opposition to the war, and the Bolsheviki were placed in the same unsavory category as the Socialists and the IWW's.

[Even more basic in creating a hostile attitude was bolshevism's unyielding emphasis on the world-wide overthrow of capitalism and the complete abolition of private property. This doctrine ran counter to all accepted American traditions of political philosophy and economy and struck terror into the heart of the average American conservative.] Already harassed by domestic radicals who advocated big changes, the nation viewed the emergence of Russian bolshevism with extremely grave concern and feared that it might portend serious domestic consequences.

For these reasons, American hostility from the beginning was vociferous. Already engaged in their violent wartime denunciations of the domestic radical, organized labor publications, church magazines, business and financial journals, and the general press now struck wildly at the Bolsheviki both for the Brest-Litovsk Treaty and for their vicious attacks on capitalism. Advocates of the Bolshevik movement were variously and interchangeably described as being "German agents," "criminals," "anarchists," "IWW's," "beasts," and "economic imbeciles." Almost overnight the word "Bolshevik" became synonomous with "treason," and anyone in the United States who by word or deed tried to hamper the further execution of the war was so named. Only a few of the nation's more liberal periodicals, such as the *Public, Dial, Nation, Survey,* and *New Republic*, dared to caution against such snap judgments or decry the erroneous impressions which were being created.[1]

The general press was undoubtedly the worst offender. Horror stories of every kind filled the columns of American newspapers. It

The Government of Russia
(Cartoonist Rehse in the New York *World*)

was claimed that in Petrograd the Bolsheviki had an electrically operated guillotine that lopped off five hundred heads an hour. Bolshevik rule was said to be a "compound of slaughter, confiscation, anarchy and universal disorder . . . the paradise of IWW's and the superlative heaven of anarchists and direct-action Socialists." [2] The nation's cartoonists had a field day; one portrayed the Bolshevik government as a smoking gun, a bomb, and a hangman's noose, while others painted scenes of wealthy and cultured women cleaning the streets, and officers of high rank, businessmen, and professors selling newspapers in order to keep from starving. The Bolsheviki meanwhile were described as riding around in automobiles, dining in fashionable restaurants, and otherwise amusing themselves. [3]

Regardless of the relative accuracy or inaccuracy of such stories, the sheer weight of their numbers and the emotional bias from which they were told so pressed down on the public mind that its reaction to the Russian Red Terror was abnormally intense. As the *Literary Digest* described it, "The rapturous joy with which America hailed the downfall of Czarism has changed into a bewildered horror at the excesses of the Bolsheviki." [4]

American radicals were not horrified; they were enthralled by the events taking place in Russia. Persecuted on all sides for their opposition to the war and to capitalism, the Bolshevik pro-peace and anti-bourgeois philosophy intrigued them. Naturally, all direct-actionists and those of like mind were immediately swept off their feet. Even the Socialist party, although basically Menshevik in its ideology, temporarily became pro-Bolshevik. Eugene Debs eulogized the Russian venture, and Morris Hillquit, who along with Berger was one of the most conservative of all Socialists, announced the revolution "has vindicated the claims of international Socialism as a living and driving force." [5] The Executive Committee of the party declared, "We endorse unreservedly the peace program of the Russian Bolshevist Government." The Socialist New York *Call* thundered praises for the new Russian order. [6]

This enthusiasm is certainly understandable. Having very little success of their own to point to and completely discouraged by their wartime persecution, American radicals were suddenly confronted with the most successful Socialist revolution the world had yet seen. And they were awed. More than that. They were revitalized. The Russian experiment immediately gave the domestic radical movement all the things it currently lacked — a fresh idea, new enthusiasm, and an example of success. It also gave the domestic movement a deeper reason for existing. The Bolshevik revolutionary philosophy contained the elements of grand strategy, not merely to fight for the new order only where and when conditions warranted, but to fight for and establish the Socialist Utopia in the whole world immediately — and the Russian Revolution represented the first step. To the average American radical, the very sweep of the program was breathtaking.

Yet, in allowing his breath to be snatched away, the domestic radical indicated just how poorly he had adjusted himself to the American environment. It is inconceivable how he, having failed thus far in his attempt to secure popular support for even a mild evolutionary socialism, could have expected more support for a violent revolutionary procedure such as the Russian venture suggested. He was being foolishly unrealistic when he toyed with the idea of employing Bolshevik methods here, and by so doing he divorced himself even more from what was either feasible or possible in the American situation.

Some radicals obviously realized this and, while they continued for a time to sympathize with the Russian Bolsheviki, they did not approve of their methods or advocate a similar plan of action for the United States. Such individuals were usually found in the conservative faction, or so-called Right Wing, of the Socialist party led by Hillquit and Berger. The other group, or Left Wing, was led by such men as Charles Ruthenberg, Louis Fraina, Benjamin Gitlow, and John Reed and loudly championed the Bolshevik program for domestic use as quickly as possible. Eugene Debs constantly flirted with this Left Wing, but at critical moments always took his place beside Hillquit and Berger.

The Socialist Left Wing was composed mainly of foreign language federations which, beginning in 1907, had attached themselves to the Socialist party. These federations were virtually autonomous groups of proletarian immigrants speaking the same language and having the same ethnic background. Since it had been almost impossible to reach such persons through the English-speaking branches of the party, they had been allowed to affiliate through these organizations of their own.

Obviously, many of the members of these federations were not at all aware of the American heritage nor did they understand or have any knowledge of American political principles. Many of these individuals merely translated American economics, politics, and law in terms of a European setting — and well they might, for many had but recently come from the Old World bringing their disillusionments and prejudices with them.

Hence, more radical in their viewpoints than Right-Wing groups, these federations easily succumbed to the Bolshevik doctrine.[7] Cheering Lenin's every success, they took their cue from *Soviet Russia*, a magazine issued by the Russian Soviet Bureau in New York, and rebroadcast its propaganda through such papers as the *Novy Mir* and *Revolutionary Age*. The *Novy Mir*, edited in 1915 by no less than Nikolai Bukharin and Leon Trotsky, began preaching the Bolshevik philosophy in the United States two years before the Russian revolution even occurred; the *Revolutionary Age*, edited by Louis Fraina and later the official organ of the Left Wing, reached an estimated 16,000 Left Wing Socialists weekly with its pro-Bolshevik assertions.[8] Other Left Wing journals such as *Obrana* (Bohemian), *Forward* (Yiddish), and *Robitnyk* (Hungarian) rapidly added to this influence by taking up the Communist chant: "Workers of the World unite, you have nothing to lose but your chains." As a result, Bolshevik phrases like "All power to the Soviets" were soon bandied about at Left Wing Socialist gatherings and some elements even formed themselves into local communes.[9]

Meanwhile, the revolutionary ardor experienced by the Left Wing Socialists was no less forcefully felt by the IWW and other direct-actionists. Although many of these shied somewhat at the Bolshevik conception of the power of the soviet, all were in sympathy with the immediate goal of the Bolshevik crusade. Indeed, immediately following the Bolshevik Revolution, both the Wobbly and the anarchist press switched almost completely to the Bolshevik line. Berkman and Goldman's *Mother Earth* and *The Blast* were decidedly outspoken in their support of the Bolshevik viewpoint and agitated for a Communist upheaval in the United States.[10] In like manner, such anarchist journals as *Naujenos* (Lithuanian) and *A. Felszabadulas* (Hungarian) sang praises to the Bolsheviki and declared the capitalistic class could no more hold up the coming American revolution "than the legendary old woman was able to sweep back the waves of the sea with her broom." Wobbly papers like the *New England Leader* (Boston), *New Solidarity* (Chicago), and the *International Weekly* (Seattle) followed in the same vein by declaring that capitalism would soon fall in the United States because "the people's hour has arrived."[11] Carried away by their enthusiasm for the new Communist order, the Wobblies invented a new chorus for their famous song "Don't Bite the Hand That's Feeding You":

> All hail to the Bolsheviki!
> We will fight for our class and be free
> A Kaiser, King, or Czar, no matter which you are
> You're nothing of interest to me;
> If you don't like the red flag of Russia
> If you don't like the spirit so true,
> Then just be like the cur in the story
> And lick the hand that's robbing you. . . .[12]

While many American radicals thus became outspoken in their sympathy toward bolshevism and the general public became increasingly convinced of its evils, the immediate problem was what to do with Russia. The disposition of this question further complicated the American position with respect to the Bolshevik doctrine and produced consequences that were unfortunate and far-reaching.

The removal of Russia from the conflict had permitted Germany to focus her entire attention on the western front and it was feared that a prolongation of the war might result. To Allied strategists, the only logical solution seemed to be armed intervention in Russia. The major support for such action stemmed from the belief that the Lenin government was held together by German influence and could not possibly last because it was not supported by the Russian people. Four days after the November Revolution, the American ambassador to Moscow, David R. Francis, declared, "This Bolshevik Government can not survive," and a short time later, DeWitt Poole, American consul at Moscow, claimed Bolshevik rule had already been "preserved beyond its natural end by German support."[13] Such sentiments were not peculiar to American officials, for the diplomats and statesmen of other Allied countries expressed similar beliefs. Therefore, as originally conceived, the Allied intervention policy in Russia was designed to neutralize German influence by reactivating the eastern front which, it was hoped, would also automatically result in the downfall of bolshevism.

On this basis a request for American participation was presented by the Allies to President Wilson in March 1918. However, the United States government moved cautiously and, although sending a token Marine force to Murmansk for the purpose of keeping that port open, refused further participation. The President renounced any armed intervention which might possibly interfere with Russian internal affairs, and the troops at Murmansk were charged to make no attempts to restore the old order.[14]

Conservative elements and the general press were not satisfied with this position of the President and in the ensuing months called for a much stronger intervention policy. Subsequent Bolshevik-German collusion in the Brest-Litovsk negotiations and the plight of the 45,000 pro-ally Czecho-Slovaks who, left stranded in the Ukraine, were slowly retreating across Siberia to Vladivostok, gave added emphasis to these demands. Atrocity stories and the various propaganda activities of anti-Communist Russian refugees further underscored the necessity for more aggressive action. As a result, by the summer of 1918, American opinion came to support increased intervention and, with repeated appeals from the Allied Supreme War Council that such a move was necessary to win the war, the President's resistance broke slightly.

Still, the Chief Executive could not reconcile a policy of aggressive intervention with his belief that the Allies should not interfere in Russia's internal affairs and hence would support only a "limited" intervention. In July 1918 the administration decided that increased American participation would be restricted to sending small forces to both North Russia and Siberia, and that even such action would be undertaken only with the express understanding that there would be no impairment of either the political or territorial integrity of the Russian people.

To carry out this decision, two contingents of American troops were landed at Vladivostok in August 1918. A month later, approximately 2000 more men under the command of General William S. Graves arrived. Simultaneously, a company of infantry, a company of engineers, and some hospital units were landed in North Russia at Archangel. Still insisting that these troops were not to be used for interference in Russia's domestic affairs, the United States had approximately 7000 soldiers on duty in Russia by late 1918.[15]

It is clear that in spite of public sentiment, the United States government accepted intervention only with the greatest reluctance. It is equally evident that its intervention policy was a hodge podge of ambiguities and contradictions. To be sure, American intervention was avowedly anti-German since it was designed to neutralize German activity in Russia and present the Kaiser with a "second front." But this anti-Germanism was so closely entwined with anti-bolshevism that the two were inseparable in the intervention situation. As long as hostilities with Germany continued, American intervention could be openly anti-German and at the same time secretly anti-Bolshevik. Even so, American participation in the destruction of Russian bolshevism was made virtually impossible by the orders given to American troops which forbade

41

their interference in Russia's internal affairs. There matters stood on November 11, 1918.

The Armistice muddied the waters further. The Germans were stopped, but what about the Bolsheviki? The Allies were really quite loath to leave the job only half-completed and thus what had originally been an anti-German device now became an anti-Bolshevik crusade. As the Soviet menace swept across Asiatic Russia in 1918–19, Japan became jittery and demanded the continuance of the intervention policy. French interests also demanded the troops remain. England, fearing the Red Scourge as much as the others, joined with France and Japan in their stand.

The position of the United States was now all the more confusing. To continue intervention would seem to abandon the traditional principle of noninterference in another nation's domestic affairs; to stop it would surely leave all of Russia to a Bolshevist fate. As one New York paper pointedly asked, "What is the American policy with respect to Russia? No one seems to know. Our Government seems unable to make up its mind." [16]

Indeed, torn between a growing fear of bolshevism, a budding isolationism, and the policy of noninterference, governmental opinion did run in different directions. Some believed that the United States should immediately "render financial and military aid to Russia, to overthrow Bolshevist tyranny and anarchy." Others believed the government should begin a complete withdrawal. The State Department reflected this confusion by expressing a desire on the one hand to remove the soldiers as speedily as possible, and agreeing on the other to wait and see what would happen.[17]

The significant point is that while this condition existed, American troops remained in Russia. The very fact that Allied troops, including those of the United States, were left there illustrated the growing fear of bolshevism, and, under such circumstances, it was extremely difficult for American troops to remain neutral. Although General Graves did a remarkable job of maintaining neutrality in Siberia, American troops in North Russia were openly used to harass the Bolsheviki. Indeed, in February 1919, at the very moment when the government announced that the troops in North Russia would be withdrawn at the earliest possible moment, newspaper headlines in the United States read: "U.S. TROOPS DRIVE BOLSHEVIK FORCES WITH HEAVY LOSSES" and "YANKS DRIVE ON REDS." [18]

Such a situation ultimately proved intolerable for the Wilson administration, which remained convinced that all American troops should be removed from Russia, and, backed by the nation's natural desire to have the boys home, it turned first to that area where friction arising from continued intervention was the greatest. In late February 1919 immediate steps were taken to remove American soldiers from North Russia and by June the last man had been withdrawn. [19]

This program of evacuation might also have been executed in Siberia had it not been for certain circumstances which prevented such action. In the early part of 1919, the danger of Russian bolshevism seemed to grow rather than lessen as, contrary to earlier expectations, Bolshevik control of Russia continued to expand. Nor did the danger confine itself to Russia. Germany was being rent with the Spartioist revolts, Poland was badly infected with the Bolshevik virus, and both Hungary and Bavaria temporarily established soviet-type regimes. The Paris Peace Conference, meanwhile, was reported to be so alarmed by the rising Red tide that, according to the New York *Times*, it had "resolved itself into a discussion of ways and means to check the spread of Bolshevism." [20]

In the spring of 1919 this mounting concern was further intensified by the formation of the Third International, or Comintern, at Moscow. Established in March, this organization was avowedly propagandistic and sought to enlist the aid of radicals throughout the world in its crusade for universal revolution. Although it was formed by the joint action of thirty-two delegates from twelve different countries, the Third International was directed and controlled solely by the Russian Communist party. Formulated by such Russian Bolshevik luminaries as Karl Radek, Nikolai Bukharin, and Gregory Zinoviev, its Manifesto was a ringing challenge to world capitalism and urged the proletariat to seize government power, disarm the bourgeoisie, arm the proletariat, and suppress private property.[21]

Aggressive though this program was, the Russian Soviet government of 1919, unlike its successor after World War II, was virtually helpless to implement it. At the time Russia was rent with tremendous internal dissension. Counterrevolutionaries, such as Admiral Alexander Kolchak and General Anton Denikin, had the Bolsheviki under attack and there was still some hope that one of them might succeed. Unable yet to maintain complete control at home, the Russian Communists found it exceedingly difficult to render any effective support to the Third International's activities outside the Soviet sphere. For all the excited talk, in 1919 the organization had to rely almost solely on ideas and propaganda to achieve its desired goal, and in no way upon external force.

Nevertheless, in the spring of 1919, such a radical and comprehensive program as that of the Third International intensified the fears of conservatives the world over. In the United States it not only heightened fear concerning the activities of pro-Bolshevik radicals, but also served as a further justification for the continuance of intervention in Siberia. At the moment Admiral Kolchak was experiencing some slight success against the Bolsheviki there, and it was hoped that with outside help and moral support he might defeat them. Hence, by the late spring of 1919, all pretext was dropped concerning the real reason for continued intervention. The issue was now joined in the firm conviction that Russian communism constituted a serious threat to world peace and to capitalism.

Under such conditions, American soldiers inevitably became the agents of counterrevolutionists despite the continued desire of President Wilson not to interfere in the internal affairs of Russia. The general press, which currently was expressing great alarm over domestic radical activity, hailed this "new look" in intervention as highly desirable and, with a sigh of relief, the New York *Times* exclaimed, "A Russian policy at last." [22]

Thus, despite a postwar trend toward isolationism and a natural desire to bring the soldiers home, the fear of bolshevism temporarily overshadowed all other considerations. American intervention in Russian Siberia continued and, according to Secretary of War Newton D. Baker, the United States in September 1919 had 8477 troops there who were going to stay because the only alternative was withdrawal which "would leave Siberia open to anarchy, bloodshed, and Bolshevism." [23]

While American soldiers remained in Russian Siberia as physical testimony both to bolshevism's continued success and the growing American concern created by this situation, there were indications that the doctrine was also making further headway among radicals at home.

For the remainder of the war and on into 1919, American radicals continued to laud the Russian Bolsheviki. While only the more violent as yet advocated a similar revolution in the United States, all domestic radicals strongly denounced Allied intervention and, after the Armistice, assailed it even more. Anarchists, Socialists, and IWW's alike proclaimed that capitalistic imperialism was seeking to destroy the only true "people's government" that existed and charged President Wilson with waging a private war against Soviet Russia. [24]

Indicative as this was of the Bolshevik philosophy's domestic success, of even greater significance was the interest shown in the American situation by the Russian Bolsheviki themselves. While nothing so melodramatic as a courier system or a spy network was yet established, the Russian Bolsheviki did attempt to extend aid and moral support to their American brethren.

Mainly this took the form of propaganda. The sympathy for the Communist cause created by the successful November Revolution, by no means peculiar to radicals in the United States, was well known to the Russian Bolsheviki and from the beginning they appropriated huge sums of money for propaganda purposes hoping thereby to extend what sympathy and support they already had.

In the American case, the Soviet government immediately enlisted the journalistic aid of two Americans who were then in Russia. Both of these men, John Reed, a leader of the Socialist Left Wing, and Albert Rhys Williams, a Congregationalist minister, were quickly admitted to the inner circle and worked for the Bureau of International Propaganda which was attached to the Commissariat for Foreign Affairs. Their job was to translate into English all decrees and decisions of the various Russian soviets and prepare them for distribution in the United States. Later, it was decided to create a separate propaganda bureau in the United States under the direction of Williams, but the plan did not succeed because the Soviet government was not recognized. Still later, there was an attempt to make John Reed, although an American citizen, the Soviet consul general to this country, but this plan also fell through.[25]

Bolshevik propaganda to the United States did not really come of age until the establishment of the Third International. Although at the time there was an irrational overrating of both the amount and the effectiveness of this propaganda, some did make its way into the country and was read by those who were interested. Such Comintern propaganda urged the creation of workmen's soviets as rapidly as possible, the destruction of public and labor support for the AFL, and the forced elimination of intervention through strikes and sabotage. The Third International also distributed for American consumption Lenin's famous, and only, letter "To the American Workers" which, although appearing in this country as early as December 1918, was not widely distributed until March of the following year. It was estimated that the circulation of this document, which simply urged American laborers to follow their Russian brethren in shaking off the shackles of capitalism, ultimately reached the five million mark. On May 1, 1919, the first issue of the Comintern's official organ, the *Communist International*, came off the Petrograd press and thereafter appeared regularly in the United States. Edited by Zinoviev, the Russian Communist party's chief propagandizer, this magazine was printed in Russian, English,

French, and German. According to its own records, the Third International distributed, besides this magazine, six other pamphlets in this country in 1919. One of these originated in the New York Russian Soviet Bureau; the rest came directly from Moscow.[26]

In this connection, Ludwig Christian Alexander Karlovich Martens must be mentioned. He appeared in the United States in the winter of 1918–19, claiming to be the representative of the Soviet Commissariat of Foreign Affairs. He promptly submitted to the State Department his instructions from Foreign Commissar George Chicherin which empowered him to negotiate for the "opening of commercial relations for the mutual benefit of Russia and America . . . at the earliest opportunity."[27]

L. C. A. K. Martens never received the opportunity. Not only did the American press greet him coldly, but the State Department refused to have anything to do with him. The government felt that since the Soviet regime had not been recognized, it did not possess the privilege of sending either diplomatic or commercial representatives to the United States. Nevertheless, Martens remained in the country and in the ensuing months established an office in the World Tower Building in New York, using it as headquarters for disseminating a favorable impression of conditions in Russia. Inevitably, he was considered to be nothing more than a Communist agent under orders from the Third International. And, as a matter of fact, it was later discovered that Martens's secretary, Santeri Nuorteva, was one of the Russian Communist party's most able propagandists and that Martens's office from time to time received large sums of money from Moscow.[28]

But whether he was here for the primary purpose of promoting a radical revolution, or merely to restore American-Russian relations as he claimed, it was true that Martens cooperated very closely with the Socialist Left Wing in the distribution of Bolshevik propaganda, and more than once he was seen at radical rallies wildly applauding such tirades as "We want an American Soviet." That such propaganda was backed by the Third International is beyond dispute, for the executive secretary, Radek, reported that the money sent to Berlin for the ill-fated Sparticist Revolution "was as nothing compared to the funds transmitted to New York for the purpose of spreading bolshevism in the United States." As to the effectiveness of this procedure, said the *Communist International,* one merely has to observe how "many of the active socialists have boldly confessed themselves bolsheviks." [29]

It was these confessions, more than the propaganda activities of the Third International or the Bolsheviki's expanding control in Russia, which provided the immediate impetus for the coming Scare. Such confessions were not secured without tremendous cost to the domestic radical movement itself. For in the heat of conflicting ideas old radical alignments melted, separated, and fused, producing a sudden change in the pattern of domestic radical development.

From the beginning of the revolution in Russia, the Right and Left wings of the American Socialist party fell to quarreling among themselves about the significance of the Russian event. Advocating an immediate revolution along Bolshevik lines, the Left Wing increasingly denounced the conservatism of the older English-speaking element of the party which, although sympathizing with the Communists in Russia, retained its belief in democratic, evolutionary action to achieve domestic goals.

Throughout 1918 and the early part of 1919, this running battle between the two factions placed the Socialist party in a constant state of turmoil. The Right Wing, which controlled the party machinery, held the whip hand and made it abundantly clear that it would not allow the party to swallow the Bolshevik program for America. This position forced Left Wing members into a rebellious attitude and, labeling Right Wingers "counterrevolutionaries" and "Kolchaks," they planned to seize party control.

In February 1919 the Left Wing section of the Greater New York Local took the first step in this direction by formulating a plan for immediate revolution and issuing a Manifesto around which all radical Socialists could gather. In the months that followed, other local Left Wing conventions were held, and by May

1919 there were approximately 30,000 Socialists who openly championed the Left Wing program. Most of these were members of the Lettish, Russian, Lithuanian, Polish, Ukranian, Hungarian, South Slavic, and Estonian federations. Said Nicholas Hourwich, successor to Bukharin and Trotsky as editor of the *Novy Mir*: "On one hand, to the left Socialist camp have gone those real revolutionary elements which . . . have not lost their proletarian banners. . . . On the other, to the right, were found those traitors to Socialism who have gone over to serve the bourgeoisie. . . ."[30]

The founding of the Third International in March with its radical Manifesto and its subsequent propaganda activities, served as a further stimulus to this Left Wing movement, and finally, unable to tolerate the actions of the Left Wing any longer, the National Executive Committee of the Socialist party suspended from the organization all those who adhered to the Left Wing philosophy. By this suspension in May 1919, the Executive Committee summarily lopped off about one third of the active party membership. Warned the New York *Call* (Socialist): "He who dreams of a 'dictatorship of the proletariat' in a single state of this country, to say nothing of the whole . . . invites all the powers of reaction and must eventually go underground."[31]

But members of the Left Wing were undaunted by either warnings or suspensions, and they called for a national convention of all revolutionary Socialists to meet in New York City on June 21. Ninety-four delegates, representing Socialist elements in twenty states, came to this meeting and rejected a proposal to form a new party immediately. The majority felt it would be best to make an all-out effort first to capture the Socialist party machinery at its national convention in Chicago in September. Before dissolving, this June meeting confirmed the principles of the Third International and wrote a new radical Manifesto: "The world is in crisis. Capitalism, the prevailing system of society is in process of disintegration and collapse. . . . Humanity can be saved from its last excesses only by the Communist Revolution."[32]

Meanwhile, the success of the Left Wing in rallying Socialists to its banner continued unabated. By the close of the summer, there were approximately 60,000 Socialists, a majority of the Socialist party, who identified themselves with Left Wing tenets. However, as so often happens with radical organizations, the unity of the Left Wing was suddenly impaired by the rise of internal factionalism. The foreign language federations, representing about 90 per cent of the Left Wing, began feuding with the native-born, English-speaking minority. The native element was charged with having garnered a disproportionate share of power and through it having illegally defeated the proposal at the June convention to form a new party.[33]

Since they had strongly backed the proposal to form a new party and were firmly convinced that they had been cheated at the June convention, the foreign language groups finally issued a call for all true revolutionary elements to meet in a separate convention in Chicago on September 1. The native-born group, meanwhile, held to the original plan to capture the Socialist party. Thus, by the late summer, the Left Wing itself was hopelessly split and, as the time drew near for the Socialist party's regular national convention, a bitter three-way struggle for power raged.

The national convention of the Socialist party convened in Chicago's Machinists Hall on August 30, two days ahead of schedule.[34] Although Eugene Debs pleaded for unity from his cell in Atlanta, under the circumstances that was impossible. Determined to make no compromise with Leftist elements, the Right Wing laid its plans carefully. As a result, those native-born Left Wing delegates who had decided at the June convention to capture the party machinery did not get the chance. They were forcibly ejected from the hall even before the business of the convention opened and the gathering proceeded with its affairs undisturbed by shoutings from the Left. Said Victor Berger, "We are the party, the others are just a lot of anarchists."[35]

Perceiving that it was no longer possible to capture the party mechanism, the ejected group brushed themselves off and made their way to a room in the same building where they immediately formed the Communist Labor party. In their Manifesto they declared the party was ". . . in full harmony with the revolutionary working class parties of all countries and stands by the principles stated by the Third International. . . . The Communist Labor Party proposes the organization of the workers as a class, the overthrow of capitalist rule and the conquest of political power by the workers. . . ."[36]

Led by John Reed, Benjamin Gitlow, and William B. Lloyd, this organization represented almost all the native-born elements of the Left Wing. The leaders illustrated the native background of the new party. John Reed was an American journalist of some note and a graduate of Harvard. Benjamin Gitlow earlier had been a member of the New York State Legislature. William Lloyd was the millionaire son of the famous Henry Demarest Lloyd. Such men were naturally suspicious of the alien-dominated language federations and, fearing that their own brand of native radicalism would be subverted by this foreign element, preferred to form their own party rather than lose themselves in the alien-inspired convention scheduled for September 1.

As previously agreed, this latter group met to form a new radical party. Dominated by Louis Fraina, Nicholas Hourwich, and Charles Ruthenberg, this convention proved so completely Bolshevik in its viewpoint that the delegates named the hall in which they met "Smolny Institute" after the Bolshevik Headquarters in Petrograd, and called the result of their labors simply the American Communist party. They completely divorced themselves from the psychology and problems of the American scene and wrote a program based solely upon the romantic aspects of the Bolshevik Revolution. The party's Manifesto, taken in large part from that of the Third International, declared: "The Communist Party is fundamentally a party of action. . . . The Communist Party shall keep in the foreground its consistent appeal for proletarian revolution, the overthrow of capitalism and the establishment of the dictatorship of the proletariat. . . ."[37]

The Socialist party was now left stripped of members. Accord-

ing to its own records, its numerical strength immediately following the formation of the two new Communist organizations fell
from 108,000 to roughly 30,000.[38] Those who remained were Right
Wingers who continued to emphasize the use of legal political
pressure to achieve Socialist goals. Led by Hillquit and Berger,
this group remained uncompromising in its opposition to the new
American Communists. Even Debs, while thoroughly deploring
the events of August 30–September 1, remained in the Socialist
ranks because he found the Communists' emphasis on violence too
much to stomach. In a time of "Reds," Debs proved himself only
"pink." [39]

The Socialist party was not alone in its despair. The IWW was
also visibly affected by the formation of the two Communist organizations. John Gambs in his authoritative *Decline of the IWW*
estimates that about 2000 Wobblies joined the new parties and
became active members. While this number seems niggardly
when compared with the losses sustained by the Socialists, it is
perhaps even more significant than the latter because the Wobbly
organization was already desperately weakened by the wartime
raids and among the 2000 who departed were many of the remaining leaders of the movement.[40] Earl Browder and James Cannon
both went over to the Communist side. Bill Shatov, another prominent Wobbly, also joined the Communists and later went to Russia where he became one of her greatest railroad builders. More
importantly, Bill Haywood himself switched to the Communists
after exclaiming, "Here is what we have been dreaming about;
here is the IWW all feathered out." [41] Indeed, so complete was his
conversion that he later left for Russia in order to observe bolshevism in action — and to escape his sentence under the Espionage Act.

Like the Socialist party, however, the IWW retained its own
identity in spite of Communist depredations. The remaining Wobblies, while sometimes evidencing much sympathy for the new
movement, continued to be deeply skeptical of the power to be
entrusted to the soviets in the event of an American Bolshevik

revolution. As an organization, therefore, the IWW proceeded on its former basis, constantly flirting with the principles of the Third International, but unwilling to surrender itself completely to the American Communist cause.

As for the Communist movement itself, it had about 70,000 members in 1919. The Communist Labor party, harboring most of the native-born English-speaking Communists, had a membership of 10,000. The Communist party, nine-tenths alien in its composition, had a total membership of approximately 60,000. On a ratio basis, the combined membership figures for both Communist parties represented less than one tenth of 1 per cent of the adult population of the country in 1919.[42]

It would be grossly inaccurate, however, to imply that the strength of the 1919 Communist movement can be represented adequately by the numbers mentioned above. Nor can the actual influence of the movement be confined to a list of statistics. Through their official organs, the *Voice of Labor* (CLP) and the *Communist* (CP), the two Communist organizations established contact with many people who were not members of either party. At the same time, other thousands of persons were reached through a large variety of Communist publications which, while having no official status, still rabidly preached the Communist doctrine. Indeed, shortly after the formation of the Communist parties no fewer than fifty domestic Bolshevik publications suddenly sprang into life, spreading the Communist philosophy in twenty-six different languages. Twenty-five of these publications circulated weekly in New York City alone.[43]

There were in addition many radical journals which, although not Communist per se, supported and propagandized the Communist program. In particular, the various publications of the anarchists and of certain small independent syndicalist groups sponsored a Bolshevik-type philosophy which was readily adaptable to Communist sale. According to Justice Department records, there were 471 radical newspapers or periodicals in the country in late 1919 advocating the violent overthrow of capitalism.[44]

Actually, these Justice Department figures are somewhat misleading because they include many publications which appeared only once or twice and therefore were more like circulars in nature than bona fide newspapers or periodicals. This still does not deny that there was great propaganda activity by the Communists and their sympathizers in 1919. Of course, such activity was in keeping with the desires of the Third International which supplied at least some of the money and brains for this purpose. It should be remembered that at no time in 1919 were the American Communists without guidance or moral support from overseas.

Since much of this literature was under Post Office ban and therefore appeared mysteriously in the folds of daily newspapers or was thrown from "el" trains in the early morning hours, it is impossible to judge accurately how many persons were reached or were affected by it. There is no doubt that in the poorer sections of the major cities, particularly where there were heavy concentrations of immigrants, the Communist line had considerable appeal. The same was true with respect to some groups of unskilled, unorganized workmen who had been abnormally affected by inflation or reconversion. Some, too, were virtually forced into an acceptance of the doctrine because of the intransigency of postwar employers. But generally, those who read such literature and reacted favorably were already decidedly radical either by background or interest and the credit for their conversion cannot be attributed to Communist propaganda alone.

This does not necessarily hold true with respect to the "parlor Reds" — a group which proved more controversial and more significant in the long run than any other. They surely represented a unique type. They were neither alien nor native-born professional revolutionists, nor could they be classified with the proletariat in any way. In the main, they were intellectuals or humanitarians — more often than not representing the wealthiest and most respected strata in society.

To explain human actions is at best a difficult matter; in the case of the "parlor Bolsheviki" it is doubly so. Why they supported the Communist cause often remains a complete mystery. Yet, some of them can be placed into rather loose categories. Some indulged in bolshevism because, being a new philosophy, it had a certain fascination about it and represented something novel to be explored. Such parlor Reds had a habit of making a fad of each new ism that came along, seeing in each one a new mental challenge or a panacea for all of society's ills. Some parlor Reds were simply middle-class idealists who had a profound and passionate dislike of even petty injustices. They found the inconsistencies of the capitalistic system theoretically unpalatable and, as a result, dabbled in communism because of its professed belief in justice for all and to each his due. Still other parlor Reds were reforming fanatics who possessed a type of religious fervor which permitted them to be overcome easily by the emotional appeal of the philosophy and the miserable plight of the poorer classes which it supposedly was designed to save.[45]

Even more remarkable were the wealthy followers of the movement. These were admittedly very few, but important because of their influence and economic power. Many in this category were wealthy widows who, wishing to use their wealth for the benefit of the masses, contributed heavily to the Communist cause foolishly believing that in this way their money would be put to a good use. On the other hand, some of these wealthy patrons contributed merely to be risqué and received a certain abnormal psychological satisfaction in associating with bona fide revolutionists and opponents of the existing order. According to Communist sources, such wealthy parlor reds more than once threw open their sumptuous Fifth Avenue or Park Avenue homes to secret revolutionary meetings.[46] In the main, however, most of these wealthy patrons were only indulging in a passing fancy and soon lost interest. Only a very few, like William Lloyd, were active party members.

Unfortunately, there are no accurate figures on the total number of individuals who, for whatever reason, aided or sympathized with the Communist cause in 1919. Some were indeed found in the schools, churches, labor unions, and most other institutions of American life. The indications are, however, that their number was not large. Perhaps the most accurate guess was made by Benjamin Gitlow, who in his *The Whole of Their Lives* stated that there were no more than a million domestic Communists and Communist sympathizers of all types in 1919.[47]

As a matter of fact it was still the 70,000 actual party members who constituted the real backbone of the movement. They were the ones who did the work and carried out the functions of the two Communist organizations. They printed the pamphlets, organized the cells, paid the dues. And, despite all the excited talk about the parlor reds, when the chips were on the table these 70,000 were the only ones who were prepared to practice fully what they preached.

Even so, it remains clear that the 70,000 members of the two Communist parties do not tell the whole story. And although the postwar trend of events, both domestically and internationally, tended to exaggerate the importance of the Communist menace, the nation's fears were not predicated entirely on mere figments of the imagination. There was some fire behind all the smoke.

4 ✱ ✱ ✱ ✱ ✱ ✱ ✱ ✱ ✱ ✱

The Road That Leads

Under normal conditions, the existence of a radical minority such as was present in the nation in 1919 would not have caused much public alarm. To be sure, such individuals would always have been recognized for what they were — potentially dangerous — but there would have been no real fear that they were about to take over the country.

As we have seen, however, conditions were anything but normal in 1919. Industrial unrest, political and moral irresponsibility, excessive intolerance, fear of opposition and change — these were but a few of the abnormalities that existed. Even so, it is highly doubtful that these aberrations could have prompted the ensuing hysteria had it not been for the aid of other causative factors which were also in operation. During 1919, there occurred a series of highly suspicious and spectacular events which so focused public attention on the issue of radicalism that all these contributing factors were ultimately welded together into a common mass from which emerged the public panic and paranoia known as the Red Scare.

Each of these incidents was particularly important because of its peculiar contribution in exaggerating the radical menace and increasing doubts concerning the essential soundness of the nation. One must admit that at a different time, or in a different background, most of these occurrences would not have elicited more than a passing response from the general public. But, occurring when they did, each of these events seemed to lay the foundations of fear for the next, and so on, until at last truly abnormal actions resulted.

[Admittedly, many of these events did contain some indication of radical activity and therefore they proved all the more conducive to the development of fear. But actually, it was not so much the existence of radical activity as the way this fact was reported which generated increasing alarm. Every conceivable technique and form of public expression and propaganda was brought into use to proclaim the existing danger. Every ambitious politician, overzealous veteran, antiunion employer, super-patriotic organizer, defender of white supremacy, and sensational journalist jumped into the fray, using the issue of radicalism as a whipping boy for their own special purposes. As a result, never before had the public mind been so atrociously assaulted — and never before was it so successfully unstrung.]

[The first of these incidents was the Seattle general strike.] American labor in late 1918 and early 1919 had already presented the nation with some cause for alarm, as we have noted. Organized labor had so intensified its insistence upon higher wages, shorter hours, and, particularly, the right of collective bargaining that industrial conflicts had become numerous. And as workers in many lines of activity walked off the job, the AFL attempted to anticipate any public suspicion by declaring that such action in no way reflected radical tendencies, but merely represented organized labor's traditional interest in protecting the legitimate rights of American workers. Samuel Gompers took great pains to attack all radical doctrines in the *American Federationist*, and insisted that American labor knew all about bolshevism and condemned it "completely, finally and for all time." [1]

In spite of such denunciations, a few guarded queries inevitably began to appear in the general press in early 1919 asking whether the strikes were actually "for wages or for bolshevism?" This was particularly true in the Pacific Northwest where IWW agitators had long been active and had capitalized most recently on the fact that wartime shipbuilding projects, especially in the Seattle area, had seriously dislocated normal industry and had caused housing shortages, extremely high prices, and general discontent. Although actually few in number, the Wobblies had proved both troublesome and noisy, and their wildcat strikes, Red flag parades, rabid speech-making, and violent propaganda had long since convinced West Coast newspapers that northwestern labor was not only insolent, but dangerously radical.[2]

In this background, 35,000 Seattle shipyard workers struck for higher wages and shorter hours on January 21, 1919. Since they had thus broken their contract with the Emergency Fleet Corporation which had two months yet to run, Director General Charles Piez flatly refused to discuss with them any matters relating to conditions of employment and ordered them back on the job. Ignoring his order, the workmen continued the strike while the Seattle press urged conciliation and pleaded for a peaceful settlement.

The evening after the shipyard strike began, the Seattle Central Labor Council, which represented all organized labor in the area, discussed the possibility of aiding the striking shipyard workers. This body was influenced to a large extent by its secretary, James A. Duncan, an aggressive labor leader who had risen to power amid the embittered industrial strife promoted throughout the Northwest by the IWW. While not technically a member of the IWW, Duncan was certainly eligible, for he was an outspoken opponent of the craft conservatism of the AFL and displayed great sympathy for Soviet Russia. Besides Duncan, there were at least twenty others on the Labor Council who were decidedly radical in their labor philosophy.[3]

Mainly at the insistence of these men, the council finally decided to conduct a general strike in Seattle as the best method of forcing a victory for the striking shipyard workers. In the desire to promote labor solidarity against the growing militancy of all northwestern employers, the various local AFL unions also accepted this idea, which, in itself, marked a serious departure from customary American labor tactics, and a General Strike Committee was immediately appointed and instructed to formulate plans. This committee, composed of delegates from 110 local unions and from the Central Labor Council, allowed real authority to rest in the hands of a small group of leaders, the so-called Committee of Fifteen. James Duncan was its leading member.[4]

At its first meeting on February 2, the Committee of Fifteen decided that a general strike should begin at 10 A.M. Thursday morning, February 6, at which time all union workmen were to leave their jobs and await further instructions. The next day, February 3, a general strike proclamation appeared in all Seattle newspapers.

The effect was electrifying. Seattle suddenly became the center of frenzied activity. Fearful of what the future portended, the public sought to protect itself against any emergency. Drugstores were deluged with buyers who wished to lay in a supply of essential pharmaceutical goods, while department stores and groceries were crowded with customers desiring to stock up on necessary clothing and food items. Evidently some citizens concentrated on articles of a less perishable quality since hardware store owners reported that they had more requests for guns than they could fill![5]

Perceiving this widespread public excitement, the Seattle *Union-Record* (spokesman for the Central Labor Council) promptly ran an editorial cautioning the public against hysteria and insisting that there was no cause for alarm. The labor paper claimed that the Strike Committee would feed the people, care for babies and the sick, preserve law and order, and run all industries necessary to the public health and welfare. Then, on a triumphant note, the editorial concluded, "We are undertaking the most tremendous move ever made by LABOR in this country. . . . We are starting on a road that leads — NO ONE KNOWS WHERE!"[6]

The ill-considered decision of the Labor Council for a general strike and certain subsequent rash statements by labor leaders and the labor press certainly did labor's cause little good. All the more convinced that Seattle labor was riddled with radicals and that the general strike was but the first step toward revolution, the city's press experienced a frenzy of excitement. From February 3 on, full-page appeals appeared in all daily newspapers begging the shipyard workers to return to work and thus forestall the threatened sympathy strike. The Seattle *Star* carried full-page editorials, captioned "STOP BEFORE IT'S TOO LATE," warning union men, "You are being urged to use a dangerous weapon — the general strike. . . . This is America — not Russia." [7] The Seattle *Post-Intelligencer* graphically described its sentiments on the situation by covering a large portion of its front page on February 6 with a cartoon entitled "Not in a Thousand Years," showing the Red banner flying above the Stars and Stripes.[8]

Despite such appeals and warnings, when February 6 came, 60,000 workmen in almost every line of endeavor struck. The economic life of the city was virtually paralyzed. Schools closed, streetcar service was discontinued, business ceased. Yet certain public services were maintained. Knowing full well that in the interest of public health and safety it could not allow a complete shutdown, the Committee of Fifteen granted exemptions to garbage trucks, laundry trucks, milk wagons, and the like. At no time during the strike was the city left without food, coal, water, heat, or light. Moreover, although an estimated 3500 Wobblies participated in the venture and radical literature appeared from time to time throughout the city urging revolution, there was no violence to mar the strike. It seemed that despite what some radicals may have had in mind, the rank and file of Seattle union labor wanted nothing more revolutionary than to force a victory for the shipyard workers and display labor's combined power in the Seattle area. Admittedly, their support of a general strike to achieve these goals was an extremely stupid mistake and can be explained only on the basis of a momentary lapse of common sense and an intense anger at northwestern employers for their intransigency. But labor's behavior throughout the strike was exemplary, not a single arrest

61

occurred, and all talk of the city being in the hands of lawless mobs was, in spite of the furor, completely unfounded.[9]

Nevertheless, the nonlabor portion of Seattle was badly frightened and quite naturally looked to the city's administration to do something. The mayor of Seattle was Ole Hanson. Born in Racine, Wisconsin, some forty-five years before, Hanson as a young man had dabbled in the law but, finding both Racine and law too prosaic for his spirited blood, had moved west in search of greater excitement and adventure. He had come into Seattle in 1902 atop a buckboard and in the ensuing years had been at one time or another a grocery store owner, a realtor, an advertising writer, and an investment broker. Politics, too, had commanded his interest and in 1908 he was elected to the Washington State Legislature. While there he was known as a friend to labor, for he sponsored much progressive labor legislation directed at eliminating labor unrest in the Pacific Northwest.

Defeated for the United States Senate in 1918, Hanson had then run for mayor of Seattle. Bearing a remarkable resemblance to the conventional Uncle Sam minus whiskers, Hanson made a hit with the voters and was elected without any definite party tag attached to him. Originally, he had been a Republican, later he had become a Progressive, and in 1916 he had supported Wilson. Indeed, when elected mayor, Hanson was considered so independent politically that conservative business interests undoubtedly would have opposed him except for the fact that his opponent was even less reliable in party attachment than he was. But even though political affiliation and party label meant little to him, Hanson certainly could not be condemned for a lack of patriotism. He had named three of his sons Theodore Roosevelt Hanson, William Taft Hanson, and Bob LaFollette Hanson![10]

Mayor Hanson had an intense hatred for the IWW. Even the most minor disturbance was, he felt, traceable to their activities. Mindful of the Wobbly phrase that "every strike is a small revolution and a dress rehearsal for the big one," he was automatically convinced that they were at the root of all labor unrest in the

Pacific Northwest. Thus, when the shipyard walkout occurred, he immediately declared it was not a strike at all, but a Wobbly plan to establish a soviet and start the flame of revolution in this country. His fears reached a crescendo when the general strike was called. There was little doubt in his mind that it signaled the beginning of an attempted revolution by scoundrels who "want to take possession of our American Government and try to duplicate the anarchy of Russia." There was also little doubt in his mind that the man who accepted this challenge might create a very promising future for himself.[11]

Hanson gladly accepted it. At his request, federal troops from Camp Lewis began to stream into Seattle in the gray dawn of February 6. With a huge American flag draped over the top of his car, the mayor personally led the soldiers into the city and directed their emplacement. On the following day, now convinced that his city was amply protected, he hurled defiance into the teeth of the Strike Committee by notifying them that unless they called off the strike by 8 A.M. the next morning he would use the troops to crush the strike and operate all the essential enterprises of the city. Then, in a proclamation to the citizens, the mayor personally guaranteed the city's safety by declaring that he had at his immediate disposal 1500 policemen and 1500 regular soldiers and that he could and would secure if necessary every soldier in the Northwest to protect life, business, and property. "The time has come," said Mayor Hanson, "for the people in Seattle to show their Americanism. . . . The anarchists in this community shall not rule its affairs."[12]

Seattle's nonlabor opinion promptly hailed the stand of the mayor. Convinced by their own fears and the grim warnings of the press that a full-fledged revolution was actually in progress, they found great solace in the mayor's words. Meanwhile, Seattle's newspapers continued their barrage of denunciation against the strikers and called for "NO COMPROMISE! No Compromise Now — Or Ever!"[13]

In reality, it was this hostile public opinion conditioned by a nagging fear of revolution, rather than the windy assertions of the mayor, which ultimately forced the Strike Committee to change its plans. Belatedly realizing that the general strike principle was foreign to traditional American labor tactics and that the public was justified in regarding it as a radical importation, the international unions applied increasing pressure on their locals in Seattle to withdraw their support from the venture. At the same time, the hierarchy of the AFL displayed a completely hostile attitude toward the Seattle experiment, fearing that labor's unorthodox action there might prove detrimental to the cause of organized labor everywhere. Indeed, the fact that Seattle organized labor had joined in the general strike movement at all disturbed conservative labor leaders no less than it disturbed the general public.[14]

In view of such conditions, it was obvious that the general strike could not possibly succeed. And realizing also that any prolongation of the scheme might ruin unionism in the city, the local AFL unions brought pressure to bear to stop the strike and quickly attempted to salvage what they could. On February 10 orders were issued for the general strike to cease.

It was a jubilant mayor who, on the morning of February 11, proclaimed, "The rebellion is quelled, the test came and was met by Seattle unflinchingly." The Seattle *Star* joyfully cried, "FULL STEAM AHEAD. . . . Today this Bolshevik-sired nightmare is at an end." The Seattle *Post-Intelligencer* covered its front page with a replica of the cartoon it had run just before the strike began, only this time the Red flag was in tatters and shreds while the Stars and Stripes were still waving proudly. "Our Flag Is Still There," the caption read.[15]

For almost a week the nation's eyes had been focused on Seattle. Caught in the tremendous excitement emanating from the general strike situation, the nation's press reprinted the exaggerated assertions of the Seattle newspapers and wildly elaborated on the indications of radicalism present. On the day the strike began, newspaper headlines throughout the country notified readers,

"REDS DIRECTING SEATTLE STRIKE — TO TEST CHANCE FOR REVOLUTION." Thereafter, editorials consistently blasted labor's action in Seattle and fed their subscribers on a constant diet of "The Seattle strike is Marxian," "a revolutionary movement aimed at existing government," and "the stepping stone to a bolshevized America." The Cleveland *Plain Dealer* claimed that in Seattle "the [Bolshevik] beast comes into the open," while the Chicago *Tribune* warned, "it is only a middling step from Petrograd to Seattle." [16]

Officialdom, meanwhile, added its weight to the mounting furor. Senator Knute Nelson of Minnesota maintained that the strike in Seattle posed a greater danger to the nation than the one faced during the war. Senator William H. King of Utah flatly declared that the instigators of the movement were confirmed Bolsheviki. "From Russia they came and to Russia they should be made to go," added Washington's Representative Albert Johnson. And although the AFL itself was currently denouncing the general strike as clearly violating the rules and regulations of the organization, various public officials went out of their way to warn the group to "go slow" and renounce its own selfish and unpatriotic designs! [17]

In the face of all such claims, Mayor Hanson's antistrike stand now acquired an even deeper significance. Despite the fact that the hostility of the AFL coupled with that of the general public was mainly responsible for ending the strike, and not Hanson, the nation preferred to believe he had slain the Goliath singlehanded. As a result, the country found itself saddled with a new hero — and no hero ever had a better press. Newspapers avidly described him as "The man of the hour," a "red-blooded patriot," and a man "with a backbone that would serve as a girder in a railroad bridge." Some journals expressed a willingness to run him as a candidate "for anything he wants," while others liberally quoted such homey "Oleisms" as this: "A man who wants a thing bad enough can get it." [18]

And what did Ole Hanson think of all this publicity? "I guess you've got to grab it when it comes along," he said. [19] Of course, to

65

liberals and radicals alike he remained "The Seattle Clown" and they later made much sport of the fact that a few months after the Seattle episode Hanson resigned as mayor to tour the country giving lectures on the dangers of domestic bolshevism — an activity which netted him $38,000 in seven months, while his salary as mayor of Seattle had been only $7500 a year.[20]

5 ★　★　★　★　★　★　★　★　★　★

Bombs, Riots, and More Bombs

IMPORTANT though it was, the issue of radicalism certainly had not been considered the most important problem facing the nation before the Seattle strike. To be sure, radical activity had created some public alarm both during and immediately following the war, but as yet there was no real fear that the nation was in imminent danger. What fears did exist in the public mind were mainly those which hung over from wartime emotionalism or grew out of a concern for the spread of Russian bolshevism in Europe and Asia. As for the American scene itself, radicalism was not yet the most crucial issue.

For this reason the Seattle general strike was particularly significant. For the first time, public attention was focused sharply and solely on the issue of domestic radicalism to the virtual exclusion of all other factors. At the same time a pattern of response and reaction was set in motion which would be standard for the rest of the Scare period. Labor was placed in the position of making some disastrous mistakes which constantly subjected it to public suspicion. Employers, in turn, were brought to the realization that the issue of radicalism could be helpful in their fight against unionism. To certain politicians it became obvious that radicalism would make an excellent political issue by which free publicity as well as votes could be obtained. The general press, meanwhile, found in the issue of radicalism an immediate substitute for waning wartime sensationalism and eagerly busied itself with reporting exaggerations instead of facts. Indeed, for the remainder of the Scare period the general press suffered a temporary lapse of accuracy and certainly did not fulfill its vaunted function in a democratic society of reporting the truth. Had it done so, the history of the period might have read differently.

But aside from these various consequences, the major fact remained that the Seattle strike had badly shaken the entire nation. Already beset by a lingering fear of radicalism, the public could well imagine that something had gone wrong in Seattle. Time would have convinced the nation otherwise; but unfortunately no lull followed in which a saner or more stable analysis of the situation could be made. Instead, throughout the late winter and early spring of 1919 the nation was not permitted to forget the great concern generated by the strike as the press, in particular, continued its exaggerated reporting. In fact, if one could believe the newspapers, where the Bolsheviki might next strike was becoming the most important question of the day.

Certain events both at home and abroad did logically keep alive some misgivings. On February 20, it was reported that Premier Clemenceau of France had been wounded by a "Bolshevik agent," and four days later, when Secret Service operatives arrested fourteen Wobblies in New York City, the fear was expressed that they, too, were involved in an alleged world-wide plot to kill Allied and American officials. In early March, much concern was voiced over the birth of the short-lived Communist regimes of Bavaria and Hungary, and dark warnings filled the press concerning Communist gains among the French and Italian populations. The formation of the Third International in March gave added weight to these indications of Communist activity and presaged even more trouble. The sequence of events did seem ominous: Russia, Bavaria, Hungary—Next?

Then came the bombs.

The word "radical" in 1919 automatically carried with it the implication of dynamite. Stereotyped in the public mind was an ever present picture of the "Red" with wild eyes, bushy, unkempt hair, and tattered clothes, holding a smoking bomb in his hands. Perhaps it was because a bomb so clearly represented the radical's reliance upon force and violence to achieve his goals that the public embraced such a concept.

There was some basis for the connection. In early February, at a time when deportation for alien radicals was being discussed, a few anarchist posters appeared in New England, declaring:

GO AHEAD

The senile fossils ruling the United States see red! . . . The storm is within and very soon will leap and crash and annihilate you in blood and fire. You have shown no pity to us! We will do likewise. . . . *We will dynamite you!* [1]

At the time no action along this line was forthcoming although a few subsequent bomb scares did arise. In early March, the Chicago *Tribune* quickened pulses by announcing that a radical plan for planting bombs in the Chicago area had been uncovered, but a veil of secrecy was allowed to shroud the entire affair and all the chief of police would say was, "The situation is a delicate one. Further than that I do not care to talk." The following month, the Department of Justice disclosed an alleged conspiracy by anarchists in Pittsburgh to seize the government arsenal and use the captured explosives to "lay the city in ruins." Shortly thereafter, it was tersely announced that eleven anarchists had been arrested in connection with this plot, but the rest of the incident was kept under a pall of mystery. [2]

Despite these early indications of the existence of bomb plots and dynamiters, it was not until April 28 that the final proof of their existence emerged. On that date, a small brown package arrived by mail at Mayor Ole Hanson's office in Seattle. Since Mayor Hanson was currently in Colorado on a Victory Loan tour, the package was left unopened on a table near his desk. However, the protective covering of the parcel had evidently been broken in transit and a fluid leaked out onto the table causing considerable damage. Upon examination, the liquid was found to be acid — the package contained a homemade bomb.

In view of radical hatred for the "Savior of Seattle," this discovery was not particularly shocking and, although the incident aroused indignation, it caused no great alarm. Hearing of it in Colorado, Hanson merely remarked, "If they have the courage why don't they attack me like men, instead of playing the part of cowardly assassins?" [3]

The Hanson bomb took on a much more serious character when, on the following day, a similar package was delivered to the home of a former senator, Thomas W. Hardwick of Atlanta. Unfortunately, this package was opened by the Hardwick's maid and in the resultant explosion she suffered the loss of both hands. Mrs. Hardwick, who was also present, was painfully burned about the head and face. Unlike the Hanson incident, there seemed to be no apparent reason why Senator Hardwick should have received such a package. Although earlier as chairman of the Senate Immigration Committee he had proposed stricter legislation to exclude alien agitators, he had never been rabid on the subject, and, in the words of the *Liberator*, was "about as near radical" as a senator could get. Hardwick, himself, could think of no reason why the bomb had been sent and wrote it off as just plain "cussedness." [4]

Two public officials in as many days had received bombs. That made headline news, and on April 30, Charles Kaplan, along with many other Americans, was reading about it as he rode the subway home from his job as a clerk in the parcel post division of the New York post office. As his eye caught the description of the packages sent to Hanson and Hardwick, he was struck with terror. Just three days before, he had laid aside sixteen such packages for insufficient postage. Hurrying back to the post office, he found them piled neatly where he had left them and immediately notified post office inspectors who in turn called the police.

Upon examination, these packages were found to be the same as those sent to Seattle and Atlanta. All were about seven inches long and three inches wide, containing a wooden tube filled with an acid detonator and a high explosive. All carried a Gimbel Brothers return address and were marked "NOVELTY — A SAMPLE." [5] Orders were immediately issued to all post offices to be on guard for similar packages and eighteen were subsequently intercepted which, added to the sixteen in New York and those already sent to Hardwick and Hanson, meant thirty-six individuals had been marked for death.[6]

The "Bomb Honor List" included such men as Frederic C. Howe (commissioner of immigration at Ellis Island); Anthony J. Caminetti (commissioner general of immigration); Senator Lee S. Overman (chairman of the Senate Bolshevik Investigation Committee); Oliver W. Holmes, Jr. (associate justice of the United States Supreme Court); Postmaster General Albert S. Burleson (who earlier had banned radical literature from the mails); Judge K. M. Landis (famous for his sentencing of Berger and Haywood); Senator William H. King (a bitter opponent of labor); Attorney General A. Mitchell Palmer; Secretary of Labor William B. Wilson; John D. Rockefeller; and J. P. Morgan.[7]

It is obvious from this list and from the timing of the mailings that whoever had sent the bombs hoped to rid the nation on or about May 1 (May Day) of government officials and important industrialists suspected of being intensely antiradical. Yet, as in the case of Senator Hardwick, the plotters had made some serious errors in judgment. Justice Holmes and Secretary of Labor Wilson were by no stretch of the imagination arch-conservatives, and Frederic Howe was considered by many to be much too liberal. But whatever went through the warped minds of those who conceived these crimes, it was fortunate that no one else was harmed. Mrs. Hardwick and her maid remained the only victims of the May Day bombs.

With blazing headlines, newspapers announced these startling events to a horrified public: "36 WERE MARKED AS VICTIMS BY BOMB CONSPIRATORS" and "REDS PLANNED MAY DAY MURDERS." Some newspapers, like the Chicago *Tribune,*

promptly gave the following advice in big heavy black type: "BE-
WARE BOX IF IT COMES THROUGH MAIL — Do Not Open It
— Call the police bomb squad." Ironically enough, such admoni-
tion helped business more than it saved lives since in the ensuing
weeks many a distraught citizen ruined perfectly legitimate packages by dousing them in water in the fear they contained hidden
explosives.[8]

Referring to the plotters as "dynamitards," and "human vermin,"
the general press clamored for immediate punitive action. Some
newspapers proposed that the nation summarily hang every bomb
thrower and bomb maker and deport every anarchist. Others
agreed that unless some such action was taken "we may as well
invite Lenin and Trotsky to come here and set up business at once."
Even certain church journals expressed deep alarm over the situation and advocated that "Every true lover of God and his country
should hit with an axe whenever and wherever appears this evil
head of anarchy."[9]

Congressmen and public officials exhibited similar concern. To
a man, they denounced the bomb plot as one of the most atrocious
crimes ever attempted in this country and demanded that suitable
action be taken. As might be expected, Mayor Ole Hanson was
particularly outspoken. Describing the government's attitude toward bomb throwers as "weak, vacillating, and changeable," he
cried, "I trust Washington will buck up and . . . hang or incar-
cerate for life all the anarchists." Then, in a burst of egotism, he
added, "If the Government doesn't clean them up I will."[10]

True, some persons and a few newspapers did not succumb to
this general alarm; unfortunately their voices were all but lost in
the din of the prevailing clamor. The Pittsburgh *Post* chided Hanson by saying that although these outrages offered a temptation to
resort to lynchings, that temptation should be zealously avoided.
Several other newspapers expressed the belief that the bomb plot
was the work of only one or two half-witted anarchists at the most,
and that to charge it to a well-organized Bolshevik plan was "to
convict ourselves of a mild form of hysteria."[11] Meanwhile, radical

and liberal journals remained quite convinced that the bombs were mere "plants" and were not the work of radicals or anarchists at all. The May Day bombs, said the *Liberator*, "were a frame-up by those who are interested in 'getting' the leaders of radicalism, and feel the need of a stronger public opinion before they can act." [12]

Working feverishly, police authorities tried to put an end to all such speculation by apprehending the perpetrators of the plot. The entire bomb squad of the New York City police, bomb experts of the city's fire department, police officials of other municipalities, private detectives, and federal agents combined their efforts in an attempt to find the culprits. Each day the public was told by their local press that these police officials had "good clues," were making "good progress," and at any moment expected to "run down the persons responsible for the outrage." But as time passed and no one was arrested, the press finally admitted that all attempts had failed.[13] Such an admission, in itself, strengthened the growing suspicion that the May Day bombs were the result not of an isolated plot but of a full-fledged radical conspiracy to overthrow the American government.

The May Day bombs had hardly become news before still other incidents occurred which further strengthened public fear of radical activity and offered further indications that there was an overall plan in operation to destroy the government. On May 1, the same day newspapers were astounding the reading public with reports of the bomb crimes, numerous riots arising from radical May Day celebrations broke out in several major American cities. Many bewildered citizens thought it more than accidental that such violent disturbances should coincide with the bombing attempts and with International Labor Day.

May Day had long been considered an international holiday for labor the world over. As a result, conservatives in nearly all countries had come to expect yearly disturbances by labor on that date. In general, however, the United States had been immune from such outbursts and had prided itself on the fact that unrest on May

Day was a Continental phenomenon which had no place on this side of the Atlantic. That was before May 1, 1919.

On that day, American radicals put on a colossal show. Using the reconsecration of their lives to international socialism as their central theme, they staged rallies, held mass meetings, and conducted Red flag parades. Of course, they quickly ran afoul of the police and incensed citizens who took exception to their activities and violent fighting usually followed.

In Boston, for example, a fierce disturbance arose over a Socialist Red flag parade sponsored by the Lettish Workmen's Association in which about 1500 persons participated. Since the paraders had no permit from the City Board of Street Commissioners to hold a parade, as was required by law, police officials immediately ordered the demonstration to stop. Defiantly, the group refused and, amid shouts of "To hell with the permit," marched on.

A riot promptly ensued between police officers, paraders, and heckling bystanders with the fighting centering around possession of the Red flags. In spite of increasing odds, the radical marchers held fast to their crimson banners while sticks and stones flew through the air, knives were brought into play, and a flurry of shots were exchanged. Three policemen and one civilian were wounded while another officer was mortally stabbed.

News of this event quickly spread to other parts of the city where other crowds soon gathered to harass any would-be marchers. When such were not in evidence they found other things to do. On Wenonah Street, one mob, finding too much time on its hands, set about demolishing the Boston Socialist headquarters. In other sections of the Boston area, angry citizens formed themselves into posses to capture stray Socialists or into vigilantes to protect life and property.[14]

Ultimately 116 paraders were arrested, charged with rioting and resisting the police, and placed in jail. Not a single non-Socialist was so charged. Later, fourteen of the marchers were found guilty of disturbing the peace and were sentenced by Judge A. F. Hayden to prison terms ranging from six to eighteen months.[15]

Boston papers quite naturally excoriated the Socialists, but made no similar condemnation of the equally indefensible actions of the non-Socialist rioters. Conversely, the radical press made no mention of the illegal activity of the Socialists, but charged that if the police had not "deliberately assaulted" the marchers there would have been no disturbance.[16]

Meanwhile, in New York City, as in Boston, riots occurred and numerous arrests were made as enraged citizens, soldiers, and sailors attempted to break up Socialist parades and raid Socialist meetings. Early on May Day, the Russian People's House at 133 East 15th Street was stormed by a group of soldiers who, after forcing their way in, compelled a Socialist gathering to sing the "Star-Spangled Banner" while they confiscated all the radical books and pamphlets they could find. Later, the new offices of the New York *Call* on Fourth Avenue were raided by about 400 soldiers, sailors, and civilians who broke up a reception (at which 700 people were present), confiscated books and literature, smashed office furniture, and finally drove the reception guests into the street with such violence that seventeen had to receive first aid for their injuries. The New York press seemingly condoned such ruthless action by its editorial silence, but the New York *Call* made its position clear. Calling the raids "orgies of brutality," this paper claimed the disturbances would not have occurred had not the police been "sympathetic" to the raiders.[17]

It was in Cleveland that May Day rioting reached its peak. The trouble here began as the result of a mammoth Red flag parade, led by Charles Ruthenberg, the famous Cleveland radical. Proceeding without incident to East 9th Street and Superior Avenue, this parade was suddenly halted by a group of Victory Loan workers and an Army lieutenant who demanded that a Socialist soldier, marching at the head of the column, drop his Red flag. When his demand was refused, the lieutenant tore the flag from the soldier's hands and violent rioting followed in which twenty Socialists were injured.

A similar situation developed in the Cleveland Public Square when another lieutenant attacked several Socialist soldiers who refused to take off their uniforms or surrender the Red flags they wore on their breasts. The resulting melee was so serious that Army trucks and a Victory Loan tank had to be used to drive wedges between the embattled rioters. According to the Cleveland press, the hero of the Public Square encounter was ex-marine John Keller who, although having lost an arm at Château-Thierry, used the other with such telling effect that "five radicals required treatment by ambulance surgeons."

Simultaneously, two other riots were gathering momentum; one in the shoppers' district on Euclid Avenue, and the other in front of the Socialist headquarters on Prospect Avenue. In the Euclid Avenue free-for-all, customers threw ink bottles, wearing apparel, shoes, and merchandise of all kinds at Socialist paraders, while over on Prospect Avenue the Socialist headquarters was raided and completely wrecked by soldiers and civilians who dumped typewriters, chairs, desks, and other office equipment into the street.[18]

As a result of all these disturbances, one person was killed and over forty were injured. The Cleveland police arrested 106 Socialists, most of whom were aliens, and charged them with the entire blame. No single antiradical, either civilian or soldier, found himself in the police line-up. The radical press immediately claimed that the May Day celebrants were martyrs. It contended that the onslaught had been instigated by the Loyal American League (local successor to the wartime Protective League) and had been financed by local capitalists with the police also being a party to the plan.[19] On the other hand, conservative sentiment placed the responsibility for the riots squarely on the shoulders of the Socialists, and the ruthless action of the anti-Socialists was upheld as having been necessary to show that "Cleveland recognizes but one flag. . . . It is the Stars and Stripes."[20]

Although other American cities also experienced some difficulty, Boston, Cleveland, and New York remained the foci of the May Day disturbances. Newspapers throughout the country concentrated on the riots in these metropolitan areas and offered editorial warnings that they might be "dress rehearsals" for an approaching Red revolution. Yet none of these papers seemed to grasp the fundamental fact that these so-called dress rehearsals had not been touched off by radicals, but by solid patriotic American citizens who supposedly championed law and order and abhorred violence. Ignoring the obvious, the press instead excitedly talked of the need for new laws to "curb bolshevism" and thus strengthen respect for law and order. Indeed, stirred by the Red threat which May Day seemed to reveal, most papers expressed the belief that "the time for tolerance is past," yet evidenced by their own attitudes that tolerance, in fact, did not exist. Even free speech was put on the auction block. "Free speech has been carried to the point where it is an unrestrained menace," said the Salt Lake *Tribune*, and from the shadow of the nation's Capitol came the voice of the Washington *Post*: "Silence the incendiary advocates of force. . . . Bring the law's hand down upon the violent and the inciter of violence. Do it Now." [21]

A few papers demonstrated that in spite of all the furor not everyone was as yet burdened by such an exaggerated fear of domestic radicalism that they were willing to advocate hasty action. The New Orleans *Times-Picayune* told its readers that comparatively little difficulty had arisen from the celebrations of International Labor Day in the United States, while the Seattle *Post-Intelligencer*, changing its tune slightly from its general strike days, declared that popular fears arising from the May Day Socialist parades were "ridiculous." The latter paper advocated allowing Red flaggers to parade unmolested; "Cracking heads is no argument," it concluded. [22] The Detroit *News* likewise advised that the public overlook such radical flag-waving and orating. Much of the May Day disturbance, said the *News*, was "but the resulting quakes and shivers and spasmodic reactions of a people just released from war." The radicals "will gradually quiet down and no heroic treatment is necessary," it added. [23]

Unfortunately for the cause of public stability, it soon appeared that certain radicals at least had little desire to "quiet down," for almost exactly a month after the May Day riots and bombs had first held the attention of a frightened and confused public, newspaper headlines again shouted, "BOMB THROWERS RENEW TERRORISM," and "TERROR REIGNS IN MANY CITIES." [24] On the evening of June 2, mysterious explosions occurred within the same hour in eight different cities, shattering both private and public buildings and killing two individuals.

Although this whole scheme was obviously a coordinated maneuver, there seemed to be even less logic to these crimes than to the bombing attempts of May 1. In Cleveland, the home of the mayor was dynamited. In Newtonville, Massachusetts, a state legislator's house was wrecked. The home of a silk manufacturer was bombed in Paterson, New Jersey. A bomb demolished the dwelling of a municipal judge in Boston. In New York City, an explosion occurred in the vestibule of a federal judge's residence, killing a night watchman who was passing by. In Pittsburgh, attempts were made to kill yet another federal judge as well as the city's police inspector. In Philadelphia, the home of a prominent jeweler was bombed, and at the same moment the Rectory of Our Lady of Victory was badly shattered.[25]

The most publicized and spectacular of all these events was the dynamiting of Attorney General A. Mitchell Palmer's house in Washington, D.C. Just as Palmer and his family had retired for the night, a terrific explosion demolished the front of his residence at 2132 R Street N.W. Windows in homes surrounding that of the attorney general's were blown in and startled neighbors rushed into the street to determine the cause. The assistant secretary of the navy, Franklin D. Roosevelt, who lived directly across the street from Palmer, assumed the responsibility for calling the police.[26]

Upon examination, it was discovered that the attorney general and his family were badly frightened but not harmed, and that the explosion had probably been premature. The bomb thrower evidently had stumbled on the stone steps leading up to the front door and had blown himself to bits with his own missile. Only fragments of his body and clothing were found, but enough to indicate that he was an Italian alien from Philadelphia. His crumpled hat bore a Philadelphia hatter's trademark, but the hatter in question could not remember to whom he had sold it.

Some other rather puzzling but fascinating sidelights shrouded the bomb thrower's identity. What resembled parts of two left legs were found at the scene of the explosion which gave rise in the press to the speculation that not one but two men had planted the bomb. As police authorities continued to insist that only one man was involved, the Washington *Evening Star* quipped that there was little wonder he stumbled and fell with such pedal equipment! [27] But regardless of his physical characteristics, there was little doubt that he was an anarchist. Near the door to Palmer's house was found a copy of an anarchist pamphlet entitled *Plain Words*: "There will have to be bloodshed; we will not dodge; there will have to be murder; we will kill . . . there will have to be destruction; we will destroy. . . . We are ready to do anything and everything to suppress the capitalist class. . . . THE ANARCHIST FIGHTERS" [28]

Naturally, the public and the press were all the more shocked and horrified by these new bombings. Although some few papers continued to remind their readers that bombs had been thrown before and that it was folly to imagine the planting of a few infernal machines was indicative of a powerful, well-organized revolutionary movement, the majority of the nation found little solace in this wisdom. Conditioned by the Seattle general strike and the May Day disturbances to suspect the worst, they assumed that the June 2 bombings were also part of an attempt at revolution and that at the root of the evil were the Bolsheviki. Attorney General Palmer buttressed such opinion by flatly declaring that the latest bombings were another attempt on the part of radical elements to rule the country. [29]

Radicals and the radical press again professed complete innocence. John Reed claimed that the bombs were planted by some reactionary who wanted to terrify the "ruling class" into destroying the radical labor movement in this country. Algernon Lee, director of the Rand School, declared that he also thought it was a "frame-up," while L. C. A. K. Martens assumed the role of the expert by remarking that the explosions were far too clumsy and ineffective to be the work of genuine dynamiters or anarchists. "The capitalist papers," concluded Max Eastman in his *Liberator*, "may shout 'Bolshevism' whenever an explosion occurs, but their shouting only strengthens the always plausible hypothesis that it was for the purpose of the shouting that the explosion occurred." [30]

Despite vigorous denials by the radicals, the responsibility for the June bombings as for the other perturbations in early 1919 remained on radical shoulders. The general public now seemed genuinely alarmed, and the majority of the press intensified its demands for vigorous repressive action by urging that "these gadflies . . . be swatted" and that there be "a few free treatments in the electric chair."

As a result, the machinery of the government began to move. In late June, Attorney General Palmer readied the Justice Department for a frontal assault on American radicalism by appointing William J. Flynn, former head of the Secret Service and one of the nation's most noted detectives, as chief of the department's Bureau of Investigation, and Francis P. Garvan, also a famous investigator, as assistant attorney general to correlate all work connected with ferreting out Reds. All the crime-hunting agencies of the government and of the nation were then placed at the department's disposal while radical halls were searched, members questioned, and a few arrests made. [31]

Congress, in turn, was also stung into action and began steps which it hoped would remedy the situation. Senator King of Utah prepared a bill making it a capital offense to transport bombs in interstate commerce or to belong to an organization favoring violent overthrow of the government. Senator Thomas J. Walsh of Montana, after reading aloud to his colleagues the pamphlet *Plain Words*, offered a peacetime sedition bill which proposed a $5000 fine or five years in prison, or both, for urging the overthrow of the

United States government, displaying in public or private the revolutionary symbols of international socialism, or distributing anarchistic literature through the mails. Other legislation of a similar nature was also proposed, especially after Attorney General Palmer told a Senate judiciary subcommittee that in his estimation the old wartime Espionage and Sedition acts could not technically be used to prevent radical activity because the nation was no longer engaged in hostilities. In the meantime, while committees were debating such matters, Congress passed a special appropriation of $500,000 for the Justice Department to carry on an extensive hunt for anarchists, bomb throwers, and enemies of law and order.[32]

While Congress and the Justice Department made these plans to curb the activities of bomb plotters and their kind, the combined police forces of the nation failed once again to trace the origin of a single bomb. As in the case of the May Day bombs, such failure lent credence to the charge that emissaries of organized world bolshevism had planned the explosions. Numerous newspapers such as the New York *Times* were piqued by the obvious lack of success and asked, "Has the gift of skill and genius in ferreting out criminals been denied to our present-day detectives?" To the *Liberator*, the answer was an easy one. "We believe," it asserted, "that the reason the perpetrators of these extensive and elaborate dynamitings have not been discovered is that some important person does not want to discover them."[33]

6 ★ ★ ★ ★ ★ ★ ★ ★ ★ ★

The Patriotic Defense

Beginning with the Seattle strike in February, the nation had experienced a bewildering array of spectacular and suspicious events. A general strike, bombs, riots, and more bombs had followed one another in rapid succession and not only had aroused intense public commotion but momentarily had relegated all else to the background. Naturally, the public had responded to these occurrences with increasing trepidation, for each one seemed to re-emphasize the danger of domestic radicalism. Indeed, each of these events had contained indications of radical action and, superficially at least, it did appear as if the nation were undergoing some sort of insidious attack.

[Yet, on the basis of the facts, there was no legitimate reason to suppose that radical activity was either extensive or well organized enough to pose a serious threat to the nation or convert any appreciable segment of the population to bolshevism. A more careful examination of the incidents themselves should have proved this point.] The Seattle general strike was basically a manifestation of postwar labor unrest and anger at the militancy of employers rather than a serious attempt at revolution. Regardless of the furor, the bombs were certainly not the result of a calculated plan to overthrow the government, but probably the work of isolated groups of terrorists who, inspired by the Russian experiment, insanely believed the unloosing of a few bombs would trigger such an upheaval here. Even the May Day riots, while displaying the

82

enthusiasm of domestic radicals for the principles of international socialism, were in no way "dress rehearsals" for revolution but rather the product of precipitous action by police and angry citizens who foolishly made martyrs of them rather than permitting them to rave and parade.

Nevertheless, through misreporting, exaggeration, misinterpretation of fact, and excessive claims and charges, what was a mere theoretical possibility of radical revolution gradually became in the minds of many a horrible reality. In fact, by the conclusion of the June bombings some citizens were prepared to believe almost anything.

It was this exaggeration which provided the matrix that held the developing Red Scare together. As already indicated, much of this came from the press because of its desire to maintain high reader interest. But also of importance were the statements and activities of prominent public officials such as Attorney General Palmer, Senators King and Thomas, and particularly Mayor Ole Hanson who, after the Seattle strike, persisted in writing articles and giving speeches which kept alive the memory of the attempted "Bolshevik revolution" in the Pacific Northwest. Moreover, the various assertions of a public hero like Billy Sunday, who reportedly described the Bolshevik as "a guy with a face like a porcupine and a breath that would scare a pole cat," did little to allay mounting public uneasiness. The great evangelist also said: "If I had my way, I'd fill the jails so full of them that their feet would stick out the windows. . . . Let them rule? We'll swim our horses in blood up to the bridles first." [1]

[In the main, however, the most flagrant overstatements and misinformation came from individuals and groups who willfully used the existence of radical activity to foster public support for their own personal postwar programs. In the long run, many of these groups actually convinced themselves that there was a danger of radical revolution, but to begin with their activities were disingenuous rather than sincere] Predisposed to overstate the danger because of the advantages they hoped to gain from resulting public fear, these groups pursued the issue of radicalism to its most ridiculous extremes and in so doing appealed more often to base emotions and prejudices than to intelligence. Some, desiring to maintain their wartime influence and prestige, continued the crusade for 100 per cent patriotism by arousing public feeling against the foreigner, the liberal, the independent, or any nonconformist through associating him with the radical movement. Some, hoping to retain white, Protestant supremacy, launched attacks on the Catholic, Jew, and Negro by insinuating they also were Bolsheviki. Others, longing to destroy the power of unions, buttressed their position by identifying union principles with Bolshevik tenets. Still others, wishing merely to destroy the reputation of those whom they hated, shouted the word "radical" at the slightest provocation.

Amply aided in this work by two governmental investigations, these various elements made absolutely no attempt to distinguish among democratic liberalism, evolutionary socialism, and revolutionary communism. Instead, they blindly labeled all persons who did not agree with them "Bolsheviki," and repeated their charges as often as possible. In that sense, they rapidly mastered the favorite technique of the demagogue or dictator — achieve by repetition and exaggeration what you cannot secure by the truth.

There existed in 1919 three organizations which were primarily interested in continuing the wartime drive for 100 per cent patriotism and which purposely intensified public fear of radicalism in order to reach that goal. The first of these was the National Security League, founded in 1914 by S. Stanwood Menken; the second was the American Defense Society, established in 1915 and headed by Elon H. Hooker; and the third was the National Civic Federation, which had originally been created in 1901 as a means of fostering greater cooperation between capital and labor but since the war had become little more than a patriotic society like the others.[2]

From the outset, these three organizations were rabid opponents of bolshevism. They advertised themselves as the public's agents in the crucial battle against Red radicalism and constantly called for "a new spirit of American patriotism" to meet the Communist challenge. They pledged their efforts to increase respect for constitutional government and, in their various fund drive appeals, urged loyal citizens to subscribe freely in order to save America by establishing an anti-Bolshevik patriotic defense.[3]

The active support which these patriotic societies received came mainly from other conservative pressure groups rather than from the general public. Specifically, their major contributions came from corporations and businessmen who saw in the patriotic crusade an opportunity to benefit the position of organized capital. The National Civic Federation had as its heaviest supporters V. Everit Macy, August Belmont, and Elbert H. Gary. The National Security League was supported largely by such men as T. Coleman DuPont, Henry C. Frick, J. P. Morgan, and John D. Rockefeller. In this respect, therefore, the real motives of the patriotic societies were not always the publicly declared ones since patriotism was definitely tied to the security of private property and more especially to the maintenance of economic conservatism. Indeed, most of the directors and officers of these societies were businessmen, which indicates a possible reason for the type of conservatism which they supported. All the patriotic organizations were hostile to organized labor and, except for the National Civic Federation which had a few trade unionists on its executive board, they were aggressively "open shop."[4]

The total membership of the patriotic societies in the postwar years was relatively small, never exceeding 25,000, but their propaganda activities were so extensive and well planned that they exerted far more influence than their memberships would indicate. Announcing that the "best antidote for Bolshevism is Americanism," these organizations thoroughly propagandized the American public on the virtues of 100 per cent patriotism and constantly warned of the dangers of domestic radicalism.

The National Security League sent extensive pamphlet literature to schoolteachers, clergymen, businessmen, and government officials, and prided itself on the fact that some of this propaganda found its way into every state in the union. Its pamphlets bore such interesting titles as "False Idealism," "Parlor Bolshevists," and "The Enemy within Our Gates," with the conclusion always reached that "when you hear a man tryin' to discredit Uncle Sam, that's Bolshevism." In every major city the league created a "Flying Squadron" of volunteer speakers to whip up public sentiment against radicalism, and by 1920 these "squadrons" had held 1000 meetings reaching an aggregate audience of 375,000 persons. In addition, the league founded Constitution Day (September 17) to commemorate the signing of the Constitution. For the first commemoration in 1919, it secured the cooperation of the governors of almost every state, the speaking services of such prominent men as Nicholas Murray Butler, Alton B. Parker, and Albert Bushnell Hart, and the wholehearted support of local chambers of commerce, the Boy Scouts, and the Sons and Daughters of the American Revolution.[5]

Except for the fact that its material was more rabid, the propaganda efforts of the American Defense Society followed much the same pattern. This organization established patriotic exercises in the schools, distributed thousands of copies of the Constitution, and furnished patriotic speakers to colleges, luncheon affairs, and fraternal meetings. It spread abroad the names of newspapers and periodicals, among them the *Nation, New Republic, Public,* and *Dial,* which loyal citizens were to boycott. It also circulated millions of propaganda leaflets which continually warned of the "hundreds of thousands of Reds" just waiting for an opportunity to overthrow the government. It offered to employers, free of charge, small pamphlets to be placed in workers' pay envelopes, pamphlets which violently denounced bolshevism. Perhaps the best indication of the basic conservative tendencies of this organization was the fact that it openly attacked the initiative, referendum, recall, and the income tax amendment as Bolshevik innovations![6]

The propaganda activities of the National Civic Federation, although not so extensive as those of either the National Security

League or the American Defense Society, were no less important. In the main, the organization's propaganda was disseminated through its magazine, the *National Civic Federation Review*. This journal, edited by Ralph Easley who had already become famous for his super-patriotism during the war, persistently invented fantastic conspiracies and imminent bloody revolutions, devoting much space to such emotionally charged articles as "My Days under the Bolshevist Reign of Terror" and "If Bolshevism Came to America." In the late spring of 1919, Easley ran a series of startling exposés on communism in the schools, press, churches, universities, and organized labor, and subsequently led a movement to scrutinize textbooks on history and political economy for breaches of loyalty. In connection with these activities, Easley always warned his readers of the dangers of public apathy and claimed that the only adequate defense against radical conspiracies was a dynamic patriotism.[7]

Easley's articles were particularly significant because of their widespread circulation. As a result of his close personal contact with both organized labor and capital, reprints of his writings appeared just as often in union journals as in business magazines. And although Easley was always quick to remind labor that many of the disloyal elements were within its own ranks, Samuel Gompers and other conservative AFL officials supported him in his patriotic crusade no less strongly than leading industrialists.[8]

[The effect of the propaganda of the patriotic societies was naturally forceful. But it was made even more forceful because in 1919 there were many other groups aiding in this antiradical crusade. Of these there were two in particular, the American Legion and the Ku Klux Klan, which, although not specifically patriotic societies, in many respects far surpassed them in the ability to promote public fear of radicalism and enforce 100 per cent loyalty.]

The American Legion was formally founded at St. Louis on May 8, 1919, by a group of delegates representing the veterans of World War I. Characterized by the Chicago *Tribune* as having plenty of "pep, punch, and democracy," this body of men bitterly upbraided all anarchists, Bolshevists, and Wobblies, and declared that one of the organization's primary goals was "To uphold and defend the Constitution of the United States of America; to maintain law and order; to foster and perpetuate a one hundred per cent Americanism." [9]

This intense spirit of patriotism was the cement which held the early Legion together. The majority of its members had already been instilled with a love of country by their Army experience and had been educated to view with suspicion all ideas or actions which seemed to compromise the prestige of the nation. Bolshevism, in particular, held an evil connotation for most veterans because of its connection with the Russian betrayal of the Allied cause at Brest-Litovsk.

The general press, which had been fearful that the American doughboy might come back from Europe tinged with the philosophy of bolshevism, hailed the antiradicalism of the newborn Legion in glowing terms. Newspapers agreed that the organization's opposition to bolshevism would be "one of the greatest forces for good this country has ever known," and that the Legion would "keep all postwar changes safe and sane." The San Francisco *Examiner* reflected this mood in a huge cartoon which portrayed the American Legion as a soldier, standing on the shores of the United States, holding a ball bat labeled "100 Per Cent Americanism," and yelling across the ocean to a long-haired Bolshevik, "Come on!" [10]

Supported by such favorable opinion, the Legion grew quickly. By the fall of 1919, its membership reached 650,000 and at the close of the year passed the one million mark. Meanwhile, a bill to incorporate the organization was introduced in Congress and was signed by the President on September 16. Two months later, in Minneapolis, the Legion held its first annual convention and at that time reiterated its hostility to radicalism and urged the immediate deportation of all individuals, whether citizens or aliens, who defamed the American way of life. Before the convention closed, the first commander, Franklin D'Olier, ordered the organization to be "ready for action at any time . . . against these extremists

"Come On!"
(Cartoonist Murphy in the San Francisco *Examiner*)

who are seeking to overturn a government . . . for which thousands of brave young Americans laid down their lives." [11]

The propaganda of the Legion, distributed to its many members and read by an untold number of others, was extremely outspoken on the matter of radicalism. The *American Legion Weekly* urged all Legionnaires to fight "Red autocracy" and give their communities constant antidotes for bolshevism by staging parades with plenty of American flags on display. The *Weekly* also featured a series of articles by Mayor Ole Hanson, who wildly magnified the extent of radical activity in the United States and underscored for Legionnaires the great danger facing the nation. In addition, the Legion's paper constantly pleaded for drastic government action in the form of jail sentences and deportations to wipe out the domestic Bolshevik menace and pledged the Legion's unfailing support for such action. [12]

Not content to wait on the government, overzealous Legionnaires sometimes took matters into their own hands. Although the Legion warned its members against violence and denounced the use of "vigilance committees," the very type of patriotic fervor which it sponsored gave rise to heightened emotions that inevitably led to rash acts. In some areas, Legionnaires assumed the responsibility of running all suspected radicals out of town after holding drumhead trials to ascertain their loyalty. In other areas Legionnaires tarred and feathered aliens who were thought to be a particular menace to the community. Indeed, everywhere in the country members of the Legion were inclined to take hasty action and brawled with Socialists whenever the opportunity arose. In Detroit, one local post prided itself on consisting of "one thousand Bolshevik bouncers," while in Denver, Legionnaires had a pact that they would reply with their fists to any malcontent who talked of revolution or anarchy. Under such circumstances, it was not strange that "Leave the Reds to the Legion" soon became a national cry. [13]

The Ku Klux Klan was a much more extreme and dangerous contributor to the patriotic crusade. The Legion organization, at least, had much to commend it and was basically sound in its principles although on the matter of radicalism it was certainly over-zealous. The Klan, on the other hand, was completely undemocratic both in structure and doctrine, and was insidious in all respects despite its many assertions to the contrary.

The modern Klan was established in 1915 by W. J. Simmons of Atlanta, Georgia. For four years it spread slowly, but in the turbulent postwar years of 1919–20 it reached gigantic proportions. To some of its members, the Klan with its Genii, Grand Dragons, Cyclops, and Furies meant excitement; to others it meant a fraternal home; but to almost all who belonged, it served as the repository for their pet fears and hatreds — the Catholic, "nigger," Jew, and foreigner.

Unlike the patriotic societies and the American Legion, the Klan was not primarily interested in attacking domestic radicalism per se, for its major interest lay not in politics or economics, but in the ethnological and cultural field. Nevertheless, in its drive against nonconformity in customs, religion, and race, the Klan also employed excessive charges of radicalism when such could be used to its advantage. Originally designed as a bulwark against anything that was contrary to "the fundamentals of the nation," the Klan was certainly suited to undertake a crusade against radicalism when it so desired. The organization's bible, the *Kloran*, abounded in expressions of 100 per cent patriotism, while one of the objects of the Klan as stated in its constitution was to "cultivate and promote patriotism toward our Civil Government . . . and conserve [the] ideals of a pure Americanism." [14]

In this respect, the Klan recommended the prominent display of the American flag in all public places and bitterly assailed the use of any foreign symbols. It denounced all aliens as "un-American" and "agents of Lenin," and, in areas of the country where such propaganda seemed feasible, it maintained that organized labor was merely the tool of "foreign agitators." The *Searchlight* and the *Fiery Cross* (neither being officially recognized by the Klan, but both speaking for it in an unofficial capacity), printed ridiculous exposés of the radicalism of all Jews and declared that they not only caused the revolution in Russia but would, unless stopped, also promote a similar revolution in the United States. These same papers charged that Negroes, too, had long since succumbed to bolshevism and that therefore drastic action was necessary in order to prevent the nation, particularly the South, from falling into their hands. Catholics, meanwhile, were condemned as being thoroughly "un-American" and extremely susceptible to radicalism because they already owed their allegiance to a foreign power! [15]

The role of the Klan in abetting the Red Scare must be equated with the fact that throughout 1919 the organization was still relatively small. In view of its subsequent phenomenal growth in 1920, it would seem that the Klan was as much a product of the Red Scare as an instigator. And yet, in those areas where the Klan was in operation in 1919, particularly in the southern states of Alabama, Mississippi, Georgia, and Texas, its claims concerning the radicalism of the Negro, Jew, Catholic, laborer, and foreigner carried considerable weight.

In the patriotic battle against domestic radicalism in 1919 there also existed various employer organizations whose anti-Red activities were of tremendous importance. Unlike the groups already mentioned, which attacked radicalism in American society as a whole, these organizations concentrated their efforts on radicalism in labor, specifically organized labor.

Rising public concern over bolshevism resulting from the bombs, riots, and the Seattle strike was made to order for the employer groups since it offered them an excellent opportunity to cripple American unionism by further emphasizing the radical menace and by identifying American labor with that menace. In so doing, they denounced organized labor's insistence upon the closed shop as "sovietism in disguise," while championing their own open-shop program as an inherent part of 100 per cent Americanism.

The major employer organizations interested in this drive were the National Metal Trades Association, the National Founders' Association, and the National Association of Manufacturers. Since the turn of the century these groups had been agitating for the acceptance of the open-shop principle, and now in the postwar year of 1919, they greatly intensified their campaign through their various publications, trade journals, and press releases. Working on the assumption that unionism and un-Americanism were synonymous, the employer groups harmonized their efforts with those of the patriotic societies, and, in that sense, depended heavily on the societies for the success of their own antiunion program. The connection between these groups was more than coincidental since many of the leaders of the employer organizations were also on the directing boards of the patriotic societies.[16]

The sentiments of these various antiunion groups were generally expressed through such outlets as the *Iron Trade Review*, the *Manufacturers' Record*, the *Open Shop Review*, and the many publications of the NAM. Of all these, the *Open Shop Review* was perhaps the most vociferous. This magazine variously charged that unionism "ranked with Bolshevism," represented a "surrender to Socialism," and was "the greatest crime left in the world." Moreover, it maintained that the Seattle general strike was caused solely by the closed-shop position of organized labor and that the AFL, itself, had the same fundamental characteristic as bolshevism — "disregard for the law." The conclusion always reached was that "unionism is nothing less than bolshevism," and that the same spirit which formed the soviets in Russia was also fomenting the closed-shop movement in this country. At the bottom of each page of every issue in 1919, the *Open Shop Review* took careful pains to remind its readers that there were at least 8,000,000 union men in the country who believed in the "insidious and radical" closed-shop principle.[17]

As this open-shop sentiment received wider support among the public and the general press, there inevitably was a growing suspicion that all of American organized labor was riddled with radicalism. Open-shop adherents eagerly seized upon every strike as an opportunity to prove that organized labor was really as radical as they claimed and that each striker was in reality an agent of Lenin. In the later months of 1919 when labor became even more aggressive and industrial turbulence grew, the influence of such propaganda upon the public mind bore bitter fruit.

While fears of radicalism were thus being intensified through the efforts of the patriotic societies, employer organizations, the Legion, and the Klan, two governmental investigations were held to determine the actual extent to which American society, and particularly American labor, was infected with bolshevism. The first of these inquiries was conducted by[the Overman Judiciary Subcommittee of the United States Senate and the second by the Lusk Committee of the New York State Legislature. In large measure both of these investigations were a direct result of the patriotic and antiunion sentiment which was so much in evidence in 1919, and their subsequent findings reflected that sentiment to a great degree. Instead of discovering the obvious fact that the radical menace was being badly exaggerated and that various interested groups were turning this fear of radicalism to their own special advantage, the investigators themselves succumbed to the emotionalism of the time and arrived at wholly erroneous and biased conclusions.]

The Overman investigation occurred first and had for its immediate background the sensational Seattle strike. On February 4, the day after the Seattle strike proclamation had been made public, the Senate unanimously passed a resolution to permit a judiciary subcommittee, already engaged in investigating German propaganda, to extend its investigation to Bolshevik propaganda as well. This action was taken not only because of the furor resulting from the Seattle situation, but also because of a radical meeting held two days before in the Poli Theater in Washington, D.C. At this meeting, Albert Rhys Williams, the chief speaker, had purportedly said, "America sooner or later is going to accept the Soviet Government, and when America discards some of the ideas current in the papers it will find it not so difficult to swallow." Already shocked by the apparent danger of Communist revolution in the Pacific Northwest, both Congress and the general public had recoiled at the idea of these doctrines being preached so near the fountainhead of American government. The press, in particular, had reacted violently and had demanded that domestic Bolshevik activity be investigated at once.[18]

The prompt action of the Senate in meeting this demand was immediately applauded and many newspapers expressed the hope that the Senate investigation would "turn inside out the cerebral convolutions of the missionaries of eternal smash." Not all papers, however, were convinced that this action was necessary, and some openly deplored the fact that one radical meeting in Washington could cause so much excitement. Cartoonist Fitzpatrick of the St. Louis *Post-Dispatch* lampooned the Senate's distress by portraying that august body as a gentleman half propped-up in bed, with the covers pulled up to his nose, his eyes bulging, and his hair standing on end. The caption read, "Trotsky'll Get You If You Don't Watch Out!" [19]

Composed of Senators Overman (chairman), King, Wolcott, Nelson, and Sterling, the committee began its hearings on February 11 (the same day that the Seattle general strike collapsed) and continued them to March 10. Its final report contained 1200 pages of testimony and evidence, but unfortunately did very little to show the extent of Communist propaganda in this country or its effect on American labor. Instead, the report represented merely another sensational exposé of Russian bolshevism and a complete denunciation of that system.[20]

During the course of the hearings, the committee received testimony from two dozen witnesses. Almost two thirds of these were violently anti-Bolshevik. They told the committee hair-raising tales of the Communist horror in Russia and impressed upon the senators' minds the dangers of such a system for the United States. These witnesses declared that the Red Army was composed mainly of criminals, that the Russian revolution had been conducted largely by former East-Side New York Jews, that bolshevism was the anti-Christ, and that a stronger policy of Allied intervention was necessary. Ambassador Francis reiterated before the commit-

Trotsky'll Get You If You Don't Watch Out!
(Cartoonist Fitzpatrick in the St. Louis *Post-Dispatch*)

tee his belief that Lenin was merely a tool of the Germans and further maintained that the Bolsheviki were killing everybody "who wears a white collar or who is educated and who is not a Bolshevik." Madame Katherine Breshkovskaya, a famous Russian anti-Bolshevik revolutionary, stated that in one year of Bolshevist rule twice as many Russian men, women, and children had been killed as soldiers at the front during the war. Other witnesses attested to the soviet decrees abolishing private ownership, confiscating land, nationalizing industry, and establishing "free love" bureaus.

Under the impact of these anti-Bolshevik assertions, those few witnesses who either were favorable to the system or even suggested a more tolerant attitude toward Soviet Russia had little chance to make their testimony sound convincing. It was not surprising, therefore, that at the close of the hearings the committee concluded that bolshevism was the greatest current danger facing the Republic. Mindful of the Seattle strike, the investigating senators thought it more than a coincidence that the Wobblies, Socialists, and Bolsheviki all used the Red flag symbol, and they were further convinced that some sort of Bolshevik revolution was impending. As a result, they recommended that more stringent sedition legislation be passed, that alien exclusion and deportation be rigidly enforced, and that patriotic propaganda to offset the Bolshevik doctrine be stimulated. "We must bring home to the people," said Senator Overman, "the truth that a compromise with Bolshevism is to barter away our inheritance." [21]

The general press reveled in the Senate investigation. Anti-Bolshevik testimony was played up in the columns of the nation's newspapers and once again the reading public was fed on highly colored tales of free love, nationalization of women, bloody massacres, and brutal atrocities. Stories were circulated that the victims of the Bolshevik madmen customarily had been roasted to death in furnaces, scalded with live steam, torn to pieces on racks, or hacked to bits with axes. Newspaper editors never tired of referring to the Russian Reds as "assassins and madmen," "human scum," "crime-mad," and "beasts." Russia was a place, some said, where maniacs stalked raving through the streets, and the populace fought with the dogs for carrion. Then, when the final report of the investigating committee was released, newspapers climaxed this sensational reporting with gigantic headlines: "RED PERIL HERE," "PLAN BLOODY REVOLUTION," and "WANT WASHINGTON GOVERNMENT OVERTURNED."[22]

Under such circumstances, the Overman investigation clearly supplemented the propaganda of employer groups and patriotic societies, and hence became a vital factor in the development of the Red Scare. Through the influence of sensational and widespread publicity, the Overman hearings further nourished public fears of labor radicalism born of the Seattle strike. More specifically, the investigation supported, if only by inference, the fear that foreign agitators were at work not only among American labor, but in American society as a whole.

The Overman inquiry served as the immediate forerunner to the even more famous and sensational Lusk investigation in New York. The immediate cause for this inquiry had sprung from a report made on radicalism in New York City by Archibald E. Stevenson, a prominent New York lawyer. Stevenson, sometimes described as "the only man in the country" whom the radicals really feared, had concluded in his report that bolshevism was rampant among New York workmen and had urged that strong remedial action be taken. This demand had gathered support from the Union League Club of New York and increasing pressure had been applied on the New York State Legislature for a complete investigation.[23]

On March 26, the legislature approved the creation of a committee "to investigate the scope, tendencies, and ramifications of . . . seditious activities and report the result of its investigations to the Legislature." Thirty thousand dollars was appropriated for the project and Senator Clayton R. Lusk was named to head the committee. Subsequently, State Attorney General Charles D. Newton was appointed chief counsel, and Archibald Stevenson was given the position of assistant counsel. The inquiry was slated to begin in New York City on July 1, but under the impact of the May and June bombing outrages, Senator Lusk decided that the investigation should start as soon as possible and set June 12 as the date of the first meeting.[24]

The investigation began amid much excitement. On June 12, while the Lusk Committee sat closeted in City Hall, twenty agents of the Justice Department and ten members of the state police conducted a daylight raid on the offices of the Russian Soviet Bureau in the World Tower Building. L. C. A. K. Martens was served with a subpoena and was whisked off to City Hall for questioning by the committee. In addition, the Soviet Bureau's offices were relieved of two tons of Russian propaganda, which was carted away in trucks and placed at the disposal of the Lusk investigators. Largely the brain-child of Counselor Stevenson, this whole maneuver was sponsored by the Lusk Committee as the best available means of securing the evidence necessary to continue its investigations.

Although the raid was given nation-wide publicity (the Los Angeles *Times* carrying an eight-column headline, "NEW YORK OFFICES OF THE RUSSIAN SOVIET GOVERNMENT ARE RAIDED"), there was little editorial comment forthcoming about the event. What little did appear was, in the main, quite cautious about the venture and expressed the hope that the Soviet Bureau raid had been undertaken with the proper authority. Yet only the liberal and radical press seemed unduly upset by the unorthodox procedure. These journals carried highly emotional accounts of the way in which the raid had been conducted, declaring that the police had rushed into the bureau's offices, pounced upon the unsuspecting occupants, cut telephone lines, and destroyed much valuable material. The New York *Call* blasted the raiders as "Black Cossacks," and Martens, who was detained only briefly by the committee and then released, asserted that his arrest was "an outrage and an uncalled for insult to the people of Russia." [25]

In view of both skepticism and open criticism of the raid, the Lusk Committee took great pains to show the public that the move had been necessary and that it had achieved remarkable success. Immediately after the raid, Senator Lusk declared that the materials seized indicated there were at least fifty radical publications in New York City alone, which he estimated were spreading the Bolshevik doctrine to at least 500,000 adherents weekly. He further claimed that the evidence proved L. C. A. K. Martens was the "American Lenin" and that huge funds had been placed at his disposal to launch an American revolution. Meanwhile, Attorney General Newton stated that the Soviet Bureau was the "clearing house" for all radical activity in the United States and that its first job was to secure the bolshevizing of American labor. Both Lusk and Newton concluded that there was a Bolshevik revolution in the making.[26]

There was just enough truth in these charges to make the Lusk investigation now appear rather important, and with the first sign of public support, the Lusk group delivered its second blow on domestic radicalism on June 21. On that date raids were conducted on the Rand School, the headquarters of the Left Wing Socialists, and the local offices of the IWW. Between two and three o'clock in the afternoon state police in plain clothes surrounded these New York City establishments, and, armed with search warrants, made a thorough search of the premises. In general, the raids were orderly, no violence occurred, and no one was arrested. Only radical literature, documents, and mailing lists were seized and were forwarded directly to the Lusk Committee. When asked by the press what the purpose of these raids was, Senator Lusk replied, "Names! — Names of all parlor bolsheviki, IWW, and socialists. They will be a real help to us later on." [27]

The raid on the headquarters of the Left Wing Socialists was somewhat disappointing. Only a few men playing cards were present when the raiders burst in, and, when a search warrant was produced, a janitor detached himself from the card players and peaceably conducted the searchers throughout every part of the premises. Despite later assertions of the Lusk Committee, little of value was found.

Likewise, the raid on the local IWW proved unproductive. Certainly there were no indications that a radical revolution was about to occur; the IWW rooms were virtually vacant when the police arrived. However, those few Wobblies who were present suffered such a severe shock when the police walked in that two, in the crazed fear that they would be arrested and tortured by the dreaded "cossacks," attempted to throw themselves out the window and had to be forceably restrained.[28]

The raid on the Rand School was by far the largest and most significant. This school had been founded in 1906 by Carrie Rand, an old-time abolitionist. It had gradually developed into a full-fledged Socialist and labor college whose methods were the same as those of any other institution of higher learning except that it offered ". . . opportunities for the general public to study Socialism and related subjects, [and gave] Socialists such systematic instruction and training as may render them more efficient workers in and for the Socialist Party, the Trade Unions and the Co-operatives."[29] Aside from the fact its owner, the American Socialist Society, had been convicted under the Espionage Act for publishing Scott Nearing's *Great Madness*, the school had never come into conflict with the law. In 1919 its enrollment was about 6000.[30]

It was against this establishment that Senator Lusk sent the majority of his raiders on June 21. Fifty men under the direction of Stevenson swooped down on the school and, much to their surprise, were peaceably admitted by its director, Algernon Lee. As a result, the search was executed in a most orderly fashion, classes were not even disrupted, and persons were allowed to come and go as they chose. The only incident to mar this tranquillity came when Lee refused to open a large safe which contained some Socialist funds, mailing lists, and other party material. Although Stevenson became disagreeably insistent, Lee remained adamant on the ground that the contents of the safe were not covered by the search warrant. It was not until two days later that the Luskers, armed with a new warrant, secured admission to the inside of the safe and received the materials they wanted.[31]

Largely on the basis of the documents seized in this undertaking, the Lusk Committee now filled the press with the most astounding revelations. Senator Lusk claimed the materials showed that radicals were in control of at least 100 trade unions and that the Rand School was cooperating with L. C. A. K. Martens and the Soviet Bureau to bring about a complete bolshevizing of American labor. Stevenson, meanwhile, told the press that the seized documents indicated radicals were also operating through the Rand School to propagandize the Negro. He claimed they planned to subsidize Negro orators, exaggerate all acts of injustice to the race, and establish radical Negro newspapers. On the basis of these alleged discoveries, both Stevenson and Senator Lusk declared that the Rand School was the actual headquarters for American Bolshevik radicals who were endeavoring to foment a revolution.[32]

These charges were almost completely without foundation; yet, frightened by its own wild assertions and believing that the time for decisive action had come, the Lusk group took steps to close this radical "haven of refuge." It filed suit to have the Rand School's charter revoked, and Governor Alfred E. Smith quickly appointed an extraordinary trial term of the State Supreme Court "for the purpose of investigating acts of criminal anarchy" arising from the Lusk disclosures.

But throughout July, the case to annul the school's charter was continually postponed while the Lusk investigators mustered their evidence. This delay, in itself, illustrated how few real facts the Lusk Committee had uncovered despite its many claims to the contrary. Finally, on July 30, when the Lusk Committee again announced it was not yet prepared to go on with the case, Supreme Court Justice John V. McAvoy threw the entire proceedings out of court.[33]

Unfortunately the collapse of the Rand School case did not mark a corresponding decline in the influence or highhanded tactics of the Lusk Committee, nor did it presage a diminution in the rigorous campaign of employer groups, patriotic societies, the Klan, and the Legion. By the summer of 1919 their antiradical crusade was in full swing and could not be stopped. Already some citizens had been taken in by their various claims and charges. But many more were soon to follow, for when subsequent events in the late summer and fall of 1919 gave the alleged discoveries of the Lusk Committee and the charges of the other groups an increasing appearance of validity, even the most cautious and levelheaded citizen paused and wondered.[34]

This, after all, represented the real significance of the patriotic defense against radicalism. While its avowed enemy was bolshevism, its ultimate victim was the general public. Herein also lies the tragedy. The patriotic defense could have served a noble purpose; certainly it was not wrong to desire the erection of a patriotic bulwark against such a pernicious doctrine as bolshevism represented. But, blinded primarily by self-interest, the super-patriots of 1919 did not realize that true patriotism cannot be maintained or inculcated by emotionally charged phrases or pledges of allegiance. Patriotism stems not from a set of forms or even from a state of mind, but from a way of life. And if that way of life commands the respect of its citizens because of the opportunities and the freedoms present, then patriotism follows as a matter of course. In emphasizing only the forms and slogans and ignoring completely the possibility of making life for the average person fuller and more meaningful, the patriotic groups missed their best opportunity to create a really formidable patriotic defense.

As it was, the defense they built was merely an illusory one. It was illusory because it was based on prejudice, hatred, and emotion, rather than on intelligence, truth, and confidence. It spawned fear, suspicion, and intolerance; it created distrust, mutual conflict, and division. It pitted Protestant against Catholic, Catholic against Jew, white against Negro, union laborer against nonunion laborer, veteran against nonveteran, neighbor against neighbor. As a result, in actual practice it was the ally of bolshevism, not its enemy. If, indeed, there was a serious threat of radical revolution in 1919, the nation escaped disaster not because of the patriotic defense but in spite of it. In the long run, it protected the nation against nothing except sane thinking, for through its activities the foundations for hysteria certainly had been well laid.

7 ★ ★ ★ ★ ★ ★ ★ ★ ★ ★

Labor and Bolshevism

IN ANY careful analysis of a social phenomenon like hysteria, one always finds in operation a tangled mass of deep-seated causative factors which interact to produce the ultimate manifestation of aberrant response.

This was certainly true in the case of the United States following World War I. As we have seen, by mid-1919 there were a host of factors in existence which were establishing the conditions necessary for the development of national psychoneurosis. The contemporary postwar scene with its war-born emotionalism, its misguided desire for normalcy, and its political and economic instability represented one such factor. The rise of Russian bolshevism, the affinity of domestic radicals for the Bolshevik doctrine, the Seattle strike, the riots, and the bombs constituted still others. Also significant were the various investigations, the sensationalism of the press, and the activities of certain politicians, employers, veterans, and super-patriots.

However, in probing into the causes for hysteria, one also is likely to discover one factor which more than any other acts as the trigger mechanism that throws the whole complex reaction of stimulus and response into operation. By mid-1919 there was one such factor in the American scene which did act as the prime mover because upon it the "scare" effectiveness of the other factors was largely dependent and by it the average American squared his thinking on the seriousness of the radical menace.

It involved the position of organized labor.

★ Red Scare

Because of such incidents as the Seattle strike and the growing success of antiunion propaganda, by mid-1919 much of the concern over domestic radicalism centered around organized labor. It was generally agreed that if domestic radicalism would succeed at all it would succeed first within the ranks of the laboring man; hence the activities of labor were watched carefully as a barometer to the real extent of radicalism in the nation. Public stability, in turn, depended in large measure upon the results of such observations, for as long as the public retained confidence in the fidelity of labor there was scant opportunity for hysteria to emerge.

Organized labor tried from the beginning to entrench itself in the public mind as one of the nation's chief bulwarks against the philosophy of bolshevism. This should not have been difficult to do. The AFL was avowedly a nonrevolutionary organization; indeed, led by Samuel Gompers and organized generally along craft lines, it was highly conservative. Its patriotism during the war had been unexcelled and its wartime cooperation with both government and industry had been unusually consistent. This is not to say that the AFL was apathetic to the workers' cause. On the contrary, it had constantly fought for higher wages, shorter hours, and union recognition, and in order to secure such gains had often used the weapon of the strike. Nevertheless, the AFL had always worked within the framework of the existing economic order and was a firm supporter of the capitalistic system. This fact had already prompted many of those who desired more aggressive action on behalf of the working class to remain outside the AFL and adhere to such other organizations as the IWW. As far as the basic conservatism of the American worker was concerned, one need only recall that while the IWW had 60,000 members at its peak, the AFL had more than 4,000,000.

In spite of later charges, basic conservatism was still the trademark of the AFL in the Red Scare era. As a matter of fact, the organization had already evidenced this when, in June 1918, it announced that although it would continue its crusade in the postwar period for the workers' right to organize and bargain collectively with employers for an adequate living wage and shorter hours of work, it would do so only within the existing fabric of the free enterprise system and without any overtones of radicalism whatsoever.[1] Obviously, a labor organization could not possibly have adopted a more inoffensive postwar program, and it was upon this basis that the historic struggle between American capital and labor was renewed.

It was true that there were a few within the ranks of organized labor in 1919 who did not share the AFL's interest in conservative action. Impressed by the recent Bolshevik Revolution in Russia, they either sympathized with the new Bolshevik philosophy or openly championed it. This was particularly the case with certain members of the various city labor councils and with recent immigrants to this country who had since made their way into the numerous unions of the AFL. Such persons believed that the AFL was moving too slowly and that the announcement of 1918 was not indicative of what the workers really wanted. James Duncan of the Seattle Central Labor Council was an example of those who entertained such beliefs.[2]

Besides these individuals, there were also some unions in 1919 which were out of sympathy with the AFL's conservative policies. Organizations such as the Amalgamated Clothing Workers, Amalgamated Textile Workers, Needle Trades International, and International Ladies' Garment Workers either refused to affiliate with the AFL because of its conservatism, or although belonging to the organization, openly opposed its postwar program. Within such unions there were indications that pro-Bolshevik radicals exerted some influence.[3]

Having already displayed an uncompromising attitude toward the Bolshevik doctrine, conservative AFL officials watched these indications of labor radicalism with growing apprehension and took immediate steps to combat it. The reasons for their resultant antiradical campaign were twofold. First of all, in view of widespread antiunion propaganda, AFL officials desired to remove from organized labor all possible taint of "bolshevism"; secondly, being conservatives themselves, they had a natural distrust and hatred for all radical labor theory.

Leading the attack was Samuel Gompers, who constantly attempted to keep union labor conservative and prevent deviations from the AFL's postwar program. Supported in this fight by other labor leaders, such as Daniel J. Tobin, Timothy Healey, Matthew Woll, and John L. Lewis, Gompers was especially caustic in his denunciation of Bolshevik sympathizers and most outspoken in his warnings to union men. Through his close relationship with Ralph Easley, Gompers drew heavily upon the propaganda of the National Civic Federation to help him in this antiradical campaign. In fact, the AFL willingly joined the super-patriotic crusade!

It is certainly ironical that at a time when antiunion elements were already meeting with some success in identifying unionism with bolshevism, organized labor cooperated with them in digging its own grave. Union journals were just as quick as employer magazines to attach any unorthodox labor procedure, such as the general strike, to the Communist philosophy, and they bitterly attacked all such innovations as "monuments of folly" and "revolutionary provoking instruments." Along with this scathing criticism, these labor journals also warned union members of the danger of "borers from within" and called upon all local unions to purge these individuals from their membership rolls immediately. The *American Federationist* and the *United Mine Workers' Journal* consistently cautioned union workers against those within the movement who wanted to plunge labor into "a sea of turmoil, hatred, and possible bloodshed." [4]

In making this attack on labor radicalism, union officials and magazines were always careful to emphasize the fact that organized labor as a whole was uninfected. There can be little doubt that most such assurances were designed specifically to offset the growing antiunion propaganda of employers. The *American Federationist*, in particular, had this as its primary goal. The magazine reiterated time and again that despite what some people said, the American trade union movement could never be "sidetracked or befogged by economic theories," and although the nation might experience some labor unrest, it would never be based on the demand for a "dictatorship of the proletariat." "American labor is loyal and true," said the journal, "and can not be swerved . . . by any such impracticable and puerile visions as are entertained by the bolshevists of Russia or of any other land." To further buttress its argument, the *American Federationist* spoke of the "Safety of Trade Unionism" and claimed that organized labor was America's chief barrier against bolshevism because workers within the trade unions were immune to that doctrine.[5]

During 1919 there were many indications that what organized labor claimed for itself was essentially true. Radicals themselves attested to the conservative tendencies of the AFL by frequently referring to the organization as the "American Fakirization of Labor" and characterizing its leaders as "traitors to the workers' cause." Moreover, many pro-Bolshevik radicals, who earlier had hoped to "bore from within," had come to realize what a difficult job it was and by the summer of 1919 had dropped out of the AFL altogether. As a further testimony to the unshakable conservatism of the organization and its leaders, no less than Lenin, himself, remarked that the AFL had to be discounted as a factor in the American radical movement. Gompers, said Lenin, was merely an "agent of the bourgeoisie."[6]

Perhaps an even better indication of the organization's conservatism was its annual convention of 1919. Convening on June 13 at Atlantic City, this gathering was permeated with an antiradical spirit from the start and indicated by its deliberations that it held no brief for Communist ideas. On the question of recommending the recognition of Soviet Russia, the delegates voted against it in no uncertain terms. The convention also refused to sanction the adoption of certain resolutions which asked for the removal of American troops from Siberia. Moreover, the assembly voted against AFL participation in a proposed general strike for Thomas Mooney, a labor radical convicted for the famous 1916 San Francisco Preparedness Day bombing. Finally, the convention reiterated the AFL's opposition to the "one big union" concept, advocated more stringent immigration laws, and overwhelmingly re-elected Samuel Gompers as president.[7]

Before the convention adjourned, however, it tempered this prevailing conservatism somewhat by espousing a few liberal ideas which, although offering no consolation to radicals, subsequently caused consternation in conservative quarters. The assembly urged the repeal of the wartime Espionage and Sedition acts and the shortening of the terms of certain political prisoners. It also unanimously adopted a resolution which stated that "the power of our courts to declare legislation enacted unconstitutional and void is a most flagrant usurpation of power and authority." In addition, over the protests of conservative leaders, the delegates endorsed the controversial Plumb Plan for government ownership of the railroads and put the convention on record as favoring the "use of every legitimate endeavor to promote the enactment of this plan into law."[8]

Nevertheless, the action of the convention as a whole was so clearly an indication of organized labor's conservatism that it could not escape general notice. Most newspapers hailed the work of the convention by contending that "reason rules American labor" and "the conservatism of American labor is a fact, not a theory." The *Literary Digest* proclaimed that organized labor had "set its face firmly against . . . a revolutionary policy," and, indeed, even the most die-hard radicals now openly admitted they saw little hope for their doctrines within the AFL. John Reed curtly described the assembly as "The Convention of the Dead," while Max Eastman declared Gomper's success in getting the delegates to adhere so closely to his policies marked the climax to "a brilliant career in the misguidance of labor."[9]

Strangely enough, at the very moment when much of the press was praising organized labor for its conservative position, some journals were claiming that union labor was actually in the hands of unscrupulous men whose "principles stand on all-fours with those of Lenin and Trotsky." [10] The reason for this contradiction does not readily appear unless the other phase of organized labor's activities in 1919 is understood. It must be remembered that while the AFL was interested in combating radicalism, it was equally interested in securing new gains from employers and its action along this line was just as aggressive.

The 1918 pronouncement of the AFL had already set forth organized labor's postwar desire for new concessions from capital and in February 1919 the *American Federationist* reiterated this position by declaring that workers had the "right to associate and organize into trade unions and to endeavor collectively to attain that economic independence essential to their welfare." A short time later, Samuel Gompers issued an open warning that labor did not intend to lose the advantages it had won during the Progressive Era and the war. "If any employer believes that industrial autocracy is going to prevail in America," he declared, "he is counting without his Host." [11]

Running headlong into the obstinacy of employers, particularly on the matter of collective bargaining, organized labor quickly girded itself for battle. Despite the unfortunate consequences attendant upon the Seattle strike in February, organized labor now relied heavily on the strike weapon, although not the general strike, to bolster its position. Resulting industrial disturbance was nothing short of phenomenal. The strike picture appeared as follows: in March there were 175 strikes; in April, 248; May, 388; June, 303; July, 360; and August, 373. The extent of this unrest was not concentrated in any special areas but was nation-wide. Woolen operatives struck in Passaic, New Jersey, in March; telephone operators in New England in April; carpenters in Columbus, Ohio, and machinists in Toledo in May; workers in the building trades of Dallas in June; Atlantic coast marine workers and Chicago street railwaymen in July; tobacco workers in Philadelphia and Allentown also in July; and silk workers in Paterson in August. In New York City alone, 20,000 harbor workers struck in March, 50,000 cloak and suit makers in May, 25,000 shirt makers and 40,000 tobacco workers in July, and 14,000 painters and 15,000 streetcar men in August.

The average number of days involved in each of these strikes was thirty-four, although a few strikes lasted more than a hundred. Actually, the total number of strikes was less than in comparable periods of 1916 and 1917, but the total number of workers involved in 1919 was much greater. As a result, there was also a much greater loss in workdays, in profits, and in wages. However, there was less loss of life in the turbulence of 1919 than in any previous comparable period of labor unrest in the nation's history.[12]

Although a few of the strikes were "illegal" and appeared to contain some evidences of radical influence, the vast majority were supported by the AFL and centered solely around the demand for higher wages, shorter hours, and collective bargaining. In many of these strikes the workers won concessions on either higher wages or shorter hours, or both, but only rarely did they succeed in securing the right of collective bargaining.[13] Employers were adamant in their stand on the latter demand, bitterly opposing it in the fear that "recognition means closing."

Though it was true that most of the strikes were orthodox and not radical in any way, the amount of unrest coupled with increasing antiunion propaganda made the public uneasy and re-emphasized the suspicions which had arisen during the ill-fated Seattle venture. Constant assurances by the AFL concerning labor's fidelity managed for a time to hold the line and "revolution hunters" had a rather difficult job in convincing anyone but themselves that any immediate danger existed. But unfortunately for the cause of organized labor one strike which occurred in May was made to order for those who were attempting to prove that labor was dangerously radical. Though not involving American labor per se, this struggle had serious repercussions on the domestic labor scene and constituted one of the gravest indications that growing antiunion charges might be true.

Just fifteen days after the May Day riots and bombs had electrified the nation, the Winnipeg Trades and Labor Council called a general strike in sympathy with the striking workers of the metal and building trades of that Canadian city. As 30,000 workers left their jobs, postal and telegraphic communication, fire and sanitary protection, transportation, and industrial production were either directly suspended or seriously curtailed. The city government ultimately fell into the hands of a strike committee which established press censorship and allowed the resumption of police and fire protection only upon its authority. A preponderance of evidence indicates that the policy of this committee was set largely by syndicalists who had hopes for radical changes in the existing economic order and employed "one big union" tactics in order to achieve that goal.[14]

Winnipeg was dominated by this strike committee for more than two weeks before the legal city council regained its lost power, and it was not until June 20 that the general strike movement collapsed. Although proponents of the strike labeled all ensuing charges of revolution as "sheer unadulterated moonshine," Canadian authorities remained convinced that the strike had been a Bolshevik experiment and, indeed, was but a continuation of the affair in Seattle. In fact, it was freely stated in the Canadian press that radical leaders, failing in Seattle, had come to Canada to try their luck and that the strike in Winnipeg had been financed and led by radical labor groups from the United States. Although this was simply not the case, in the record time of one hour the Canadian Parliament passed an emergency measure on June 6 to permit the immediate deportation of the miscreants to the United States should they be apprehended.[15]

In the United States, meanwhile, the Winnipeg incident was reported in a most sensational manner. Eight-column headlines announced to a shocked public the events taking place there, and wide circulation was given exaggerated Canadian press releases which described babies suffering from lack of milk and the city's inhabitants living in filth because of the suspension of sanitation services.

Naturally, the whole affair was bitterly denounced. American newspapers called the venture "Russian sickness" and a "Bolshevist interim." Most other agents of public expression readily admitted that the Winnipeg struggle was radicalism at its worst. Labor journals, in particular, vehemently criticized the action of Winnipeg labor. The *United Mine Workers' Journal* called the "one big union" concept, which underlay the strike, the "One Big Failure," and Samuel Gompers in the *American Federationist* labeled the Winnipeg affair "evil," "ill-advised," and "a complete fiasco." [16]

In spite of American labor's rabid denunciations of the Winnipeg incident, the damage had been done, and suspicious eyes once again turned in organized labor's direction. It is understandable why some citizens by mid-summer 1919 held a highly suspicious attitude concerning the aims of organized labor. It is equally understandable how such suspicions could be held in spite of labor's professed conservatism and its antiradical crusade. Constantly open to attack because of its insistence upon labor's rights, organized labor found its support waning as antiunion conservatives made the most of labor's peculiar dilemma. And at a time when general strikes, riots, and bombs were much in evidence it was easy for the enemies of unionism to connect industrial unrest with radicalism and thus cover the whole organized labor movement with the Communist label.

The Winnipeg strike was only the first, and least important, of three major factors operating in the summer of 1919 which helped to crystallize attitudes on the position of organized labor and undermine public faith in its essential soundness. The other two were organized labor's relationship to the proposed nation-wide general strike for Thomas Mooney, and labor's insistence on the Plumb Plan for government ownership of the nation's railroads.

Throughout the spring of 1919, plans for a nation-wide strike had been discussed by radicals and various liberal labor groups as a protest against the allegedly unjust conviction of Mooney, a radical labor agitator who along with Warren K. Billings had been arrested in July 1916 and sentenced to death for a bomb explosion during a San Francisco Preparedness Day parade in which nine persons were killed and forty wounded. With their sentences later commuted to life imprisonment and because of lingering doubts concerning even their guilt, these two men, particularly Mooney, had become a symbol of the working class's fight for equal justice. Radicals especially had embraced Mooney's cause, and it was felt that a general strike, more than any other action, might force his early release.

Pressure had been applied on the AFL for its aid in conducting this strike, but from the beginning that organization expressed antipathy to the scheme. Conservative AFL officials had refused to sanction any consideration of the general strike action, and, in April, the *American Federationist* illustrated this sentiment by denouncing the whole project.[17] At its convention in Atlantic City in June, the position of the AFL was further clarified by the defeat of the general strike resolution and the organization thereafter officially washed its hands of the entire matter.

The defeat of this proposal, however, indicated only the sentiment of the central organization, not that of the individual unions. Under the rules, the Federation had no power either to call or to forestall a strike of its member unions and hence the latter were still free to handle the Mooney situation in any way they chose. As a result, there was some doubt as to what the separate unions would do, especially since there was considerable sympathy for Mooney among their members.

The Mooney general strike had been set for July 4 and for weeks prior to Independence Day newspapers and conservative labor journals cautioned workers against any participation in this folly. As the day drew nearer and radical agitation for the general strike increased, their appeals became all the more insistent. The public press, meanwhile, burdened its readers with wild stories about the horrible event to come, with the result that the public became greatly alarmed. Having already experienced two general strikes, the public could easily believe a new and more terrible one was on the way. Furthermore, since it had but recently witnessed two horrifying bomb plots, the public could also imagine that the

July 4 strike would probably be accompanied by renewed attacks on property and life. A reflection of the rising fear appeared in newspaper headlines: "REIGN OF TERROR PLANNED," "STOLEN EXPLOSIVES TO BE USED," and "PLANS FOR WIDESPREAD VIOLENCE AND MURDER." [18]

As a result of these unsubstantiated warnings, many citizens and public officials actually became so terrified that they frantically prepared for the July 4 onslaught. In New York City, 11,000 police and detectives were kept on twenty-four-hour duty, guarding all federal, state, city, and county buildings, as well as the Stock Exchange and the homes of prominent men. Hundreds of private citizens were sworn in as special deputies and all meetings of an emotional nature were suspended for the day. Indeed, so great was the fear of the city's authorities that they even refused the use of Carnegie Hall to the American Defense Society because its proposed Independence Day rally might incite both radicals and patriotic partisans to lawlessness. [19]

The pattern was essentially the same in other American cities. In Chicago, two companies of the Fourteenth Infantry were brought into the city to forestall possible trouble, and the entire police force plus 1000 volunteers were placed on the alert. In Boston, thirty armed soldiers were stationed at the Federal Building. In Philadelphia the streets were literally "filled with policemen." In San Francisco, special precautions were taken in view of the city's connection with the Preparedness Day bombing and the Mooney trial, and in Oakland known Reds were arrested and incarcerated for the day as an "insurance device." Meanwhile, in the Pacific Northwest whole areas were alerted against threatened Wobbly uprisings and federal agents were stationed there to meet any emergency which might arise. [20]

What happened was anticlimactic. Independence Day came and went. Nowhere in the nation was there any undue disturbance. Liberal labor elements and radicals remained quiet and let the Eagle scream. The Mooney general strike with its attendant bombings and bloodshed simply failed to materialize. Even in the two areas of the country where one might have expected some disorder, none was forthcoming. In both Seattle and San Francisco the day passed quietly except for the usual sound of exploding fireworks.

Blushingly, most newspapers tossed off the fact that nothing had happened with the claim that widespread precautionary measures had prevented outbreaks. But a few journals were frankly skeptical. These implied that the whole sensational situation might have been built up by conservative interests for its calculated effect on the public mind. Said the *Christian Register*: "The preponderance of evidence leads to the conclusion that the predictions of an organized assault upon American institutions on the occasion of the anniversary of American independence had been considerably overemphasized in an attempt to impress public opinion with the gravity of an ultimate danger." [21]

Since no general strike occurred, public confidence in the conservatism of American workers should have been quickly restored. But the mere possibility of the general strike had given antilabor elements such an excellent opportunity to lodge their propaganda more firmly in the public mind that suspicion of labor actually increased. Furthermore, the sensationalism of the press in promoting the July 4 scare so heightened antiradical emotions that the adverse effect on public faith in the fidelity of labor did not quickly disappear.

This situation was further worsened by the fact that organized labor was currently championing the controversial Plumb proposal for government ownership of the nation's railroads. This plan, drafted by Glenn R. Plumb, a counsel for the Railroad Brotherhoods, first received wide attention in February 1919. It called for the purchase of the railroads by the United States government, the establishment of an operating corporation of fifteen men (five representing the public, five management, and five labor), and the division of the profits between the government and managerial and classified employees. [22] The four Railroad Brotherhoods had immediately endorsed this plan, as did all others who, on principle, desired government displacement of private control. And while the liberal press hailed such action by claiming that the railroad unions had "stuck in their thumbs and pulled out a Plumb," the conservative press branded the scheme "'Plumb' Bolshevistic." [23]

Throughout the spring of 1919, the Railroad Brotherhoods vigorously defended the proposal while conservatives continued to take pot shots at the program. Plumb wrote and spoke in behalf of his project and strongly urged all labor to support it. By the summer of 1919, the proponents of the plan claimed it had at least three million supporters and a Plumb Plan League was formed to elicit even more support. The primary objective, of course, was to secure the backing of the AFL and considerable pressure was brought to bear on that organization. Conservative AFL officials were not sure they wanted to associate with the project and Samuel Gompers openly opposed it. But favorable sentiment among organized labor in general proved too much for AFL leaders, and at its June convention, as we have seen, the AFL endorsed the scheme. Of all the decisions made by the convention, this one seemed to many conservatives to be the most onerous. "Better things were to have been expected of the American Federation of Labor," complained the *Wall Street Journal*.[24]

In the meantime, Congress itself was wrestling with the knotty railroad problem. It seemed only logical that the government, which had seized the railroads during the war, should return them once again to their private owners. There was considerable hostility even in Congress against the railroad companies because of their previous mishandling of the lines. However, even though many congressmen insisted that certain public safeguards be established before the return of the railroads, few subscribed to the Plumb Plan. Indeed, many members thought the plan "might well have been formulated by a Lenin or a Trotsky," and some simply called it "a bold, bald, naked attempt to sovietize the railroads of this country." [25]

Despite such opposition, the Plumb movement snowballed, and, on August 2, a bill embodying the plan was formally introduced in Congress by Representative Thetus W. Sims of Tennessee. The Railroad Brotherhoods backed this action and made it increasingly clear they would fight with everything at their disposal to prevent the return of the railroads to private ownership. They immediately asked their members to contribute $2,500,000 for a Plumb Plan sinking fund and announced they would elect a "Plumb Plan Congress" if necessary. According to Plumb, there were roughly eight million workmen in August 1919 who were fighting for his plan and he warned that unless his proposal or something like it was adopted, there might be serious trouble. Other spokesmen for public ownership darkly prophesied that even if the roads were returned to their owners, "they wouldn't stay there very long." [26]

But by this time conservative and antiunion elements had fully mustered their forces and through their own publications and their chief ally, the general press, unleashed a murderous counterattack. The railroad companies themselves undertook a vigorous advertising campaign against the plan, calling it the first step along the road to bolshevism. Employer and business magazines urged the nation to resist firmly such a "revolutionary proposal." Editorials appearing in the public press echoed these assertions and further suggested that the principle might next be applied to banks, natural resources, and public utilities. Meanwhile, the very opposition which conservative AFL officials displayed toward the whole project served to accent these charges. [27]

By the close of the summer, organized labor was definitely on the defensive with respect to charges of "bolshevism." Despite its many endeavors to prove that American labor was basically antiradical, its own actions in some respects seemed to contradict its protestations. By continuing its relentless crusade against employers and by underwriting such proposals as the Plumb Plan, labor created situations which worked seriously to its disadvantage. The large body of sentiment which had hailed organized labor's conservatism at the time of the AFL convention rapidly disappeared as antiunion groups met with increased success in their attempt to connect organized labor's postwar program with the radical philosophy of bolshevism.

This decline in public confidence could not have come at a more unfortunate time since labor was just then in the process of intensifying its drive against organized capital for higher wages, shorter hours, and the right of collective bargaining. It undoubtedly would have been wiser for labor leaders to have kept rein on their unions and bided their time until a later date. Their success might have been better; at least it could have been no worse. Under the circumstances it is difficult to see how labor could have expected much public support for its undertakings and it was a mistake for labor leaders not to have realized it.

At the same time, there were also other factors working against labor's chances for success. In September, in connection with the birth of the two Communist parties, many radicals who heretofore had remained aloof from the trade union movement now reversed their position and began to assume a more direct interest in organized labor's affairs. Under the guidance of the two Communist factions, these radicals, along with the radical press, began to identify themselves with organized labor's efforts to wring concessions from employers. Indeed, the Communists championed all the the major fall strikes no less vigorously than if such struggles had been their own in the hope that they might turn them to good advantage. Said the Communist party Manifesto: "Strikes of protest develop into general political strikes and then into revolutionary mass action for the conquest of the power of the State. . . . The Communist Party shall participate in mass strikes, not only to achieve the immediate purposes of the strike, but to develop the revolutionary implications. . . ." [28]

Although such radicals still bitterly opposed the conservatism, leaders, and structural arrangement of the AFL, the fact that they now openly supported organized labor's strike actions made the public even less receptive to labor's insistent claims concerning its fidelity. Quite naturally, antiunion groups seized this new opportunity to undermine still further public support for union labor.

Meanwhile, constant warnings by conservative labor leaders to "pay no attention to agitators who are now trying to disrupt our splendid movement," were taken as additional proof that radicalism, and not justifiable demands, was to blame for much of the labor unrest.

Thus, having attempted from the beginning to run with the hounds on the issue of domestic radicalism, by the fall of 1919 organized labor found itself identified with the hare instead. Its position had become increasingly precarious as the disappearance of public confidence made even the wildest antiunion charges seem believable. In fact, by the fall of 1919 all strikes, regardless of their nature, had come to be considered "crimes against society," "conspiracies against the government," and "plots to establish communism."

★ ★ ★ ★ ★ ★ ★ ★ ★ ★

When Policemen Strike

THE fall of 1919 was a particularly dreary season. The nation was blanketed in an unusual amount of fog and excessive rainfall made life generally uncomfortable in many areas. The normally beautiful New England landscape was limp from repeated drenchings, while local newspapers in the habitually dry Midwest complained of excessive precipitation and predicted it augured a long, cold winter.

This dampness, however, did not seem to deaden the public fear of domestic radicalism which had been growing steadily since the Seattle strike of some months before, nor did it render less volatile the explosive struggle in the making between capital and labor. If anything, the miserable weather tended to fray nerves a little more and make tempers even shorter. In fact, in the long run the climate of public opinion proved to be even uglier than the weather.

It was under these foreboding conditions that three of the most spectacular labor disturbances in modern American history occurred. As an aid in promoting the Red Scare their significance can scarcely be overstated. Each of these strikes greatly augmented the growing charges of labor radicalism which were so common by the late summer of 1919, and each was especially instrumental in crystallizing public sentiment on the alleged Communist danger. All three of these disputes were widely and sensationally reported and all three indicated how drastically and rapidly public confidence in organized labor had declined.

The first was the Boston police strike.

The Boston police strike had been brewing for some time. Throughout 1919, Boston police had become increasingly disgruntled with their low salaries, long hours, and poor working conditions. On numerous occasions, they had requested some relief from the city administration and in May, the city had made a slight gesture in their direction by granting them a $200 yearly increase and raising the annual salary maximum to $1600. Even so, the Boston policemen remained woefully underpaid, and their demands for shorter hours and better working conditions were ignored.[1]

As a result the Boston police considered the possibility of more direct action. In June, the local policemen's organization, known as the Boston Social Club, tentatively laid plans for affiliation with the AFL. It was hoped that this action would elicit organized labor's support for the Boston policemen and specifically enable the Social Club to intensify its efforts in their behalf.

This certainly was not a novel development. Police had already been unionized in numerous American cities without any great outburst of public opposition or feeling. But now, because of rising fear of labor radicalism, the Boston police met bitter hostility — many persons believed that police unions in particular might become powerful weapons in the hands of radical labor leaders.[2]

Championing this latter viewpoint was Boston's police commissioner and former mayor Edwin U. Curtis who as early as 1895, while serving as one of Boston's youngest mayors, had displayed an unfriendly attitude toward labor unionism. A conservative lawyer-banker, he now bridled at the prospect of having to deal with a police union and, upon hearing of the policemen's plans, issued a general order which declared that "a police officer cannot consistently belong to a union and perform his sworn duty." Subsequent orders were then issued by the commissioner's office which specifically prohibited Boston policemen from joining any group composed of members of the force which affiliated with a larger organization outside the department unless it was a post of the Grand Army of the Republic, United Spanish War Veterans, or the American Legion.[3]

The Boston police remained undaunted. Agitation for affiliation with the AFL increased, and, on August 1, officials of the Boston Social Club announced that in spite of the commissioner's orders they were going ahead with their original plans. Ten days later they formally asked the AFL for a local charter, and on August 15, such a charter was granted. In the meantime, the Central Labor Union of Boston passed resolutions pledging to the police "every atom of support that organized labor can bring to bear in their behalf." [4]

Seeing his authority so boldly challenged, Commissioner Curtis acted with dispatch. On August 26, he tried nineteen leaders of the new union for violation of his orders, found them guilty, but gave them suspended sentences. Meanwhile, because of a curious arrangement whereby the commissioner of police and the mayor both had concurrent jurisdiction over the city's police, Mayor Andrew J. Peters appointed a Citizen's Committee, headed by James J. Storrow, to find a permanent solution for the police union problem. After due deliberation, this commission decided that although the policemen should not affiliate with the AFL, no objection could be had to their "forming their own independent and unaffiliated organization."

This decision of the mayor's committee was flatly rejected by Curtis who refused to consider not only police association with the AFL, but also any type of police unionism. His stand on this matter was firmly supported by the major Boston newspapers which declared that if the policemen made unionism the price of peace, the city would have none of it. All the more convinced that his position was sound, Commissioner Curtis on September 8 suddenly revoked the suspended sentences of the nineteen union leaders and summarily removed them from the force. [5]

The Irish tempers of the Boston policemen seethed. They quickly held a caucus and by a vote of 1134 to 2 agreed to walk off the job at evening roll call, 5:45 P.M., Tuesday, September 9. The reasons they gave for undertaking such a drastic move were these: to lodge a strong protest against Curtis for the arbitrary manner in which he had acted, to compel the return of the nineteen suspended leaders to the force, and to cause the city administration to recognize the Social Club's right to affiliate with the AFL.[6]

The Boston press now surrendered itself to sensationalism. It begged the policemen not to leave the city defenseless and spoke of the dire consequences if they should. Also, despite the fact there was nothing to indicate the Boston police were subject to any radical influence, all major Boston newspapers immediately labeled the strike decision "Bolshevistic," and warned that the venture was foredoomed to failure because "behind Boston in this skirmish with Bolshevism stands Massachusetts, and behind Massachusetts stands America." The Boston *Herald*, in particular, lamented the fact that bolshevism should thus evidence itself in the very city which had cradled American democracy and had given the American Revolution birth.[7]

In view of these assertions and the threatened absence of the policemen, the public frantically took steps to protect itself. Private citizens quickly established means for safeguarding their own lives and property, and banks and businesses organized security guards from among their employees. At the same time, the recruiting of a volunteer police force was begun by certain farsighted civic leaders. Even Harvard contributed its fair share to this force when President Abbott L. Lowell assured any student who wanted to volunteer that his marks would not suffer should he be required for police duty. Besides these "vacationing" students, there was also a considerable number of ex-soldiers and Legionnaires who offered their services.[8]

City officials, meanwhile, did very little to meet the walkout threat. They made almost no preparations and hence all the precautions taken remained of a purely unofficial and amateur character. Commissioner Curtis later claimed that he really had not expected the police to strike and therefore did not see the need for any elaborate defense preparations. This does not explain, however, why on the very eve of the strike he was quoted as saying, "I am ready for anything." [9]

Neither the commissioner nor anyone else was prepared for what happened. When, on September 9, 1117 of the city's 1544 police left their posts, the meager precautions which had been taken proved wholly inadequate. On that evening shortly after dark, little bands of hoodlums gathered, and, noticing the absence of bluecoats, began removing spare tires from parked automobiles and knocking off the hats of innocent pedestrians. In one instance, a trolley car was stopped, stoned by an unruly group of rowdies, and the passengers forcibly ejected. Later, in the downtown district, other lawless elements smashed windows, took the goods on display, overturned fruit stands, and defiantly held dice games on the Boston Common. Other small groups of rowdies and excited citizens rioted in Roxbury, South Boston, and the West End, while elsewhere loyal policemen and citizen volunteers found themselves jeered and pelted with mud. The latter, completely untrained in their new duties, proved totally unable to cope with these minor disturbances and, in view of the possibility that some really grave disorder might result, the Provost Guard of the Boston Navy Yard was rushed into the city at midnight and helped maintain order until morning.[10]

Although the striking policemen desired nothing more revolutionary than affiliation with the AFL, this blundering action of leaving a whole city devoid of police protection seemed radical enough in itself and opened the strikers to serious attack. Having labeled the strike "bolshevism" even before it started, Boston conservative elements and the city's press now were all the more convinced of its revolutionary character, and therefore completely misinterpreted the aims of the striking policemen. On Wednesday, every major Boston newspaper referred to the strike's radical basis by quoting prominent citizens, business leaders, and chamber of commerce members who branded the strikers "deserters," "agents of Lenin," and "bolshevists." At the same time, the local press exaggerated the real extent of lawlessness in the city. The *Evening Transcript* carried large pictures showing several looted stores and implied that the destruction on Tremont Street, opposite Boston

Common, was worse than on Newsky Prospect, Petrograd, during the Bolshevik Revolution. Other papers described the night just passed as a "Bolshevist nightmare" filled with such "lawlessness, disorder, looting . . . as was never known in this city." [11]

While the illusion was thus created that the city was entirely in the hands of Bolshevik mobs, city officials sprang into action. The citizen volunteer police force was quickly given official status and placed under the command of those loyal policemen who had stayed on the job. New appeals were then issued for more recruits, and the inhabitants of Boston were requested to cooperate with the volunteer force by remaining off the streets after dark. Stern warnings were issued to all hoodlums concerning the serious consequences of being caught committing lawless acts during the period of crisis.

However, on the question of what further steps were necessary to relieve the situation, the city's administration was badly divided. Commissioner Curtis, with the backing of Calvin Coolidge, governor of Massachusetts, now insisted that the affair was under control and favored continuing the fight to the finish. On the other hand, Mayor Peters, who was also no great friend to labor but who was a Democrat and therefore of the opposing political party to both Curtis and Coolidge, advocated immediate arbitration to settle differences with the striking policemen and tendered the opinion that the stiff-necked attitude of the commissioner had been the major cause for the strike. The mayor further believed that unless arbitration was begun at once, the city should be more carefully protected. When it became apparent that neither the governor nor the commissioner intended to arbitrate the matter, the mayor personally called out 5000 soldiers of the State Guard to aid the volunteer police in patrolling the streets. Hence, among other things, the strike had become a political football. [12]

In spite of the added precautions, disorders continued and, indeed, temporarily increased. On Wednesday evening, two men were killed and several were wounded by machine gun and rifle fire in South Boston. In Scollay Square, another riot broke out in which one man was killed. Banks and business offices stayed open all night while employee guards sat ready with nervous hands on cocked rifles. Millions of dollars' worth of valuables were removed to Springfield and Worcester for safekeeping, and many businessmen boarded up their stores to prevent looting.

Fortunately, this Wednesday night rioting marked the peak of unrest in Boston and by Thursday morning, September 11, the volunteer police force together with contingents of the State Guard had the city well under control. Henceforth, there was no further bloodshed or undue disturbance. Except for the three deaths which resulted mainly from the inexperience of the volunteer police, the furor over the extent of lawlessness in the city appears rather foolish since the total cost to the city of Boston for the two-day rioting and looting was $34,000, or roughly the cost of a small fire.[13]

Since the beginning of the strike there had been the fear that a general sympathy strike might be called to aid the striking policemen. That fear was well founded. Even before the strike began the Boston Central Labor Union had pledged its support to the disgruntled police, and immediately after the walkout, it underscored its sincerity by ordering a vote of its affiliated unions on a general strike proposal. It appears that liberal and radical labor elements within the Central Labor Union provided the primary impetus for such a plan and a few of these undoubtedly hoped for aggressive radical action.

With good cause, however, the local unions in Boston refused to be stampeded into a repetition of the earlier ill-fated Seattle affair and used utmost caution in handling this problem. Although their sympathy with the striking police was keen, they permitted their decision to hang fire while union officials discussed the degree of success such a strike would probably have. Perceiving finally that the possibility of victory was slim since public opinion was already decidedly unfavorable to the strikers, union leaders made the only wise move they could. On Thursday evening, September 11, the general strike proposal was defeated and the Central

Labor Union declared, "the time is not now opportune for the ordering of a general strike." [14]

It was certainly not difficult for Boston labor leaders to ascertain the climate of public opinion. Not only Boston, but the whole nation had been aroused by the action of the city's policemen. From the moment the strike began, newspapers throughout the country kept their readers fully informed of developments in Boston. Citizens on the other side of the continent were no less acquainted with the details of the incident than were those in neighboring Massachusetts towns and villages. On September 10, the San Francisco *Examiner* ran an eight-column headline: "POLICE STRIKE: RIOTS IN BOSTON — Gangs Range Boston Streets, Women Are Attacked, Stores Are Robbed, Shots Are Fired," and other American newspapers followed suit: "TROOPS TURN MACHINE GUNS ON BOSTON MOBS," and "TERROR REIGNS IN CITY." [15]

Newspapers outdid one another in the amount of editorial execration heaped upon the Boston strikers. They immediately took up the cry of "radicalism" emanating from the Boston press, and vied with each other in pointing out the most "facts" which proved the strike was nothing less than revolution. Scare words such as "Bolshevist," "soviet," "radical," "chaos," and "terror" were used indiscriminately and served as the framework around which exaggerated stories were built. Cartoonists depicted Boston as being completely under the control of thugs as the city's police stood idly by, and editorial phrases such as "Boston and Bedlam," "'Sovietism' in Boston," and "Desertion — Not a Strike" were commonplace. The policemen, agreed the press, had absolutely no right to strike and by their action indicated what would happen all over the country if more workers became inspired with communistic ideas. "Bolshevism in the United States is no longer a specter," warned the Philadelphia *Public-Ledger*, "Boston in chaos reveals its sinister substance." "Lenin and Trotsky are on their way," screamed the *Wall Street Journal*.[16]

In Washington, meanwhile, government officials seemed no less upset by the strike situation than the nation's press. Many congressmen were in agreement that the police strike was a bald-faced attack on American government by organized radicalism and a logical continuation of the Seattle strike and the May Day riots and bombs. Senator Henry L. Myers of Montana, a most vociferous antiradical spokesman, warned that unless something was done, "the nation will see a Soviet Government set up within two years." Of course, all such official statements were widely circulated by the general press through the use of sensational headlines: "BOSTON STRIKE CAUSES GRAVE WASHINGTON FEAR — Senators Think Effort to Sovietize the Government Is Started." Even the great liberal himself could not withstand the rumors, or the journalistic pressure, and added his voice to the din. Currently on his western speaking tour for the League, President Wilson digressed from his main topic long enough to declare that the action of the Boston police was "a crime against civilization." [17]

Events now moved rapidly toward a climax in Boston. Although the city was already well under control, the animosity which had arisen between Mayor Peters and Commissioner Curtis over the proper handling of the strike crisis prompted Governor Coolidge to take personal command of the situation on September 11. On the following day, Samuel Gompers, who had just returned from an international labor conference in Europe and who realized what a colossal blunder the Boston police had made, urged the strikers to return to their posts and await the outcome of possible mediation. When the policemen voted unanimously to accept this suggestion, the AFL president sent telegrams to both Mayor Peters and Governor Coolidge requesting that the strikers be reinstated pending arbitration "to honorably adjust a mutually unsatisfactory situation." [18]

The nation now anxiously awaited word from the city and state administrations, and, thoroughly convinced that the strike had a radical basis, a majority of the press called for no compromise. Such papers believed that it would be a "national calamity" for Boston to grant the request of the AFL chief and agreed that the

SWORN TO UPHOLD THE LAW AND STRIKING TO PUT THE UNION ABOVE IT.
POLICE
BOSTON
GALE

Strikers
(Cartoonist Gale in the Los Angeles *Times*)

striking policemen "should consider themselves lucky if they are permitted to escape with only the loss of their positions." Concluded the *Ohio State Journal*: "When a policeman strikes, he should be debarred not only from resuming his office, but from citizenship as well. He has committed the unpardonable sin; he has forfeited all his rights." [19]

It was no surprise, therefore, when on September 13, Commissioner Curtis, over the protest of Mayor Peters, announced that the striking policemen would not be reinstated and that a whole new police force would be recruited. On the following day Governor Coolidge declared that he would back this decision to the limit and quickly dispatched a telegram to Gompers refusing arbitration and maintaining, "There is no right to strike against the public safety by anybody, anywhere, any time." [20]

It is often strange how fate, because of some seemingly insignificant incident, marks a man for fame and fortune while others are left to toil on in relative obscurity. Before Coolidge penned his reply to Gompers, he had already served two thirds of a term as governor of Massachusetts without attracting much attention. But now, he suddenly became news. Seventy thousand letters and telegrams flooded the governor's office as newspapers from Florida to Washington, from California to Maine, reprinted his message. Coolidge's picture appeared in a thousand different dailies, while editors waxed eloquent with effusive praise. In an age of exaggerated fears and widespread industrial unrest, what Coolidge had written immediately made him a Jack-the-Giant-Killer, a hero, another Ole Hanson. He was the new savior of the country.

One commentator later declared that the governor's telegram ". . . struck fire from the Americanism of the entire country. Wires relayed it to the remotest regions, and it thrilled the United States. Men breathed more freely. At last a universal issue was defined. Either you stood for the public safety or you stood against it." [21] Therein lay the appeal of the Coolidge message. The governor had done something more than write down a few well-chosen lines. He had given character and personality to the mind of an

America which had reverted from the mood of social and economic adventure to one of conservative self-interest. Coolidge, with his rigid ideas on the sanctity of private property and his respect for convention, was merely representative. He had spoken for the great mass of ordinary citizens who, alienated by the excesses of strikers and filled with an exaggerated fear of radical activity, had been pushed into believing that labor had become a real menace. Unknown to Coolidge at the moment, the simple sentence "There is no right to strike against the public safety . . ." started him on the road to the White House.

Coolidge's message to Gompers and his firmness in supporting Commissioner Curtis struck the death blow to the already dying police strike. And, while Boston papers chanted "Much as we pity individuals, no striker should under any circumstances ever again be a policeman," Commissioner Curtis recruited his new police force. Because of a Massachusetts law which gave veterans civil service preference, this new force was composed mainly of ex-servicemen who, during the first few weeks of their employment, could be seen patrolling the streets clad in old army coats and breeches with police caps, badges, and holstered revolvers.

Meanwhile, because of the appreciation of "citizens in all walks life," a fund of $500,000 was raised to recompense members of the State Guard who had patrolled the city during the crisis and also to help those few loyal policemen who had stayed on the job. The disloyal police were left to shift for themselves. These ex-policemen were regarded with extreme suspicion by prospective employers, and they found employment difficult to secure. When a few of these discharged patrolmen, fed up with the treatment they were receiving, brought suit to force the return of their old jobs, the Massachusetts Supreme Court upheld the earlier dismissal action of Commissioner Curtis and refused their plea for reinstatement.[22]

As the conclusion to the police strike was thus brought about, the nation's press continued to discuss the incident solely as an attempt at revolution. Public expression agreed that labor had at last "gone too far" and that it now posed the question of "whether our system of government represented in the Constitution is to be abandoned or not." Governor Coolidge and Commissioner Curtis were universally praised for the stand they had "so stoutly taken against the Bolshevists in their city," and were given the credit for having prevented "the beginnings of Soviet government." [23]

As a result of such misstatements and misrepresentations, the general public never did receive a truthful or clear picture of the situation in Boston. The police strike died with the majority of the nation believing that revolutionary radicalism had been involved and that somehow a great catastrophe had barely been averted. Yet, it is clear that the Boston police were guilty of radicalism only in their willingness to leave a community unprotected and not in what they wished to gain thereby. They might be convicted of gross stupidity but they most certainly could not be indicted for bolshevism. In no instances were the riot disturbances caused by the striking policemen nor were radical aims or designs ever mentioned by police leaders at any time during the strike. What hullabaloo existed concerning bolshevism was to be found in the nation's press, not among the strikers.

In the final analysis, with all the camouflage removed, the Boston policemen's real "crime" remained their original desire to join the organized labor movement in America.

9 ★ ★ ★ ★ ★ ★ ★ ★ ★ ★

Big Steel—Gray or Pink?

THE Boston police strike was only two days old when the press announced that a nation-wide steel strike would begin on September 22.

The groundwork for this conflict had been laid in August 1918, when a conference of twenty-four trade unions met in Chicago and established a National Committee for Organizing Iron and Steel Workers with Samuel Gompers as its honorary chairman, John Fitzpatrick as acting chairman, and William Z. Foster as secretary-treasurer. Throughout the following months of 1918 and 1919, this committee had achieved remarkable success, particularly within the ranks of unorganized immigrant steel workers. It had organized steel men in Johnstown, Youngstown, Chicago, Cleveland, Wheeling, Buffalo, and, to some extent, in Pittsburgh, the stronghold of the United States Steel Corporation.

The steel organizers had met with bitter resistance from the steel interests who retaliated by discharging known union men and prohibiting local union meetings. Steel agents even went so far as to kidnap union organizers and run them out of town before they could talk to prospective union men. Nevertheless, Foster, who was the director of the campaign and who had been run out of a number of steel towns himself, continued the drive on the basis that the "industry could be organized in spite of all the Steel Trust could do," and it was claimed that by the summer of 1919 he had a steel union in every important mill town.[1]

135

William Z. Foster was not a typical AFL organizer. While most of the Federation's leaders were conservatives, Foster exhibited a background and held economic philosophies which ran counter to the pattern. He had been born into a poor laborer's family in 1881 and lived the formative years of his life in the Kater Street section of Philadelphia's worst slum. There, among the ramshackle dwellings, the crime, the disease, and the "rum-dumbs," young Bill developed his first ideas on the capitalistic system.

He attended school for only six years after which he struck out for himself. For three years he served as a sailor on square-rigged sailing ships, encircling the globe once. Then for three years he worked in several fertilizer plants in the United States. For varying periods he also was employed by the building, mining, and lumbering industries, and for a time even tried his hand at homesteading in Oregon. His longest period of employment was as a railroad worker.

Always interested in the plight of the common working man, Foster was a natural-born agitator. In 1894, when but a lad of thirteen, he participated in his first strike, called by streetcar workmen in Philadelphia. Thereafter, he was constantly involved in agitational activities wherever he went. While employed by the mining and lumbering interests of the West he came into contact with the IWW and for a time was enamored of that organization. But he soon became convinced that dual unionism was a mistake and that militant elements ought to stay in the old trade unions.

Foster had also dabbled with socialism for a while, but he abandoned all such ideas in 1916 for "pure and simple" trade unionism. During the war he displayed a real conversion by giving patriotic service in Liberty Bond drives and by participating as a four-minute speaker. However, in spite of these appearances, he retained a sufficient amount of his earlier radicalism to desire the overthrow of the conservative labor machine "by the mass organization of the unorganized." To this end, he had served as a leader in organizing unskilled railroad workmen into the Brotherhood of Railway Carmen and in 1918 was also instrumental in organizing the meatpacking industry. Therefore, even prior to the steel union movement, many workers could attest to the militant, although somewhat unorthodox, organizing procedures of Bill Foster. To the National Association of Manufacturers he was always better known as "Red" Foster.[2]

Foster's crusade to organize the unorganized could not possibly have found a better milieu than that of the steel industry. Many of the steel workers were uneducated immigrants of a dozen different nationalities who were completely at the mercy of the steel trust. Living conditions for such workmen were often wretched, many of their homes being "mere unpainted shacks without running water or plumbing." Almost half the men worked twelve hours a day, seven days a week; the average workweek for the whole industry was slightly under sixty-nine hours. An unskilled steel laborer's average annual income was only $1466, while the estimated minimum subsistence for a family of five in 1919 was at least $1575.[3]

As a result of these deplorable conditions, steel workers were extremely interested in bettering their economic position and joined the new steel union movement to force action. The AFL, in turn, backed the steel workers in their demands and, on June 20, 1919, asked Judge Elbert H. Gary, chairman of the United States Steel's Board of Directors, for a conference to discuss conditions in the steel industry and possible improvement of the workers' position. When no reply was forthcoming, the steel union leaders circulated a strike ballot among the local steel unions, all of which by August 20 registered a desire for a strike, the exact date to be determined by the National Committee for Organizing Iron and Steel Workers. With this warning to the steel companies that they were serious in their demands, Fitzpatrick and Foster on August 26 requested of Judge Gary an arbitration conference to settle all differences. His reply of the following day declared that because of the open-shop policy of United States Steel, "The officers of the corporation respectfully decline to discuss with you, as representatives of a labor union, any matters relating to employees." Fitzpatrick and Foster immediately asked Judge Gary to reconsider but he again refused.[4]

In view of these events, it was obvious that a tremendous industrial struggle was in the making. Organized labor had been rebuffed in securing what it felt were legitimate demands, while Judge Gary was firm in his desire to hold the line against the growing power of steel unionism. President Wilson, acting in the interest of industrial peace, immediately appealed to both sides to stay the conflict and on August 31, in a Labor Day message to the nation, declared that he was going to call an industrial conference in the near future "to discuss fundamental means of bettering the whole relationship of capital and labor."[5] It was the President's hope that a steel struggle might be thereby averted.

But neither Gary nor the steel union leaders showed any willingness to avert the impending strife and, despite the plea of the President, refused to change their original positions. On September 10, under tremendous pressure from the local steel unions, the National Committee for Organizing Iron and Steel Workers voted for the strike to begin on September 22. Two hundred thousand copies of the strike call were immediately issued in seven different languages: "STRIKE SEPTEMBER 22, 1919. The Workers in the iron and steel mills and blast furnaces . . . are requested not to go to work on September 22, and to refuse to resume their employment until such time as the demands of the organizations have been conceded by the steel corporations."[6] The basic demands for which the strike was called were the right of collective bargaining; reinstatement of all men discharged for union activities with full pay for time lost; the eight-hour day with one day's rest in seven; abolition of the twenty-four-hour shift; an American living wage; double pay for overtime; the check-off and seniority; and the abolition of company unions.[7]

Given to the public at a time when the sensational Boston police strike had not yet been settled, this steel strike announcement caused national consternation. The business world, in particular, was shaken as steel stocks wavered on the exchanges. Again President Wilson frantically urged conciliation and appealed directly to Samuel Gompers to use his influence to postpone the strike at least until after the President's proposed industrial conference had convened in early October. The conservative Gompers, who reluctantly continued to serve as honorary chairman of the organizing committee, suggested to Fitzpatrick and Foster that they abide by the President's request, but they immediately replied "that any vague, indefinite postponement would mean absolute demoralization and utter ruin" for the steel union movement. They also informed President Wilson of this fact, further buttressing their decision with a recital of instances of oppression and of denial of workers' rights by the steel companies.[8]

It has since been asserted that Gompers, although favoring postponement, refused to force the hand of the steel union leaders because he feared certain hotheaded radicals might promote the strike anyway. There is certainly an element of truth in this contention, for the radical views of some steel organizers were well known. For some time newspapers had been parading the "bolshevism" of these persons by quoting Fitzpatrick as saying, "We are going to socialize the basic industries of the United States," and also by publicizing excerpts from Foster's earlier syndicalist writings. Newspapers such as the New York *Times* continually cautioned Gompers against this "'Red' element" within the AFL and early declared that the proposed steel strike was not a strike for wages and hours but a "strike for power, for control of the industry." Meanwhile the Washington *Post* warned, "The public is not in a long-suffering mood just at present," and suggested that the AFL keep its membership firmly in line.[9]

At first glance it would appear that the general public and the press had already lined up against the steel workers, and yet closer examination reveals that Judge Gary was not faring too well at their hands either. Indeed, his arbitrary stand on the open-shop principle and his absolute refusal to confer with the union chiefs had aroused considerable animosity. Even such normally conservative newspapers as the Springfield (Mass.) *Republican* and the

Chicago *Tribune* thought Gary was acting like an "extreme reactionary" and predicted that his actions would drive even the conservative unionist into the arms of the Reds. The liberal press, as represented by the *Survey*, the *New Republic*, and the *Nation*, agreed with these papers and declared that Gary was utterly in the wrong in his drive to "smash unionism." It was inevitable, of course, that the *Wall Street Journal* should assert that these charges were wholly false and that Judge Gary was actually "fighting the battle of the American Constitution." [10]

Amid these conflicting opinions as to the real purport of the antagonists, the steel strike began on September 22. Although the steel companies minimized the extent of the walkout, and conservative AFL leaders withheld wholehearted support, an estimated 275,000 steel workmen left their jobs on that day. Shortly thereafter their ranks were swelled by thousands of other steel workers, and, by the end of the first week, the strikers numbered in excess of 365,000. According to Foster, the strike was about 90 per cent effective, although he did admit that in the Pittsburgh area only about three fourths of the plants were shut down. [11]

The magnitude of the strike was a shocking revelation to the nation. Up to the very moment of the walkout, the public, along with the President, had hoped that the struggle would somehow be averted and that conservative AFL officials would hold the steel zealots in line. Now it appeared to many observers that radicalism had gained the upper hand. Cartoonists portrayed the steel industry as undergoing a radical attack, and some papers, such as the Boston *Evening Transcript* and the *Ohio State Journal*, even expressed the fear that the primary goal of the strike was to change the character of the government. Other newspapers, only a shade less perturbed, declared that the struggle at best represented "another experiment in the way of Bolshevizing American industry." Even those papers which did not believe that the steel strike was a "revolution" agreed that it was indeed a "serious mistake" and that organized labor would be the chief sufferer from the consequences. [12]

Coming Out of the Smoke
(Cartoonist Kirby in the New York *World*)

On the other hand, greatly influenced by the recent formation of the two Communist parties, the radical press hailed the steel strike in glowing terms and completely identified itself with the conflict. The Cleveland *Socialist News* declared that the strike threw a "HALF MILLION WORKERS IN OPEN CLASS WAR." The Chicago *New Solidarity* (IWW) maintained that "possibilities of revolution are in what may develop during the strike," and the Chicago *Communist* (CP) immediately urged all laborers to support the steel workers for a final battle to "crush the capitalists." Meanwhile, the *One Big Union Monthly* (IWW) exclaimed: "We are cooperating with Foster at every step in the fight. Many of our members [Wobblies] are in the Steel Workers' Union; some of them sit in the councils of that body. . . . Let Foster build his one big union; may it grow, may it increase, may it win its battle with the Steel Trust." [13]

In such manner, the illusion was created from the beginning that the steel strike was another attempt at revolution. And yet, in spite of the exaggerated assertions of both radicals and conservatives, it appeared that many citizens at first were basically sympathetic to the strikers' demands for better working conditions and opposed to the arbitrary actions of the steel trust. The steel companies were certainly aware of this fact and their most pressing problem therefore was to promote a more favorable public opinion toward their own position. Perceiving that their greatest ally was the latent public fear of the strike's radicalism, the steel interests realized that much of the current animosity to Judge Gary's actions would disappear and the strike would fail if the public could be convinced that "bolshevism" was the *only* strike issue. With the Seattle general strike and the Boston police strike as their guides, steel officials and antiunion conservatives began a concerted drive to mold public opinion along this line.

The ruses used were many. The fiction was spread through the press that steel workers received up to $70 per day, and certain newspapers even carried reports "that the more luxurious New York hotels expected an influx of striking steel workers who would use the occasion to take a vacation and spend their 'high wages'." The inference, of course, was that the strike could not possibly be for higher wages.[14] It was also consistently maintained that the strike would not prove successful because native American workmen were refusing to leave their jobs and that their action was causing many foreign strikers to return to work. The native element, it was said, was opposed to the radicalism of the foreign workers and considered the strike "disloyal" and "un-American." A whole host of false reports were then made upon this assumption, for at a time when Foster claimed the strike was 90 per cent effective, newspaper headlines read as follows: "CONDITIONS ALMOST NORMAL IN ALL STEEL PLANTS," "WORKERS FLOCK BACK TO JOBS," "STRIKE CRUMBLING." Pittsburgh papers — the *Dispatch, Leader, Chronicle-Telegraph, Post,* and *Press* — kept up a constant barrage of such propaganda.[15] Later it was estimated that the total number of returnees involved in all these back-to-work stories was 4,800,000. Supposedly that number re-entered mills where only a half million had worked before! [16]

Then, too, between September 27 and October 8 no fewer than thirty full-page advertisements appeared in the various Pittsburgh papers, condemning the strike and asking the steel workers to return to their jobs. These appeals were printed in as many as nine different languages and, in addition to exhorting workmen to "GO BACK TO WORK" and to "STAND BY AMERICA," maintained that the native workers who clearly understood the radicalism involved were already back. Through such advertisements the idea was also circulated that the United States in the name United States Steel, meant the corporation was actually a part of the federal government and that a strike against it was a rebellion against the United States. As the strike progressed, similar advertisements also appeared in other newspapers asking labor to "SHOW UP THE RED AGITATOR FOR WHAT HE IS" and warning workers to "BEWARE THE AGITATOR WHO MAKES LABOR A CATSPAW FOR BOLSHEVISM." [17]

Important as this propaganda was, it was William Z. Foster who bore the brunt of the steel companies' attack. Steel officials widely circulated copies of his *Syndicalism,* a pamphlet written in 1911 while he was still a member of the IWW, in which he declared: "In his choice of weapons to fight his capitalist enemies, the Syndicalist is no more careful to select those that are 'fair,' 'just' or 'civilized' than is a householder attacked in the night by a burglar. He knows he is engaged in a life and death struggle . . . and considers his tactics only from the standpoint of their effectiveness. With him the end justifies the means." [18]

While these views had been publicized prior to the strike, it was after the strike began that they gained their widest notoriety. Under the tutelage of antiunion conservatives, the press of the country, with few exceptions, centered on Foster's radical past and made of him a thoroughly revolutionary leader. Although Foster constantly denied such charges and declared that no radicalism of any kind was involved in the steel strike, the majority of the press remained firm in its conviction that he was "an avowed syndicalist," "an uncompromising enemy of the existing political order," and "a revolutionist." He engineered the steel strike, agreed the press, "not for the purpose of improving labor conditions, but for the purpose of revolutionizing industry." [19] Meanwhile, not only the press, but government officials as well gave Foster's background careful scrutiny. Senator Henry L. Myers of Montana characterized Foster as "a notorious syndicalist, revolutionist, and enemy of organized government." Senator Charles S. Thomas of Colorado labeled him a radical who wanted economic chaos in the United States. Representative John G. Cooper of Ohio branded him as a man unfit for "the name of an American citizen and the protection of that flag." [20]

Had no violence occurred during the strike, it might have been more difficult for the general public to accept wholeheartedly these charges of revolution, so cleverly built up by conservative antiunion forces and strengthened by press assertions and the statements of public officials. However, as riot after riot ensued between embattled strikers, nonstrikers, and law enforcement officers, charges of bolshevism gained credibility. The public became increasingly convinced of the radical nature of the strike without realizing such disturbances were often the result of police belligerency or of insidious action on the part of steel representatives.

The day before the strike began, headlines in the Washington *Post* declared "STEEL MILLS READY TO FIGHT STRIKERS — POLICE PLANS RUSHED." Three days later, headlines read: "RIOTING SPREADS IN STRIKE," "GUARDS RAID PENNSYLVANIA MILL PICKETS," "MANY SHOT—2 DEAD." [21] Such headlines tersely explain what happened throughout the strike. From the very beginning the steel companies openly prepared for war and surrounded their plants with guards armed with rifles and riot guns. Also, because of their control over local politics, particularly in western Pennsylvania, the steel corporations strengthened and assumed charge of the law enforcement agencies in many local communities where citizens were sworn in by the droves as special deputies and were armed to prevent picketing and violence. It was estimated, for example, that along the Monongahela from Pittsburgh to Clairton (a distance of twenty miles), 25,000 men were under arms at the onset of the strike and that in some areas there was a deputy sheriff for almost every striker. [22]

Such a condition merely opened the way to violence. Police officials and local deputies were often overzealous in displaying their authority. In certain areas, union meetings were summarily broken up, picket lines were dispersed, and orderly participants were clubbed. In some small mill towns, the local mounted police rode over pedestrians on the sidewalks, injuring peaceful groups of men and women. When strikers attempted to defend themselves against such brutality, they were treated ruthlessly. For example, at Farrell, Pennsylvania, in a skirmish between strikers and police arising from the latter's oppressive curtailment of free speech, four strikers were killed and eleven badly wounded. The net result of such police activity was that in many areas civil liberty became a dead letter. [23]

Besides this use of special deputies and police, the steel companies' employment of labor spies and strikebreakers also served to inflame hatred and incite violence. Probably of all the weapons used by the steel interests to quell the strike, these two were the most reprehensible. Virtually every local union had at least one company spy in its midst and even the National Committee for Organizing Iron and Steel Workers was not immune. Later it was discovered that there had been one company agent in that body. Through such agents, the steel companies purposely aroused racial hatred and prejudice by instructing them "to stir up as much bad feeling as you possibly can." This was also achieved by using Negro strikebreakers wherever possible against white pickets.[24] As a result of such nefarious activities, brutal riots broke out in some mill towns between nationalities and between races. In Donora, Pennsylvania, a riot between Negro strikebreakers and foreign strikers cost two of the strikers their lives. Similarly, in Braddock, twenty persons were injured and one killed in a riot involving two excited foreign mobs.[25]

The ruthless methods employed by the steel companies were not described to any extent in the press. Instead, reports of riot disorders were written in such a manner as to make it appear that steel officials were always on the defensive against those who were attacking law and order. Newspapers dwelt mostly on the evidence of radicalism involved and related all other factors to it. The public, therefore, received a completely biased picture of the strike situation.

Actually, the vast majority of the riot disturbances contained no traces of radicalism whatsoever. However, there was one which did possess some evidence of radical activity and hence was all the more publicized in the press and capitalized on by the steel companies. Occurring at Gary, Indiana, on October 4, this incident increased the fear of labor radicalism, hurt the steel strikers' cause, and added support to all the various misstatements of the steel interests.

From the beginning of the steel struggle, press reports from Gary had emphasized the radicalism of the strike leaders in that city. They were quoted as making such extreme statements as

"The strike won't stop until the steel workers become the law-makers at Washington, D.C." [26] As a result, even the federal government had become alarmed and sent federal agents into the area to prevent radical elements from capitalizing on the strike.

The situation at Gary had become increasingly tense as the steel companies decided on a showdown and imported large numbers of Negro strikebreakers in order to break the influence of the strike leaders in that city. On October 4 violent rioting inevitably ensued. Governor James P. Goodrich of Indiana immediately ordered eleven companies of the state militia into East Chicago and Gary, and these soldiers plus 500 special police and 300 deputies set about to restore order, filling the city's hospitals with wounded and its jails with arrests. [27]

This restoration of order proved short-lived, for on the following day rioting flared anew when 500 strikers stormed the Tyler Street gates of the United States Steel Corporation's plant, and another group attempted to force its way into the Buchanan Street entrance. Again militiamen were hurried to the scene, but this time they were unable to quell the disturbance before a number of persons were killed and many injured. In desperation, the Indiana governor now appealed for federal troops. A pouring rain on the afternoon and evening of October 5 tended to cool heated tempers until the arrival the following day of regular army soldiers under General Leonard Wood. [28]

Immediately after his arrival, the general placed Gary under martial law, forbade assembly in the city's streets or parks, and made the carrying of firearms a major offense. He then asked Army Intelligence to begin a thorough investigation of the alleged radical influence among the workmen in the city. The sifting process purportedly uncovered those who were attempting to make the steel strike a revolution. According to Army Intelligence, radical pamphlets were found which had been circulated freely among the strikers, and which reportedly advised them to "capture the power of the state" and "establish the dictatorship of the workers." Furthermore, evidence of a bomb plot designed to blow up the

147

homes of prominent Gary citizens was discovered, and it was rumored that the perpetrators of the infamous May and June bombings might be involved. As a result of these discoveries, a whirlwind raid on known nests of Gary radicals was conducted by the Army on October 15, netting scores in arrests and much Bolshevist literature.[29]

Although steel strike leaders immediately denied all connection with this radical element, and General Wood's investigation showed that most of the Gary radicals were neither regular steel workers nor organizers, the damage to the steel strikers' cause had been done. Newspapers throughout the nation seized upon the Army raid and the various Gary riots as further proof of the radicalism of all steel workers. Most newspapers agreed that these incidents at Gary proved the steel struggle was "an attempted revolution, not a strike," and advanced the belief that the Gary workers represented a "Red Guard" in American industry. Concluded the Boston *Evening Transcript*, "[The Gary incident] shows the extraordinary hold which 'Red' principles have upon the foreign born population in the steel districts."[30]

Meanwhile, the manner in which bona fide radicals reacted to the situation in Gary did little to allay mounting public fear. Some radicals readily admitted their complicity in the Gary riots and openly urged strikers to kill police and soldiers. One of their pamphlets demanded that laborers everywhere arm themselves and take reprisals "for every worker killed." Mother Jones, a well-known agitator, shouted to a radical meeting in Gary that in spite of all opposition "We're going to take over the steel mills and run them for Uncle Sam." The Chicago *Communist* shrieked, "RESIST THE TERROR!" and added, "Armed force must not prevail! . . . Workers, act! Out of your mass strikes will come . . . a state of the workers, proletarian dictatorship, which will crush the capitalist as the capitalist state now crushes the workers."[31]

Unfortunately for the cause of industrial peace, the Gary turmoil served as the backdrop for the President's National Industrial

Conference which supposedly was to allay much of the current industrial unrest. Convening in the Pan-American Union Building in Washington, D.C., on October 6 (the day that General Wood declared martial law in Gary), this body was composed of representatives of capital, labor, and the public, and had as its chairman Secretary of Interior Franklin K. Lane with William B. Wilson, secretary of labor, as a special adviser. Although the general press hailed the conference as "the only method that can produce a better understanding" and fervently hoped it would succeed, the meeting really had little chance for success. Capital was in the driver's seat and could afford to be obstinate. Labor was on the defensive and somewhat belligerent. As usual, the public sat uncomfortably in between.[32]

For several weeks the conference paid lip service to industrial cooperation. However, when Samuel Gompers offered a resolution on October 21 declaring for "the right of wage earners . . . to bargain collectively . . . in respect to wages, hours of labor, and relations and conditions of employment," the conference fell to pieces.[33]

Here, after all, was the central issue of the industrial discord, *not* radicalism. Capital was determined not to allow its predominant position to be compromised by the collective bargaining power of labor, and organized labor was equally determined to force capital to concede. The representatives of the public, meanwhile, held the balance of power, and by their action illustrated that the constant charges of labor radicalism and the propaganda of antiunion elements were achieving their goal. By a coalition vote of capital and the public, Gompers's resolution was voted down. Immediately thereafter, on October 22, the AFL president declared, "I have sung my swan song in this conference . . . and with a feeling of regret that I am not able with a clear conscience to remain longer, I go."[34]

The next day's headlines of the Chicago *Tribune* briefly told the story: "LABOR QUITS, CAPITAL FLITS, PUBLIC SITS!" Although some papers, such as the Washington *Evening Star*,

149

thought the employer group was just as guilty as labor in the breakup of the conference, general sentiment placed the blame squarely on Gompers's shoulders. The Baltimore *Sun* declared that "Labor's action was not justified," and the *Rocky Mountain News* said its withdrawal made of the conference "An industrial Sarajevo." Gompers's action, concluded the *Wall Street Journal*, was merely further proof that organized labor was succumbing to "the IWW's and Russian Bolshevists." [35]

From the time of the Gary riots and labor's withdrawal from the Industrial Conference, the steel strike was doomed. Although the struggle dragged on for two more months, public sentiment had become so adverse to the strikers that they could not hope to win. During this two-month period, conservative pressure groups and government officials continued to emphasize the strikers' supposed radicalism, not only because of their own real fear, but also because of the calculated effect which such propaganda would have on the public mind. The National Security League and the *Open Shop Review* persistently reiterated the charge that the steel struggle was purely "an effort of anarchists . . . to destroy the government," while government officials such as Washington's Senator Miles Poindexter openly avowed that unless something were done "there is a real danger that the Government will fall." [36] Newspapers continued to present the public with an entirely false picture of the strength of labor radicalism by filling their columns with phrases like "a bolshevist campaign," "the bolshevism in it," and "not an ordinary labor dispute." Conservative AFL officials, who had been cool to the strike from the beginning, now also fanned the flames of public fear by stating that some of the strike leaders were indeed "noted IWW's and Anarchists . . . and outspoken Bolshevists from the tops of their heads to the soles of their feet." [37] The radical press itself helped this fear of bolshevism along by declaring that of course there were radicals in the steel strike who "do not need the newspapers to tell them that they are Bolsheviki." [38]

Since it became increasingly obvious to all concerned that these widespread charges of bolshevism were strangling the strike, two investigations of the real purpose of the conflict were watched with particular interest. One was made by the Senate Committee on Education and Labor, the full results of which were made public before the strike officially closed.[39] The other was handled by a special commission of inquiry of the Interchurch World Movement, and, although its final report did not appear until the fall of 1920, its summary findings were also given to the public while the strike was yet in progress.[40]

While admitting that the steel companies were guilty of industrial despotism in their arbitrary refusal to bargain collectively with the steel union leaders, the Senate report placed special emphasis on organized labor's shortcomings. Besides assailing union leaders for refusing to postpone the strike on the President's request, it declared the AFL had committed a colossal blunder in permitting Foster to conduct the strike and that the evidence showed he had not renounced his earlier syndicalist views. The Senate report boldly concluded that behind the strike was massed "a considerable element of IWW's, anarchists, revolutionists, and Russian Soviets" who were using the conflict "as a means of elevating themselves to power." [41]

The findings of the Commission of Inquiry exactly reversed the emphasis by minimizing the extent of radical influence among both strikers and strike leaders, and placed special blame on the steel interests. It declared that although a few workers may have wanted "big changes," these had no voice in the strike. It vigorously attacked the part played by the steel companies in using "strikebreakers," "undercover men," and "labor spies." It further charged that the grievances of the steel workers were just and that the steel interests used their control over the press and police agencies to abrogate free speech and restrict an airing of the true causes of the struggle. The strike, it continued, was conducted in an orthodox fashion according to the rules of the AFL, and Foster, regardless of his earlier bent for syndicalism, had harmonized his actions perfectly with those of the AFL in the steel fight. The church report concluded that under the influence of the steel companies, the general press and other interested elements had built up false Red charges to make the public lose sight of the real issues.[42]

The report of the Commission of Inquiry was much closer to the truth than that of the Senate committee. But, regardless of the many possible points of difference, one fact was universally agreed on — the words "revolution" and "bolshevism" had killed all chance of the strikers' success. This fact was no more obvious to the investigators than to the strike leaders themselves, and, on January 8, 1920, at a time when fewer than 100,000 men were still out and when steel production was about 70 per cent of normal, the National Committee for Organizing Iron and Steel Workers voted to end the battle.[43] The men had gained not a single concession, twenty lives had been sacrificed, and approximately $112,-000,000 had been lost in wages. The tremendous loss to the steel companies cannot be calculated, but they obviously considered the expense well worth the defeat of the steel union movement. After the strike Foster resigned from the AFL and rapidly gravitated toward the Communist party, while conservative union leaders vainly attempted to repair the damage done by ruthlessly continuing their purge of all suspected radicals from the organized labor movement. On the other hand, the United States Steel Corporation, with its vast resources and its control over subsidiaries, independent companies, banks, and mines, emerged from the struggle as the recognized champion of the American conservative tradition as well as the primary industrial bulwark against unionism. Backed by a favorable public opinion which was based on an exaggerated fear of bolshevism, this corporation proved that not even 350,000 strikers could prevail against it.

Coal—Black or Red?

Just six weeks after the steel strike announcement was made, the third of the great fall strikes — the coal strike — began.

This expression of discontent on the part of the nation's coal miners stemmed largely from the fact that although the coal industry had prospered tremendously during the war, miners' wages had remained fairly stationary because of a wage agreement made in September 1917 which was to run for the duration of the war but not beyond April 1, 1920. The coal operators preferred to think this 1917 agreement was still binding, for although hostilities had ceased with the Armistice, the war had not yet been officially declared terminated. The miners, in turn, chose to believe that within the meaning of the agreement the war was at an end and therefore they had begun agitation for a new wage contract.

As a result, unrest in the coal fields had become more serious as the postwar months of 1919 slipped by, and United Mine Workers' officials, most of whom were urging caution, found it increasingly difficult to keep union members in line. Wildcat strikes called by independent unions kept the coal fields in a constant state of insurgency and by the fall of 1919 some miners were openly advocating a complete nationalization of the industry because of their extreme dissatisfaction with both the coal operators and conservative UMW officials.[1]

At its annual convention held in Cleveland in September 1919, the United Mine Workers Union recognized that in view of the widespread unrest some action had to be taken and proceeded to consider the possibilities. Finally, under the leadership of John L. Lewis, acting president of the union and a bitter anticommunist, the convention decided to reject all proposals to nationalize the mines, but did endorse such novel demands as a nation-wide contract, a 60 per cent wage increase, a six-hour day, and a five-day week. Also, the convention resolved to terminate the wartime contract on November 1, 1919, and call a nation-wide coal strike unless their demands were met and a new agreement signed.[2]

Although the UMW earnestly contended that these demands were justifiable, much of the general public regarded them as being far too excessive and radical. The coal operators refused to consider them at all, and declared that no negotiations would be undertaken with the UMW before April 1, 1920. However, under pressure from Secretary of Labor Wilson, both the mine union leaders and representatives of the operators were brought together in Washington, D.C., on October 21 for the hopeful purpose of reaching at least a temporary understanding. But when it finally became clear that the mine operators would agree to nothing more than a modified wage increase with a postponement of all the remaining issues to April 1, Lewis snorted at the whole procedure and declared, "In the language of Elbert H. Gary, I cannot discuss arbitration at this time."[3]

Consequently the UMW issued a strike call for November 1. In announcing this action Lewis declared, "The United Mine Workers of America are now embarking upon the greatest enterprise ever undertaken in the history of the trades union movement." Then, anxiously eyeing the dying steel strike, he added: "In calling this strike the United Mine Workers have but one object in view, and that is to obtain just recognition of their right to a fair wage and proper working conditions. No other issue is involved and there must be no attempt on the part of anyone to inject into the strike any extraneous purposes."[4]

John L. Lewis may have hoped that "no extraneous purposes" would be injected into the coal struggle, but his hopes were certainly in vain. For once in his life, his timing was bad; it was almost inevitable that at a time when steelworkers were being condemned for their "Bolshevik" actions, striking miners should be similarly censured.

As with the steel workers, there was some basis for these claims since there were a few in the mine unions who advocated sweeping reforms in the industry and hoped for revolutionary action. Even though such individuals at no time controlled the strike or even received any degree of miner support, the mere fact of their existence added greatly to public concern. The same applied to the radical press which, already supporting the steel strikers, now championed the miners' cause as well. Various radical pamphlets declared, "MINERS! REMEMBER! In this Republic of sharks and 'pimps' nothing can be obtained without violence. Tooth for tooth and FORWARD!" One proclamation of the Communist party shouted, "Workers, rally to the support of the miners. Make their strike general. Unite for a struggle against industrial slavery." [5]

Super-patriotic and antilabor elements naturally made the most of the situation. From the moment the strike decision was announced, congressmen were deluged with telegrams from businesses, American Legion posts, the National Security League, and the American Defense Society begging action to prevent a "Bolshevik revolution" in the coal industry. Mine owners themselves flocked to Washington demanding that something be done to quell the proposed "insurrection." T. T. Brewster, chief spokesman for the coal operators, released to the press wholly untrue reports which claimed the coal strike was being undertaken on direct orders from Lenin and Trotsky and that Moscow gold was financing the whole project. Following the example of the steel interests, the mine companies quickly distributed other forms of exaggerated or false propaganda with considerable effect. [6]

Government officials, both state and federal, soon took up the cry of "radicalism." Congressional leaders flatly declared that the proposed coal strike was a radical innovation and that the strike decision showed radical labor had "a stranglehold upon the throat of the country." Still others gloomily predicted that unless some action was taken the nation would revert "to a state of barbarism." Though less hysterical in his approach, even President Wilson bitterly denounced the coming conflict from his sickbed in the White House. Describing it among other things as "one of the gravest steps ever proposed in this country," "the most far-reaching plan ever presented," and "a grave moral and legal wrong," the President concluded that a coal strike in the face of approaching winter was "not only unjustifiable, it is unlawful." [7]

Already engaged in circulating exaggerated tales of bolshevism in the steel strike, the general press reiterated with zeal all these expressions of official and conservative sentiment on the dangers of the proposed coal strike. Moreover, in connection with such headlines as "STRIKE A CRIME — WILSON" and "CONGRESS IS READY TO ACT IN EMERGENCY," many newspapers ran highly emotional editorials which emphasized the radical aspects of the situation and demanded swift action. Some papers, such as the New York *Tribune*, were so carried away that they characterized the miners as "thirsting for a strike. . . . Thousands of them, red-soaked in the doctrines of Bolshevism, clamor for the strike as a means of syndicalizing the coal mines . . . and even as starting a general revolution in America." [8]

Once again radicalism had been made the crux of a great industrial struggle. And yet, it would be difficult to say just how much of the government's subsequent action was based on a fear of radicalism and how much on the need for coal. It is clear that those few newspapers which did not subscribe to the belief the strike was radical still called for government intervention on the basis that the nation would be deprived of a much-needed commodity. In any event, there can be little doubt that the radical factor played some part in prompting government action, for this question was undoubtedly discussed when Attorney General Palmer, who was currently seeing Reds everywhere, conferred with the President on October 29.

What actually was said at this meeting is not known. However, we can guess what happened. Palmer impressed upon the President the seriousness of the impending strike, pointing out its unquestionable effect on the nation's economy and its radical overtones. He then urged the President to take a strong stand and suggested that the government enjoin the miners from striking. Whether President Wilson accepted this latter proposal willingly or reluctantly is a matter for conjecture. Josephus Daniels, secretary of the navy, later maintained that had Wilson been a well man he most certainly would never have consented to Palmer's suggestions.[9] It is true that the President was still very ill from the stroke he had suffered, and on the insistence of his wife and his doctor, Admiral Cary T. Grayson, he was permitting most domestic matters to be settled directly by the department head concerned. In the coal strike situation, only the President and Palmer were involved since at no time was the full Cabinet summoned to discuss the impending struggle. And although Joseph Tumulty, the presidential secretary, later claimed President Wilson took a great interest in the strike and kept in daily contact with the details of the situation, there is every indication that he actually left the major decisions up to Palmer.[10] Moreover, contrary to his later assertions, the attorney general never received official Cabinet sanction for what he did, and, indeed, some Cabinet officers were bitterly opposed to his actions.[11]

In any event, immediately following the conference between the President and Palmer, the Chief Executive reactivated the wartime Fuel Administration which had been created by the Lever Act, and Attorney General Palmer applied to Federal Judge Albert B. Anderson of the Indiana District Court for an injunction based on the Lever Act to prevent the walkout. On the following day, October 30, Judge Anderson issued a temporary order enjoining the UMW leaders from any participation in the proposed struggle.[12]

Labor was shocked. During the war, the AFL had acceded to the passage of the Lever Act only after it had received concrete assurances from Woodrow Wilson himself that the law would not be used to interfere with labor activities. Now, however, it was employed against labor and labor sentiment was vehement. Samuel Gompers, who up to this point had urged Lewis to "avert the strike or at least postpone it," began to support the miners' cause vigorously. The Federation's president declared that the injunction represented a "broken pledge" and that such action was "replete with possibilities." John L. Lewis, meanwhile, charged that President Wilson and his cabinet were the allies of "sinister financial interests" and that the injunction represented "the most sweeping abrogation of the rights of citizens . . . that has ever been issued by the Federal Court." [13]

Attorney General Palmer parried all such thrusts by claiming that the injunction was the only action open to the government if it was to forestall a condition which might lead to the paralysis of government. The majority of the press wholeheartedly agreed with him. Most newspapers maintained that the coal strike, simmered down to its essentials, represented a plain case of law and human rights on the one side and defiance of law and public welfare on the other. They contended that it was merely a question of whether the will of the people or the will of a minority should prevail. Speaking for the general press, the Portland *Oregonian* claimed the main issue was who will rule: the strikers or the government? Concluded this paper, "The public . . . is nerved to a great test. It would better be faced now." [14]

The test came. Although UMW officials technically complied with the restraining order, 394,000 leaderless miners left the mines on November 1. The fact that such a colossal walkout occurred in spite of the federal injunction convinced the press all the more that bolshevism was involved. Newspaper headlines read, "REVOLUTION IS STAKE RADICALS PLAY FOR IN STRIKE OF MINERS" and "APATHY OF MEMBERS, IT IS SAID, ALLOWS REDS TO CONTROL LABOR UNIONS." Front pages were filled with such phrases as "bolshevism rears its ugly head" and "Red Bolshevism directs this blow against the nation." Cartoonist

Fung, of the Seattle *Post-Intelligencer*, expressed a widely held opinion when, below the caption "Rough Shod," he portrayed a monstrous foot labeled "Coal Strike" just ready to step on and crush the Capitol Dome, representing the "Government." [15]

In the midst of this consternation and confusion, the commonwealth of Massachusetts held its gubernatorial election. Ordinarily a state election would not have much influence on national affairs nor would it call forth much comment. In this case, however, the Massachusetts election became the battleground for the contending forces in American society and it was only natural that public interest in the outcome was keen. More importantly, the final result directly affected the fortunes of both the steel and coal strikers.

Calvin Coolidge, who was the unanimous choice of the Republican party for re-election as governor, was bitterly opposed by Richard H. Long, a well-known and highly respected Democrat. Liberal labor elements, progressives, and radicals alike scathingly denounced Coolidge's past administration, and certain politically minded Boston ex-policemen stumped the state in an effort to defeat him. Conservative groups, on the other hand, strongly backed the governor and used as the central theme of their campaign the claim that he had saved Boston from bolshevism. A vote for Coolidge, they said, was a vote for "law and order."

Since the major campaign issue was Coolidge's action during the police strike, the nation turned to watch developments in Massachusetts. Even the Los Angeles *Times*, on the day of the election, November 4, ran an eight-column headline, "REDS RUN ELECTION ISSUES . . . BATTLE IN BAY STATE" and asked, "Shall the State of Massachusetts be governed by law or mob rule?" [16] The answer was given in no uncertain terms. Receiving a plurality of 125,000 votes, Coolidge was elected governor for the second time. The nation's press was extremely gratified by this decision and the news of the coal and steel strikes was pushed temporarily into the background by such headlines as "WHOLE

NATION HAILS MASSACHUSETTS," and "MASSACHUSETTS FOR LAW AND ORDER." Editors lavished their praise on the state's voters by claiming Coolidge's victory brought reassurance to loyal Americans everywhere that legitimate government would be sustained and that "radicalism is not to rule." The Los Angeles *Times* declared the election was "A Defeat of the Soviets" and entoned, "Massachusetts — God bless her — again and amen!"[17] Even President Wilson, a good Democrat, expressed his satisfaction by sending the Republican governor a telegram which said, "I congratulate you upon your election as a victory for law and order. When that is the issue all Americans stand together."[18]

This election proved a serious blow to both the steel and coal strikers. In the face of such definite evidence that the public was fed up with industrial unrest, disaffection spread among labor's ranks and some striking miners followed disheartened steel workers in returning to their jobs. As one newspaper put it, Coolidge's victory had given the coal strikers and their leaders a bad case of "indigestion."[19] On the other hand, the action of the voters of Massachusetts gave added encouragement to all those antilabor conservatives who, perceiving that public opinion was strongly supporting them, pushed even more relentlessly for the defeat of labor unionism. Specifically, Coolidge's success served to speed the plans of those officials who were currently advocating more stringent action against the striking coal miners.

Just four days after the Massachusetts election, Judge Anderson, on a motion by Attorney General Palmer, made the original temporary injunction permanent and ordered the UMW leaders to cancel the strike order by 6 P.M. on November 11. The coal union leaders were now faced with a serious situation. To be restrained from actively participating in the strike was one thing; to be ordered to call it off was another. For two days the nation waited while the union chiefs debated what to do. Meanwhile, the AFL Executive Council met under the direction of Samuel Gompers, denounced the latest mandatory injunction, pledged to the miners the full

(Cartoonist Morgan in the Philadelphia *Inquirer*)

support of the AFL, and appealed to the citizens of the country to endorse the miners' cause.[20]

In this instance, the mine union leaders, particularly John L. Lewis, displayed a far keener perception of current popular sentiment than did Gompers or the leaders of the AFL. After a seventeen-hour session of the UMW Executive Committee on the night of November 10–11, UMW officials agreed that the strike should be terminated. Lewis ordered the strike call canceled and appended the following statement: "We are Americans, we cannot fight our government."[21]

Lewis's words were enthusiastically received throughout the country and the decision of the UMW officials was complimented in glowing terms. But this enthusiasm proved only short-lived. In spite of the fact that UMW officials had canceled the strike order, many miners simply refused to return to work. Some strikers were extremely reluctant to abandon a struggle upon which they had staked so much. Alexander Howatt, president of the Kansas miners, on hearing of the court order, exclaimed: "The strike can't be stopped," and added, "We'll call their bluff." [22] So persistent was this feeling among many of the miners that the strike continued, unauthorized, for almost a month. During that time, as coal piles dwindled, the Fuel Administration had to enact more rigid coal-saving regulations, some schools closed for lack of heat, factories shut down, the workday in many areas was cut to six hours, electric signs were permitted to burn only one hour per day, and rail transportation was drastically curtailed.[23]

The general press, which but a few days before had been so pleased with the UMW Executive Committee's decision, now heaped further condemnation upon the coal workers and fiercely berated the mine chiefs for not being able to stop the strike. During the following month the press spread abroad ever wilder claims of Bolshevist sentiment among the miners, and in certain quarters it was freely stated that the continuation of the strike indicated a Moscow-spawned plot to overthrow the United States government. Public officials were especially dismayed at the lawless action of the miners, and some, like Attorney General Palmer, remained convinced that the basic object of the strike was revolution.[24]

This gnawing fear of radicalism, coupled with the growing clamor for coal, ultimately forced the government to act once again. In a final attempt to halt the coal strike, Judge Anderson, on December 3, cited Lewis and eighty-three other UMW officials for violation of the injunction and bound their cases over to a grand jury for investigation. Meanwhile, President Wilson authorized the Fuel Administration to offer the striking miners a flat 14 per cent wage increase with the promise that an arbitral commission would be established to investigate their other demands. The

President then appealed directly to the strikers to accept his proposal.[25]

In the face of impending contempt proceedings against UMW officials, the President's conciliation plan, and an increasingly adverse public sentiment, the solidarity of the insurgent miners rapidly weakened, and on December 10 the President's plan was accepted and the strike ended. The wage increase contained in the proposal became effective immediately, and the arbitral commission was appointed shortly thereafter. Three months later, this commission recommended a 27 per cent wage increase, but no change in hours or working conditions. On that basis, a two-year contract was finally signed by the miners and operators on March 31, 1920.

[As in the case of the Boston police strike and the steel strike, the important result of the coal strike is not to be found in terms of unsatisfied demands or workdays lost, but in the effect of the strike on the public mind. The net result of all three of these great fall strikes was a marked increase in public fear of domestic bolshevism and there can be little doubt that adverse public sentiment killed them.]The New York *Evening Post* was very near the truth when it claimed that the force of public opinion in late 1919 was "more impressive than the demonstration of the power of the courts . . . or of the Government."[26] That antiunionites were well aware of this fact is undisputed, and labor learned the same fact through bitter experience. Shortly after the steel and coal strikes, organized labor demonstrated its increasing awareness of the indispensable asset of a favorable public opinion by establishing the Federated Press, the first national news service owned and operated by labor unions.[27]

But no number of Federated Presses could undo the damage already done, and the future fortunes of organized labor suffered immeasurably. Coal and steel unionism, in particular, were adversely effected. For example, of the 250,000 steel workers organized in the 1918–19 whirlwind campaign, only a handful remained in the unions by mid-1920. And although membership in the AFL as a whole did not decline to a similar extent, the defeats just experienced also sapped much of its strength and vitality. In November 1919, the number of strikes dropped to 145 and in December hit a six-year low of 94. Fewer and fewer workers expressed a willingness to brave the storm of public criticism and charges of "radicalism" which were almost certain to greet any new labor dispute.

Leaders of the AFL, meanwhile, were both disappointed and hurt by the attitude of the public and the actions of the government. Such widespread opposition seemed to them to show a lack of recognition for labor's patriotic wartime services. At the same time, labor leaders shared the deep-seated antagonism of the general public toward radicalism and continued their own crusade against it wherever it appeared within the organized labor movement. As a matter of fact, at the height of the coal strike, when it was already obvious that the striking miners were losing because of exaggerated charges of "bolshevism," the *American Federationist* was busy lambasting that doctrine and calling upon union laborers to be wary of the Bolshevik agents in their midst.[28]

Naturally, those antilabor forces which primarily had brought labor to this unfortunate position continued their unrelenting crusade and open-shop adherents, in particular, wrung every advantage they could from the strike situations. Mainly as a result of Judge Gary's successful stand on the open-shop principle in the steel struggle, open-shop activity increased tremendously in the late fall. The open-shop principle was now completely identified with American democracy, the implication being that all organized labor was openly opposed to the American system. Concentrating therefore on labor's "un-Americanism," open-shop proponents furthered their campaign by creating additional means for supplying the press, churches, schools, colleges, businesses, and local chambers of commerce with their antiunion propaganda. For example, the NAM established a separate Open Shop Department which launched an *Open Shop Bulletin*, prepared an *Open Shop*

Encyclopedia, and acted as a clearinghouse for most other open-shop literature.[29]

Public opinion was inevitably affected. Daily newspapers reprinted open-shop arguments and in their editorial columns declared that anything less than the open shop was "un-American" and "un-patriotic." Some clergymen, such as Dr. David J. Burrell of the Marble Collegiate Church of New York City, drew upon the Bible to prove that the closed shop was not only "un-patriotic to the last degree," but "un-Christian" as well.[30] Prominent citizens, such as former President Taft, issued statements that organized labor in its closed-shop demands was really "embracing Soviet methods," while certain congressmen branded the closed shop as "tyrannous" and "wholly in conflict with the fundamentals of American freedom."[31]

Along with the three fall strikes, the effect of all such propaganda in sharpening the Red Scare is obvious. Through the various techniques used in playing up the radical aspects of the police, steel, and coal strikes, the general public was finally brought to believe that almost every union man was opposed to the American way of life and was the unwitting, if not deliberate, dupe of dangerous radicals.

Still, the real issue was never radicalism and even the closed versus the open shop struggle involved the simple and much more basic question of union versus no union. It was on this latter basis that employers really made their devastating raids on the power of organized labor.

Yet the fact remains that to the general public the basic issue *was* radicalism and as its faith in the loyalty of union labor finally tottered and collapsed, the last remaining barrier to hysteria disappeared.

11 ★ ★ ★ ★ ★ ★ ★ ★ ★

The Gag and the Mob

By the late fall of 1919 bolshevism actually had a stranglehold on the nation. But, ironically enough, this was not the result of any revolutionary activity on the part of Bolshevists or the ideological appeal of their program. Instead, it represented the willful action of the American people themselves. Through their unintelligent thinking and intolerant actions they were rapidly accomplishing what no number of domestic radicals could have achieved by themselves.

It is remarkable how thoroughly the fear of domestic bolshevism permeated the body politic by late 1919. As we have seen, much of this was based on the action of organized labor. But there was no element or phase of the nation's life which had not also fallen under similar frenzied scrutiny or had not given some cause for alarm. In this respect, the widespread propaganda activities of the various patriotic and conservative pressure groups paid off handsomely. "You're a Bolshevist" soon was on the tip of every tongue and the phrase "He ought to be in jail" followed after the word "radical" like the tail follows the dog.

There was no attempt at any time to understand what the word "bolshevism" actually meant or what its relationship was to other isms such as socialism or anarchism. Instead, all such isms were lumped together as being the same. Also there was no endeavor to separate liberals from radicals, progressives from revolutionists, or legitimate reformers from irresponsible crackpots. It was auto-

166

matically assumed that anyone who was not a "conservative" was a "radical," and hence even those who advocated the mildest reforms were dumped into the "Red" classification. In fact, in popular parlance a Bolshevik was anybody "from a dynamiter to the man who wears a straw hat in September," while the name "radical" covered all those whose shades of opinion ranged "from a mild wonderment over 'what the world is coming to' to the extreme extremists of the left wing." [1] Specifically, by late 1919, a radical was anyone suspected of being pro-German, a Russian or other foreigner, a person who sent bombs through the mails, a believer in free love, a member of the IWW, a Socialist, a Bolshevist, an anarchist, a member of a labor union, a supporter of the closed shop, or anyone who did not particularly agree with you.

[In the long run, therefore, bolshevism was translated not so much in terms of a specific political philosophy as in terms of the average citizen's own emotions, especially his pet hatreds and fears. Hence, it was easy for him to associate with the concept of bolshevism all those, both individuals and groups, with whom he personally had differences and in this way assuage his own conscience as well as protect his own interests. In this sense the average citizen was no better than the sensational journalist, the opportunistic politician, or the antiunion employer. And, in spite of the deleterious influence which their propaganda had upon him, morally he too was to blame for the unfortunate consequences that followed.]

Such indiscriminate thinking on the part of the average citizen inevitably fostered the assumption that there were many more domestic Bolshevists in operation than actually existed and that some of them, particularly the so-called parlor Reds, occupied responsible positions and wielded great influence. As the definition of a Bolshevist was constantly broadened, estimates of the number of such individuals became quite ridiculous. For example, Sherman Rogers, who ran several exposés of the parlor Reds in the New York *World,* made the "conservative estimate" in the late summer of 1919 that there were approximately five million such persons in the country and at least ten to fifteen million others who were subjected almost daily to their influence and teachings.[2]

Along with the three fall strikes, this proclivity to define a Bolshevik emotionally rather than rationally fanned public fear to the point where hysteria ultimately became manifest. Parlor Reds were thought to be everywhere and came to be regarded as even more dangerous than the labor radical or the bona fide revolutionist. Declaring such persons were "lower than the man who hurls or plants a bomb," many newspapers illustrated the temper of the day by crying, "Round up the Parlor Reds!"[3]

Unfortunately not only the real parlor Reds but individuals in all circumstances and walks of life were adversely affected. As the poison of suspicion seeped through every pore of society, many Negro leaders, public school teachers, college professors, clergymen, public officials, prominent citizens, and others were subjected to outrageous criticism from super-patriots and indeed from the public at large for supposed deviations from the accepted line. Insinuation, slander, character assassination, and smear were the methods most often used to compel conformity or enforce silence. Sometimes, the desire to force compliance precipitated ruthless action and mob violence or was used as the excuse for condoning such lawlessness.

The great tragedy was that in all this the concept of "Americanism" suffered greatly. No longer was it a word rich in significance and inspiration. No longer did it denote a way of life which encouraged new ideas. Instead, it had been emptied of its meaning and robbed of its unique power, since through the efforts of the patriotic societies "Americanism" was now used mainly to support a wide variety of reactionary ideas and condone a diversity of illiberal actions. In fact, "Americanism" was applied to anything which represented the *status quo* and which either directly or indirectly served to stifle progress. In this sense, "Americanism" became the great ally of "bolshevism" because, while the former was used to stymie liberal and progressive thought, the latter was employed as the clincher to any and all unwanted opinions:

I mustn't call you "Miky" and you
    mustn't call me "wop,"
For Uncle Sammy says it's wrong
    and hints we ought to stop;
But don't you fret, there's still
    one name that I'm allowed to speak,
So when I disagree with you I'll call
    you Bol-she-vik! veek! veek!
It's a scream and it's a shriek;
It's a rapid-fire response to any
    heresy you squeak.

You believe in votes for women? Yah!
    the Bolsheviki do.
And shorter hours? And land reforms?
    They're Bolshevistic, too.
"The Recall" and other things like that,
    are dangerous to seek;
Don't tell me you believe 'em or I'll
    call you Bolshevik!
Bolshevik! veek! veek!
A reformer is a freak!
But here's a name to stop him, for it's
    like a lightning streak. . . .[4]

Inevitably, this indiscriminate use of the word "Bolshevik" and
the deterioration of a wholesome concept of "Americanism" encouraged excessive intolerance and furthered the manifestation of
hysteria. Much of this, as we shall see, was evidenced by the state
and federal governments. But even more was displayed by the
general public itself. Naturally, the unwarranted restriction of
free speech and action which resulted from this situation cannot
be calculated accurately. Nevertheless, there is enough substantial
evidence to indicate that such restrictions represented one of the
most damning aspects — if not the most damning — of the entire
Red Scare.

Because of its professed desire to foster open-mindedness, the
educational system was second only to labor in the amount of

criticism which it received and the suspicion which it aroused. As early as the spring of 1919, super-patriotic and conservative journals, such as the *Manufacturers' Record* and the *National Civic Federation Review*, claimed that Bolshevistic doctrines were being spread through the schools, and certain newspapers rebroadcast these assertions or ran their own exposés of radicalism in American educational circles.[5] All these accounts were highly colored and totally misrepresented the real situation.

It was widely claimed that such colleges as Barnard, Wellesley, and Radcliffe were "hotbeds of bolshevism," while Chicago, Yale, Vassar, and Smith were denounced as "radical institutions" because they made the writings of Marx and Engels required reading for their students. President Henry N. MacCracken of Vassar was openly accused of being a "Soviet defender." Professors Felix Frankfurter and Zechariah Chafee, Jr., of Harvard, were declared to be leaders of a "parlor pink seminary." Other professors, such as N. B. Gras (Minnesota), E. C. Hayes (Illinois), E. A. Ross (Wisconsin), James Harvey Robinson (Columbia), John Dewey (Columbia), Dean Roscoe Pound (Harvard), and J. R. Commons (Wisconsin) were also labeled as "radicals" and placed in the parlor Red category.[6]

Inevitably, this drive for educational conformity on the college level caused public school teachers also to be suspect. As public fear of radicalism increased, teachers in some localities were suspended indefinitely for discussing bolshevism in any way, while in other areas immediate and arbitrary dismissal was the procedure. The classroom was regarded more and more as a holy shrine where only the goddess of 100 per cent patriotism, and not truth, was to be worshiped and where no conflicting ideologies were to be either presented or discussed.

Examples of intolerance against public school teachers were many. In Baltimore, a teacher was dismissed because she had explained to her students the philosophy of bolshevism and then had compared it with democracy. In Cambridge, Massachusetts, a young graduate of Radcliffe was suspended from her teaching duties when it was learned that she had formerly been a leader in the Radcliffe Liberal Club, an organization which promoted an open-minded study of bolshevism.[7]

New York City, with its environs, was the chief area where witch hunting for "Red" schoolteachers was undertaken. William L. Ettinger, superintendent of the city's schools, acted on the premise that there was no such thing as "9 to 3 patriotism" and emphasized the fact that the New York City system had no place for any teacher whose "personal convictions" made it impossible for him to be a "patriotic example to his students."[8] As a result of his and others' endeavors to find out "Who's Red and Who's True Blue" among the city's teachers, there were numerous dismissals throughout 1919.

Probably the most celebrated case involved Benjamin Glassberg, a Brooklyn high school history teacher who had been a director of the Socialist New York *Call* and a lecturer at the Rand School. He was dismissed in May 1919 for stating that the Soviet regime had been unduly maligned and for quoting several noted Bolshevists in answer to the question as to whether Lenin and Trotsky were German agents. The Lusk Committee (which was the direct instigator of many such dismissals) and the New York press first demanded and then applauded his removal. On the other hand, the *New Republic* met this action with "The Tsar is gone; the Kaiser is gone; but the little tsars and kaisers of our educational system continue in their ways of tyranny." Said Benjamin Glassberg, "Because I am a Jew, a Socialist and a member of the Teachers' Union I have been dismissed."[9]

Throughout the late spring and summer of 1919 the concern of the public and the press over radicalism in the nation's schools caused considerable talk on how the situation might be remedied. Many journals felt that increasing teachers' salaries might make many educators less susceptible to radical philosophies. The New York *Times* pointed out that Yale instructors received less than the college's furnace men. In a survey of certain rural areas, the *Literary Digest* found that public school teachers received less for instructing farm children than the average farmer paid a hired hand to swill his hogs. In similar fashion, the *Christian Science Monitor* discovered that in some areas of Illinois (where the average monthly income for a miner was $217) teachers were receiving only $55.[10]

Whether this factor of low salaries actually caused any appreciable amount of radicalism among teachers is doubtful. However, the fact remains that in the fall, as labor unrest grew, fear increased that the nation's schools were indeed the breeding grounds for communism. The patriotic societies intensified their demand for absolute educational conformity and the general press circulated ever wilder claims concerning bolshevism among educators. At the height of the steel strike, the Portland *Oregonian* maintained the spread of radicalism had been so thorough that American youths were "the prey of theoretical propagandists in our institutes of education." In the midst of the coal strike, the Toledo *Blade* charged that "publicity seekers among college professors who have picked up Bolshevism as a heaven-sent opportunity to spill flapdoodle" were as guilty as the radical labor agitator in stirring up social and industrial unrest.[11]

Although throughout 1919 the overwhelming majority of teacher dismissals for radicalism were based on hysteria and not on fact, there were a handful of removals which appeared quite justifiable. In November, Sonia Ginsberg of New York City Public School 170 was dismissed because she possessed a Communist party card and was active in the affairs of that organization. Six other women teachers in the schools of that city were found to be members of the Communist party and were removed by Superintendent Ettinger. Meanwhile, in Boston, an elementary school teacher was dismissed for attending Communist meetings and for making the remark, "Give us one generation of small children to train to manhood and womanhood and we will set up the Bolshevist form of the Soviet Government." In like manner, a sociology professor, Arthur W. Calhoun, of Ohio State University was removed for writing: "I want no mere puttering reforms. If the radicals will stick for ultimates and confiscation, I'll stay with them. One of the things that will hasten the revolution is to spread the notion that it *can* come soon." [12]

It was such expressions as the latter, along with the apprehension of a few bona fide Communists within the nation's educational system, that supported ever increasing pronouncements by the general press and the patriotic societies that there was "hardly a school or college in the country in which a Communist nucleus . . . has not been established." Those who were in a position to be well informed knew that such wild claims were erroneous. Even Superintendent Ettinger finally had to admit that among the vast number of the country's teachers the percentage of radicals was probably so small as to be negligible.[13]

However, throughout the late months of 1919 the fear remained that many teachers were followers of Lenin and Trotsky. As a result the teaching profession was temporarily rendered impotent because it could no longer carry out its function of truth-seeking and inquiry with any degree of safety. This was particularly unfortunate because if there was ever a time when the nation needed keen intellectual guidance it was at a moment when the country was confronted by a vicious foreign ideology. Yet, the nation preferred to stumble along with the guardians of its intellect mired in a "safe" but unrewarding and unproductive rut of conformity. For a time at least, no one dared live on the bright mountain tops of intellectual curiosity; everybody hurried into the shelter and the shadows of the valleys. While teachers on all levels of instruction retained their theoretical right to free speech, they were abject fools if they exercised it.

The situation with respect to clergymen and church organizations was much the same. Never at any time was there any reason to believe that radicals had taken over organized religion. Nor were the activities of those few religious "Pinks" who existed of sufficient importance to have caused any furor. The vast majority of ministers were completely patriotic and church journals such as the *Watchman-Examiner, Congregationalist and Advance, Christian Register,* and *United Presbyterian* bent over backwards during 1919 to assure their readers that loyalty to their country and godliness went hand in hand. In fact, church opinion as a whole mirrored public opinion to a large degree in its violent denunciation of the Bolshevik system.

And yet, because organized religion displayed a growing interest in social and economic problems and advocated certain changes in the pattern of American life to reduce unemployment, economic suffering, and the autocratic power of employers, the religious movement also became suspect. As early as March 1919, Ralph Easley claimed in the *National Civic Federation Review* that radicals were misleading the churches about the rights of labor and remarked that this was not difficult to do in view of the number of clergymen who subscribed to such "radical magazines" as the *New Republic, Nation, Public, Dial,* and *Survey.*[14]

Church agencies such as the National Welfare Council, the Federation for Social Service of the Methodist Church, and the Commission on the Church and Social Service of the Federal Council of Churches of Christ in America were particularly denounced by super-patriots and antiunion conservatives as "leaning toward bolshevism" because these organizations openly opposed employers' attempts to destroy unionism. This was especially true in the case of the Commission of Inquiry of the Interchurch World Movement, which was bitterly maligned as "Bolshevistic" because of its favorable attitude toward the steel worker in its investigation of the steel strike.[15]

The many prominent clergymen who were connected with these groups were immediately charged with being either sympathetic to radicalism or avowed radicals themselves. Bishop Francis J. McConnell (president of the Federation for Social Service of the Methodist Church), Dr. Harry F. Ward (secretary of the same organization and a professor of Christian ethics at Union Theological Seminary), Rev. S. Parkes Cadman (head of the Federal Council of Churches), Rev. Arthur C. McGiffert (president of

Union Theological Seminary), Rev. Charles R. Brown (dean of the Yale School of Religion), Rev. William A. Smith (editor of the *Churchman*), and Rabbi Stephen Wise were at one time or another placed in the parlor Red category.[16] Dr. Ward, in particular, was condemned by super-patriots because he had once claimed in his writings that the creation of a state composed entirely of producers and controlled by producers was "manifestly a Scriptural aim." Indeed, so great was the clamor raised over this statement that the Publishers' Section of the Graded Sunday School Syndicate (interdenominational) refused to reprint various teachers' manuals and Sunday school textbooks written by him.[17]

Through such misinterpreted statements as that by Dr. Ward, charges of religious radicalism slowly gained credibility in the public mind, and many people were brought to believe that even within organized religion "Bolshevism lifts its ugly head." Conservative antiunion groups, hostile anyway to the role the church was playing in passing moral judgment on economic issues, supplemented this growing fear by drawing wholly unfounded conclusions about connections between this alleged religious radicalism and the current labor unrest. As in the case of schoolteachers, resultant public intolerance soon precluded the free exercise of ministerial opinion and in many localities forced either a pattern of sullen conformity or arbitrary dismissal.

Again it was the nation which was the ultimate loser. Perhaps what the country needed most during the Red Scare period was the maintenance of moral and spiritual faith, yet it could hardly expect to safeguard it under these conditions. Rather than lead, the clergy now followed and as a result the nation's moral perceptions became duller not sharper. Temporarily, organized religion was forced to abandon its normal crusade for human equality and justice and consequently lost its primary social reason for existence. Gradually, it became afraid to take a stand and sank into the cowardice of noncommitment. For a time the nation had to be content with having the money-changers in the temple; no one dared drive them out.

Although education and religion were the two most obvious fields affected by the fear of radicalism, schoolteachers and clergymen were by no means alone in their inability to exercise free opinions by the late fall of 1919. Many other individuals and organizations also fell under the spotlight of suspicion. Thorstein Veblen, the famous economist, was considered a radical because of his unorthodox views on the evolution of the capitalistic system. Charlie Chaplin was held to be a Bolshevist because of his peculiar affinity for odd economic and social ideas. Jane Addams, a liberal thinker along social reform lines and one of the founders of Hull House, was charged with being part of the domestic Red network. As a result of his novel views concerning the connection of law with social and economic progress, the brilliant lawyer Clarence Darrow was denounced as a parlor Red.[18]

As might be expected, certain government officials were also subjected to super-patriotic attack and scrutiny. Said the *Wall Street Journal*, "We talk of parlor Bolshevists, but what of those other Bolshevists, in the Cabinet, or at any rate near the throne?" [19] Indeed, as the Red Scare heightened, all government officials who displayed a liberal streak of any kind were regarded with suspicion. Senators William E. Borah (Idaho), Robert M. LaFollette (Wisconsin), and George W. Norris (Nebraska) were particularly singled out for attack because of their firm support of minority rights and their opposition to the mounting Red Scare hysteria. Norman Hapgood, United States minister to Denmark, was charged with aiding the Reds since earlier, as editor of *Colliers' Weekly*, he had displayed certain liberal tendencies. William C. Bullitt, who had been sent on the 1918–19 peace mission to Russia, was thoroughly castigated for his supposed sympathy for bolshevism. George D. Herron, a delegate to the ill-fated Prinkipo Conference, was placed under suspicion both because of his own liberalism and because his wife was connected with the Rand School. Frederic C. Howe, commissioner of immigration at Ellis Island, was branded a radical because of his lenient attitude toward immigrants and deportees. Secretary of Labor William Wilson was considered in many conservative quarters as being tinged with radicalism because he was a union man and hence an "unconscious ally of bolshevism." Louis F. Post, the assistant secretary of labor, was regarded with suspicion since he had originally been editor and owner of the liberal journal the *Public*. Indeed, some super-patriots even went so far as to label President Wilson, himself, a parlor Red.[20]

Charges of bolshevism were directed into yet other fields as many liberal civic organizations were attacked for their radical leanings. The American Civil Liberties Union was condemned by 100 per cent patriots as a "Bolshevist front" and "a supporter of all subversive movements." Besides the Civil Liberties Union, the National Information Bureau, the Russian Famine Fund Committee, the National Council for the Reduction of Armaments, the National League of Women Voters, and the Foreign Policy Association were charged with being "tools of the radicals" and unpatriotic in their actions.[21]

Even the journalistic world did not escape the onslaught. The *Nation, New Republic, Dial, Public,* and *Survey*, as well as their complete staffs, were charged with being in sympathy with radicalism and condoning revolution. The Lusk Committee, for instance, branded the *Survey* as having the "endorsement of revolutionary groups," and the Toledo *Blade* claimed that the *Nation* and the *New Republic* were as guilty of the riots, bombs, and industrial unrest as the radical agitator. Paul V. Kellogg, editor of the *Survey*, was consistently denounced as a "radical sympathizer," and Oswald G. Villard, editor of the *Nation*, was misrepresented by the general press as a dangerous radical. It seemed Villard was the favorite target for journalistic jibes in 1919; the Philadelphia *Inquirer* at one time even suggested that he be deported to Russia. By late 1919, current hostility toward such editors and their publications caused the average citizen to think twice before he permitted it to be known that he subscribed to these journals.[22]

The weed of wild suspicion bore even bitterer fruit. At a time when irresponsible charges of radicalism were being leveled against certain educators, clergymen, public officials, and others, that whole segment of the nation's population which did not conform in skin color was brought under suspicion for ideological nonconformity as well.

The groundwork for such suspicion had been laid by the sensational Lusk disclosures in June. At that time, Lusk and his cohorts had stated that radical activity already had made significant progress among the Negro race and that a more active radical program of indoctrination was contemplated. The general press had met such claims with fear and trembling and had agreed that of all the reprehensible actions of radicals none surpassed this attempt "to undermine the loyalty of the Negroes." [23]

Unfortunately, such pronouncements were the immediate prelude to a series of race riots which electrified the nation in the summer of 1919. In particular, Washington, D.C., and Chicago, Illinois, fell under the sway of mob violence as Negroes and whites spilled through the streets fighting and slaughtering one another. Naturally, the question uppermost in the minds of all citizens was what had caused these brutal incidents. A myriad of factors were suggested. Continued wartime intolerance, the advent of Prohibition, sudden wartime migration of many southern Negroes to the North, inadequate Negro housing, high rent, inefficiency of the police, white-black economic competition, and a new feeling of independence on the part of certain Negroes were listed as the more important ones. Inevitably added to this list was bolshevism.

From the outset of the race riots in both Washington and Chicago (in which more than forty persons lost their lives), the fear was expressed that these disorders might be the result of Red propaganda. Some newspapers even ran such headlines as "REDS TRY TO STIR NEGROES TO REVOLT," and the New York *Times* declared that there was "no use in shutting our eyes to facts . . . Bolshevist agitation has been extended among the Negroes." One newspaper cartoonist depicted Lenin smiling and nodding his head while reading a news release of the American race riots and remarking to himself, "They're learning." Although other newspapers refused to believe radicalism among the Negro was the primary cause for the bloodshed, they were willing to admit it was entirely possible that radical influence had played a part. "There may be, as is intimated," said the Cincinnati *Enquirer*, "insidious and sinister agitation of revolutionary character back of these phenomena." [24]

If one could believe the Negro press, there was some slight basis for these exaggerated fears. Although the older Negro journals such as the *New York Amsterdam News*, *Negro Age*, and *Half-Century Magazine* rarely, if ever, broke with conservative precedent, other publications — the *Challenge*, *Crusader*, *Messenger*, *Negro World*, and *Veteran* — evidenced decidedly radical tendencies. Displaying the restless spirit of the "new" Negro in their crusade for greater social, economic, and political justice, these latter journals were naturally prone to seize upon bolshevism as a helpmeet, and in their despair over the painfully slow advances made under the democratic system closed their eyes to the even greater injustices inherent in the Bolshevik order. For example, in July, the *Negro World* told its readers that it devolved upon all oppressed peoples "to avail themselves of every weapon [Bolshevism] that may be effective in defeating the fell motives of their oppressors." A month later, the *Challenge* remarked, "Bolshevism is not bad. . . . Sovietcy takes away nobody's freedom. It gives a larger freedom." The August 30 issue of the *Veteran*, supposedly presenting the views of returning Negro soldiers, displayed a cartoon depicting a Negro in uniform, armed with a sword and a rifle, standing on a rope which led to the background where the United States was portrayed as a tree against which broken fragments of the Statue of Liberty were leaning and by which was the figure of the Devil. At the Negro soldier's feet was a large head of a white man surrounded by the labels "Jim Crow Him — Burn Him — Lynch Him — Kill — Mob — Starve." [25]

Since, by the fall of 1919, such radical Negro statements were widely publicized, a growing number of people accepted the claim that the racial unrest was due, in large part, to Bolshevist agitation.

The summer race riots therefore supplemented the other suspicious events of 1919 as a further indication of domestic Bolshevist activity and underwrote the assumption that no element in American society was immune to radical attack. For many persons, it seemed bad enough that organized labor, the press, religion, education, and government were infected — but also the Negro . . . !

This charge of Negro radicalism was definitely exaggerated. On the basis of the evidence, it is clear that radicalism, at best, played only a subsidiary role in the race riots and that such factors as inadequate housing, high rents, and Negro-white competition for industrial jobs were infinitely more important. But, in view of suspected labor radicalism and the alleged widespread activities of parlor Reds, overrated charges of bolshevism among the Negro seemed plausible. Unquestionably some of this exaggeration sprang from an entirely sincere fear on the part of certain individuals that bolshevism was making great progress within the race. However, it must be pointed out that most of these charges stemmed not from sincere hearts, but from believers in white supremacy, white riot participants, and their various sympathizers who wished to manufacture a clear justification for the white position by placing the entire blame on the Negro. It is enough to add that the rising Ku Klux Klan was the primary manufacturer and distributor of such propaganda.

Regardless of the various reasons for the race riots, these occurrences amply indicated the extremely ugly mood of the nation in 1919 and pointed to the increasing proclivity for lawless mob action which the Red Scare phenomenon encouraged. More importantly, such incidents illustrated a growing callousness toward injustice and a public indifference toward maintaining basic liberties. In their misguided desire to safeguard the nation, many citizens seemed prepared to throw away their traditional liberties and either countenance or participate in lawless acts. In this respect, such citizens were not one whit better than those against whom they fought and were themselves furthering radical aims.

Of course, such individuals consoled themselves by claiming that they were protecting liberty and sustaining the nation's traditional values. But they were either foolish or naive; you cannot save liberty by constantly denying it, nor can you maintain values by devaluing them. Mob action never has been nor will it ever be a successful guardian of democratic freedom.

Instances of mob violence were fairly frequent throughout 1919, although not so frequent as the liberal and radical press would have one believe. Nevertheless, the *Nation* was being more than just facetious when it once suggested that newspapers ought to print a special section listing all radical, Socialist, and liberal meetings so the public would know "Where To Get Mobbed To-nite." [26] Such incidents arising from local mob action were usually touched off by radical or Socialist gatherings (as in the case of the May Day riots), or by seditious utterances of one sort or another. Once in New York City, when a man shouted "To hell with the flag," there was such a free-for-all fight in the Waldorf-Astoria Hotel that the police had to be summoned to restore order. Again, at a Madison Square Garden Socialist rally, a fight ensued between Socialists and ardent patriots which necessitated police action to quell it and no small number of the rioters required medical attention. Subsequently, during the steel strike, a mob of enraged citizens forced 118 striking foreign steel workers at Weirton, West Virginia, to kiss the American flag. Too numerous to mention here are many other similar examples of local mob action, the frequency of which can be seen in the American Civil Liberties Union estimate of at least fifty for the year 1919.[27]

There was, however, one further example of mob violence which must be mentioned because it surpassed all others in calculated brutality and was so clearly expressive of the extent to which anti-radical thinking and propaganda had affected the public mind by late 1919. Occurring at the height of the labor unrest in the steel and coal industries, this action — the Centralia Massacre — marked, in a sense, the beginning of a truly hysterical public reaction to domestic radicalism.

In November 1919, there were only two IWW halls operating in the entire state of Washington, the rest having been suppressed or closed by either the police or local mobs. One of these two halls was located on Tower Avenue in the small town of Centralia. It had but recently been reopened, since the year before, in 1918, it had been raided and closed by an excited mob during a Red Cross parade.

The Centralia community was quite concerned about the re-opening of this radical refuge in the late summer of 1919, and on October 20, a group of local businessmen formed the Centralia Protective Association in order to safeguard the town from further infiltration by such undesirable individuals. Rumors then made the rounds that the IWW meeting hall would again be raided, possibly on Armistice Day, and the IWW, fearful lest such violent action actually take place, issued an appeal asking for tolerance and charging that "the profiteering class of Centralia have of late been waving the flag of our country in an endeavor to incite the lawless element of our city to raid our hall and club us out of town." [28]

Armistice Day in Centralia was raw and damp; a clinging, persistent fog had rolled into town during the night and even at noon the atmosphere had the appearance of dusk. Hoping to make up in patriotic fervor what the day lacked in weather, an American Legion parade formed in the Centralia city park shortly before 2 o'clock. Leading the parade were the members of the local Elks Lodge, then came a band, the Boy Scouts, the members of the Chehalis Post of the American Legion, and finally the members of the Centralia Post led by Warren O. Grimm, post commander and a leading figure in the Centralia Protective Association.

Meanwhile, almost certain that this parade boded ill for their safety especially since the proposed route of march lay directly past the IWW hall, the town's Wobblies undertook frantic defense measures to protect their headquarters from possible attack. Some members were stationed inside the hall itself; several were deployed directly across the street in the Avalon Hotel; and still others were placed about 400 yards away on a height of ground called Seminary Hill which stood approximately seventy-five feet above Tower Avenue. All were armed with either revolvers or rifles.[29]

At first it appeared that violence would be averted. The paraders passed by the hall peacefully enough, although several of them were seen carrying pieces of rope which they later claimed they had taken along only "as a joke." Then, for some unknown reason, the marchers decided to retrace their steps and pass the Wobbly Hall a second time. In so doing, they had to make a sharp turn at the junction of Third Street and Tower Avenue, and at that point considerable confusion resulted because the paraders were unable to maintain their proper lines. Some marchers later claimed that despite the confusion only shouts of "Halt, close up," were heard; but others declared there were also cries of "Let's go, Up and at 'em boys." In any event, at that precise moment, a few Legionnaires moved in the direction of the IWW Hall, which was only a few yards distant, and a flurry of shots immediately poured forth from the Avalon Hotel, Seminary Hill, and the Hall. Warren Grimm was felled in the middle of the street with a bullet through his stomach; Ben Casagranda, another Centralia Legionnaire, was killed as he reached the curb; and Arthur McElfresh, also a Legionnaire, was shot through the head just as he broke through the door of the IWW Hall.[30]

The Wobblies responsible for the shooting were quickly apprehended and placed in jail except for Wesley Everest, a local IWW agitator and himself an ex-soldier, who escaped from the Wobbly headquarters and sped toward the Skookumchuck River. A posse was quickly dispatched to track him down and finally managed to overtake him just as he was attempting to ford the stream. Up to his waist in water, Everest still refused to surrender, stood his ground, and in the process emptied his revolver into the oncoming crowd. As a result, still another Centralia Legionnaire, Dale Hubbard, succumbed to IWW fire. His gun now empty and no longer able to defend himself, Everest was quickly seized, beaten, kicked, cursed, and had his teeth knocked out by a rifle butt before he was carried back to town and thrown into jail with the rest of the captured Wobblies.[31]

Tragic as all these events were, they served merely as the prelude to even more reprehensible activity. That same night, as Everest lay bleeding on the floor of his cell, the lights went out all over Centralia. Under cover of darkness an enraged mob broke into the jail, seized Everest, and carried him into the street where he was again beaten unmercifully. He was then thrown into a limousine and en route to the Chehalis River was emasculated by one of his kidnappers in an orgy of brutal sadism. At the river, he was dragged from the car and amid his pleas of "Shoot me, for God's sake, shoot me!" he was hung by a short rope from the girders of a railroad bridge. This rope, however, did not satisfy his tormentors and he was pulled up and hung by a longer one. This also was regarded as too short and so he was pulled up a second time and fitted with still a longer rope. Somehow Everest remained alive throughout this ghastly process and in a last desperate effort clung to the edge of the bridge as he was pushed over the side for the third time. Someone growled, "Tramp on the bastard's fingers," and down Everest went, this time permanently. Making sure their work was well done, his murderers then turned the car lights on his dangling body and riddled it with bullets before driving back into the now peaceful town of Centralia.[32]

Several days later, the sodden corpse of Wesley Everest was cut down and was taken to the Centralia jail where with its foot-long neck it was laid out in full view of the other Wobblies as an example of Centralia's dislike for radicals. Shortly thereafter, since the town's undertakers refused to care for the body, four of Everest's comrades were taken from their cells and were forced to dig a grave for it in potter's field. No inquest was ever held to determine the exact cause of death. The incident was allegedly summed up by the Centralia coroner as follows: "Everest broke out of jail, went to the Chehalis River bridge, and committed suicide. He jumped off with a rope around his neck and then shot himself full of holes."[33]

The Centralia Massacre immediately set off a chain reaction of police action and mob violence all along the West Coast. Declaring a "War to the Death" on all such radicals, local, state, and federal law enforcement officers began a series of raids on November 12 to rid the area of the "Bolshevik menace." In Tacoma, thirty-four Wobblies were seized. In Spokane, members of the local American Legion, acting as deputy sheriffs, rounded up seventy-four more. In Oakland, an uncontrolled mob demolished what radical meeting places and halls they could find in order to prove that in Oakland "law and order shall prevail." In Seattle, a similar drive to "eliminate Reds" netted thirty-eight persons; publication of the Seattle *Union-Record*, official organ of the city's AFL unions, was suspended and three members of its staff were arrested for an editorial which had the temerity to suggest that the IWW be allowed to present its side of the Centralia affair.[34]

Indeed, almost all expressions of opinion not only bitterly lamented the deaths of the four Legionnaires, but condoned the Everest lynching and the subsequent raids. Not one of these accounts mentioned the fact that Everest also was an ex-soldier and had, in fact, served overseas. Instead, repeated applause rocked the national House of Representatives as Representative Albert Johnson (Washington) read to his colleagues telegram after telegram from American Legion posts and 100 per cent patriots condemning the Centralia murders as having been committed by "IWW draft-dodgers and traitors" and memorializing the dead Legionnaires as "victims of a long premeditated conspiracy to bring about an armed revolution in the United States." In the Senate, Senator Wesley L. Jones (Washington) received the plaudits of his fellow legislators when he cried, "The shots that killed these boys were really aimed at the heart of this Nation by those who oppose law and seek the overthrow of Government." Shouted Senator Miles Poindexter (Washington), "This detestable outrage is the fearful penalty which Centralia has paid for the over-lenient policy of the National government toward anarchists and murderous communists."[35]

The nation's press, meanwhile, reported the Centralia occurrence and the resultant West Coast raids in its typical sensational fashion. Eight-column headlines read: "RETURNED HEROES SLAIN BY IWW," and "'WAR TO DEATH' IS DECLARED AGAINST IWW." Editorials bulged with venomous phrases and emotional assertions. "An Unbelievable Deed," said the Portland *Oregonian*. "Radicalism Run Mad," shouted the New York *Times*. "An Act of War Against the United States," exclaimed the Boston *Evening Transcript*.[36]

Radical sentiment, of course, told a different story. Ralph Chaplin, just released from Fort Leavenworth after serving two years for his wartime Wobbly activities, maintained that the IWW in Centralia had been "framed." "Big Bill" Haywood branded the Centralia Legionnaires as "cooties" and believers in "the rope and the lamp post." The Chicago *New Solidarity* flatly declared that the businessmen in Centralia had started the chain of events which led to the shooting and that the IWW's "were decidedly not the aggressors."[37]

However, despite anything which radicals could say, majority opinion was convinced that the responsibility for the lawlessness in the West rested squarely on their shoulders and that it was "Time for a Showdown." Newspapers urged that the roundup of IWW members on the Pacific Coast be made "a national movement" and that all radicals whether "active or philosophical, parlor or outhouse" be vigorously suppressed. The cartoonist of the Washington *Evening Star* indicated the four Legionnaires would not have died in vain if Uncle Sam now doubled up his fist and really got down to the business of eliminating Reds. The Pittsburgh *Post* even went so far as to proclaim that "the sooner the firing squad is got into action the better," while certain church journals, such as the *United Presbyterian*, urged that every Bolshevist be made to "change his course or swing at the end of a rope."[38]

It was not until several months later that the concluding chapter to the Centralia affair was written. In February and March 1920,

They Have Not Died in Vain

(Cartoonist Berryman in the Washington *Evening Star*)

eleven of the captured Centralia Wobblies were tried for murder in Montesano, some forty miles northwest of Centralia. This change of venue was deemed necessary because of the existing prejudice in Centralia, but emotions proved to be just as high in the Montesano area. Legionnaires packed the courtroom, and federal troops had to be stationed in the region to maintain order.

Throughout the trial, the main question was whether the shooting had occurred before or after the Legionnaires began their assault on the IWW hall, and on that precise point testimony was hopelessly mixed. Nevertheless, on March 12, after deliberating for twenty-two hours, the jury acquitted two of the Centralia Wobblies, declared one insane, and found the remaining seven (one other having been released during the trial) guilty of second-degree murder. The sentences imposed ranged from twenty-five to forty years. A few weeks later the Washington Supreme Court unanimously upheld both the verdict and the sentences.[39]

Strangely enough, the outcome of the Montesano trial was universally denounced. Conservative opinion blasted the jury for not returning the death penalty based on first-degree murder. On the other hand, the IWW thought the verdict "one of the greatest judicial outrages of Modern Times." With due regard for conservative opinion, it does seem that if the defendants had not been avowed radicals the outcome of the trial might have been somewhat different. Subsequent to the trial, one juror in a sworn affadavit said, "I verily believe . . . that if these men had not been affiliated with the IWW organization they would never have been convicted."[40] Meanwhile, a so-called "labor jury," which was composed of six men elected by the various labor bodies of the Northwest to attend the trial and report their findings, claimed that on the basis of the testimony the defendants were not guilty, that business interests had conspired to raid the hall, that the hall was in the process of being raided when the shooting began, and that W. O. Grimm was the chief conspirator.[41]

Regardless of the differing opinions involved, the Centralia Massacre was the classic example of the antiradical public hysteria, hate, and intolerance which had been rising steadily since the Bolshevik Revolution of 1917. Centralia glaringly portrayed what disastrous events can befall a people and a community when unreasoning and emotional thinking supplants sanity. Moreover, Centralia showed that by the late months of 1919 indifference toward both civil liberty and violence had almost become a national virtue.

And what of Wesley Everest who had fallen prey to this insane public hatred for radicalism and whose killing had been submerged by the nation's sympathy for the four dead Legionnaires? Said one journal calmly, "Too bad to swing there, Wesley, for being a fool." [42]

12 ✶ ✶ ✶ ✶ ✶ ✶ ✶ ✶ ✶ ✶

The Quaker and the Ark

P<small>RIOR</small> to the late fall of 1919, the federal government had moved rather slowly against the domestic Bolshevik menace. Because of the press of other postwar problems and a preoccupation with the League question, most officials in Washington had not been able to concentrate their thinking on the radical danger. To be sure, politicians talked now and again about the evidences of radicalism in the country and the newspapers played up such statements with zeal. But only a few politicians had yet become really demagogical. In fact, there was every indication that most officials in Washington were less concerned about the radical menace than were their constituents. They had not lost their heads nor for the most part had they espoused hasty or ill-advised action to attack a nebulous Red threat.

However, in a democracy what the general public thinks and does also in the long run vitally affects the government. Hysteria, therefore, is particularly dangerous to the democratic system because it always represents a two-edged sword. Not only does such aberrant emotionalism unhinge public sanity, but ultimately it also destroys intelligent action by the government.

This was certainly the case in 1919. The events of the late summer and fall together with mounting public fear had a marked effect on official Washington and prompted a reorientation of thinking. This was true of both Congress and the administration. The June bombs, the Lusk disclosures, and the race riots (particularly the one in Washington itself) rapidly forced the adoption of a much more serious attitude toward the radical problem. And then the three major fall strikes stimulated even greater governmental interest. Moreover, mounting claims concerning the activities of parlor Reds, particularly with respect to their infiltration into high political office, created widespread official alarm. As a result, by the late fall of 1919 many government officials were also succumbing to rising hysteria and in so doing automatically caused the federal government to play a leading role in the Red Scare drama.

The person most responsible for the subsequent action of the federal government was Attorney General A. Mitchell Palmer. Under his direction the federal police power was set in motion so zealously against domestic radicalism that the months of November 1919 to January 1920 have sometimes been labeled "Government by Hysteria" or "Palmer's Reign of Terror."

A. Mitchell Palmer was born at Moosehead, Pennsylvania, of Quaker parents on May 4, 1872. As a boy he received a very thorough indoctrination in the Quaker faith and reached the age of maturity with his religious beliefs intact. Mitchell Palmer had an exceptionally quick and retentive mind, and proved well suited for his chosen profession, the law. At the age of 19 he graduated from Swarthmore with the highest honors and two years later, in 1893, was admitted to the Pennsylvania bar. He then became active in the local affairs of Stroudsburg, Pennsylvania, and finally became interested in state and national politics as well. He was elected on a reform ticket as a Democratic representative from the Twenty-Sixth District to the Sixty-First, Sixty-Second, and Sixty-Third congresses, and in 1912 served as vice-chairman of the Democratic National Committee. In that same year Palmer also acted as chairman of the Pennsylvania delegation to the Democratic National Convention and was chiefly instrumental in swinging the votes of that delegation to Woodrow Wilson.[1]

For this and other political services rendered, President-elect

Wilson offered Palmer the portfolio of secretary of war in February 1913, but Palmer graciously declined by saying, "I am a Quaker. . . . And the United States requires not a man of peace for a war secretary, but one who can think war. . . ." [2] However, President Wilson kept in touch with the Pennsylvania lawyer-politician, appointing him first to a judgeship on the United States Court of Claims and then, in October 1917, to the job of alien property custodian, a post created by the 1917 Trading with the Enemy Act. Palmer continued in this latter capacity until March 5, 1919, when he was finally brought into Wilson's official family by a recess appointment as attorney general. [3]

It has often been charged that Attorney General Palmer undertook his subsequent one-man crusade against the Reds to further his own personal political ambitions. The Quaker from Pennsylvania did, without a doubt, have his eye on the White House and along with many other followers of the New Freedom hoped to be the heir apparent. His qualifications were certainly better than average. He was an ardent Wilsonian, he was a strong supporter of the League, and, for the moment at least, he had the confidence of the President. Moreover, he was an able administrator, a diligent worker, and a proof-tested reformer, having consistently opposed the infamous Penrose machine in Pennsylvania.

There is every indication that by the spring of 1920 Palmer played the Red Scare for all it was worth, hoping to use his aggressive stand against the Reds as the primary means by which he could project himself into the presidency. But in the fall of 1919 it appeared that the attorney general began his attack on radicalism partially to satisfy mounting clamor for the government to act and partially to sooth his own very real fear that the Reds were about to take over the United States. As alien property custodian, he had already gained a wide knowledge of anti-American and antidemocratic propaganda, and hence was much more sensitive to radical outbursts than he otherwise might have been. Moreover, in that capacity he had been made acutely aware of the problem of sabotage and fifth-column activity, and therefore was more suspicious than normal. Then, too, as a Quaker, Palmer was especially opposed to both the godlessness and the violence of the Bolshevik program and thus easily developed an abnormal attitude toward it. It would be difficult to estimate accurately the tremendous effect which the bombing of his own home had on his thinking. The June 2 incident unquestionably heightened Palmer's proclivity for exaggerating the radical menace anyway, and it is understandable how he came to scent "a Bolshevist plot in every item of the day's news." [4]

Shortly after the bombing of his home, Palmer asked for and received an appropriation of $500,000 from Congress to facilitate the Justice Department's apprehension of those who sought to destroy law and order. Palmer now began his crusade in earnest. On August 1, he established within the Department's Bureau of Investigation the so-called General Intelligence, or antiradical, Division. As its head he appointed young J. Edgar Hoover, charging him with the responsibility of gathering and coordinating all information concerning domestic radical activities. Under the general guidance of bureau chief Flynn and through the unstinting zeal of Hoover, this unit rapidly became the nerve center of the entire Justice Department and by January 1920 made its war on radicalism the department's primary occupation. In fact, there are some indications that both Flynn and Hoover purposely played on the attorney general's fears and exploited the whole issue of radicalism in order to enhance the Bureau of Investigation's power and prestige. [5] Certainly, the hunt for radicals during the 1919–20 period "made" the Bureau of Investigation and started it on the road to becoming the famous FBI of the present day.

In any event, shortly after the creation of the GID, an elaborate card index system was established; over 200,000 cards contained detailed information concerning all known radical organizations, societies, associations, and publications. Set up by Mr. Hoover on the basis of his earlier experience as an employee of the Library of Congress, this index was so constructed that a card for a particular city not only showed the various radical organizations in that area but also their membership rolls, names of officers, and time and place of meetings. By the late fall of 1919, according to Attorney General Palmer, this index also contained the complete case histories of over 60,000 dangerous radicals and housed "a greater mass of data upon this subject than is anywhere else available." [6]

Under the direction of Hoover, the GID became the Justice Department's personal antiradical propaganda bureau as well as a vast repository of radical information. This was particularly true after the formation of the Communist parties in September. In the ensuing months, the division sent to all major newspapers and periodicals letters signed by the attorney general which began with the statement, "My one desire is to acquaint people like you with the real menace of evil-thinking, which is the foundation of the Red Movement," and ended with exaggerated accounts of domestic Communist activity. The division also distributed copies of the manifestoes of the Third International, the Communist party, and the Communist Labor party, and warned Americans against falling for this Bolshevik claptrap.[7] At the same time, the division, with the attorney general's full acquiescence, circulated much propaganda connecting the major fall strikes and the summer race riots with the Communists. It need hardly be added that such propaganda was widely circulated by the general press and that under the circumstances the United States Department of Justice was, itself, one of the major agents fostering Red Scare hysteria in the fall of 1919.

Strangely enough, in spite of this vigorous propaganda campaign, the Justice Department did not immediately show any inclination to undertake specific action against the Red menace. Such reticence stemmed to a large degree from experience already gained in connection with the Seattle strike a few months earlier, when a group of fifty-four alien radicals from the Seattle area had been apprehended by Justice Department agents and sent East for possible deportation. Carried on a special train, derisively called the "Red Special," this group had been hurried off to Ellis Island and held incommunicado while the majority of the nation's press howled for their immediate expulsion.[8] But some intense opposition to this proposed action had developed. The *Nation* spoke long and loud of the great evils of deportation and called for legislation to protect aliens against such arbitrary action. The New York *Globe* warned the government that there might be such a thing as carrying this "anti-red business" too far, while the Duluth *Herald* wondered if the nation was not already "beginning to over-do it." Said the New York *Call*, "To-day it is the IWW; tomorrow the Socialist Party. . . ."[9]

This opposition to hasty governmental action caused the Justice Department to proceed cautiously, and, in the final analysis, the department shied away from mass deportations. After careful reexamination of the cases, a large portion of the "Red Special" group were released for insufficient evidence, and twelve others were given their freedom because they voluntarily repudiated their Red tenets. By May 1919, only three of the original fifty-four had actually been deported. Ruefully, the New York *Times* declared, "At the water's edge an indulgent Government hesitates. By official magic some of the goats are transformed into probationary sheep."[10]

Those who urged caution won only a temporary victory. The pressure of ensuing events in the summer and fall of 1919 definitely tipped the scales in favor of more aggressive action and agitation for the deportation of radical aliens became more vociferous while the failure of the government to deport caused increasing comment. Petitions from state legislatures, business organizations, and patriotic societies flooded Congress demanding that the government do something and that the Justice Department, in particular, be shaken out of its lethargy. Such sentiment became sufficiently strong by early October that Senator Poindexter rose in the Senate and publicly denounced the Justice Department for not creating new "Red Specials" and securing the immediate deportation of all radical agitators.[11] Such assaults on the Justice Department reached a climax when, on October 19, the Senate unanimously adopted a resolution which requested the attorney general ". . . to advise and inform the Senate whether or not the Department of

Justice has taken legal proceedings, and if not, why not, and if so, to what extent, for the arrest and punishment [or deportation] . . . of the various persons within the United States who . . . have attempted to bring about the forcible overthrow of the Government. . . ." [12]

This resolution, together with mounting public clamor, served as the immediate reason for Palmer's turning from less talk to more action. Realizing that in view of the cessation of hostilities with Germany it would be extremely difficult to proceed against radical citizens on grounds of either espionage or sedition, he centered his efforts on the apprehension of radical aliens who would be subject to the deportation provisions of the Alien Law of 1918. This procedure seemed at the moment to be most expedient anyway since the General Intelligence Division estimated that about 90 per cent of all domestic radicals were aliens, and it was believed that the native-born element, if left alone, would never prove really dangerous. On this basis, orders were sent to Bureau of Investigation agents and confidential informants that their major activities "should be particularly directed to persons, not citizens of the United States, with a view of obtaining deportation cases." [13]

On November 7, one day before the coal strike injunction was extended and four days before the Centralia murders, Attorney General Palmer gave the public and Congress the action they had been waiting for by unloosing a nation-wide raid against the Union of Russian Workers. Founded in 1907, this organization had its headquarters in the Russian People's House, 133 East 15th Street, New York City, and, according to its own statements, was composed of "atheists, communists and anarchists." It believed in the complete overthrow of all institutions of government and the confiscation of all wealth through the violence of social revolution. The estimated membership of the organization was 4000.[14]

Although 250 officers and members of the URW were seized in simultaneous raids in eleven other cities, the main blow fell on the New York headquarters. The People's House raid was conducted with mathematical precision, bureau agents remaining outside the building in parked cars until the signal was given. At that moment, they closed in rapidly and took the establishment by surprise. Several huge truck-loads of radical propaganda were confiscated, and about 200 men and women were violently assisted out of the building by a special riot squad and driven away to Justice Department headquarters at 13 Park Row for questioning. The New York *Times* reported that some of the occupants had been "badly beaten by the police . . . their heads wrapped in bandages testifying to the rough manner in which they had been handled." [15]

As a result of the questioning, only thirty-nine of those seized were finally held. Of the others, a few were found to be American citizens and were immediately released; the rest were simple workingmen of Russian nationality who spoke little or no English and who belonged to the organization for almost every conceivable reason except to promote revolution. Nevertheless, despite their obvious ignorance concerning the real aims of the URW, certain of these prisoners were held for excessively long periods of time before they were given their freedom. This was particularly true at Hartford, Connecticut, where some arrested members were kept in jail five months before even receiving a hearing. [16]

In the meantime, state and local officials regarded the attorney general's November 7 raid as the signal for them to act also and throughout the country local raids were made on suspected nests of alien radicals. Once again the activity was greatest in New York City where on November 8 the Lusk Committee, with the aid of 700 police, raided seventy-three radical centers, arrested more than 500 individuals, and seized tons of literature. Of the number arrested, thirty-five citizens were held on state criminal anarchy charges (among them, Benjamin Gitlow and Jim Larkin); all others who were aliens and thought to be in a deportable category were turned over to federal authorities for disposition. All in all, as a result of the federal raid and these various local raids, some 246 aliens were ultimately detained and adjudged to be deportable radicals, most of them being members of the Union of Russian Workers. [17]

In spite of the obvious injustices involved and the small catch of truly revolutionary characters, the nation seemed delighted with the raids. To the government, and especially to Attorney General Palmer, went unstinting praise for having acted "In the Nick of Time" and having nipped "a gigantic plot" in the bud. Suddenly, the attorney general became the most popular figure in the nation and found himself enthroned as the third in a triumvirate of great saviors of the country — first Hanson, then Coolidge, now Palmer. His prestige was perhaps all the more enhanced since the government was temporarily leaderless; Woodrow Wilson lay stricken in the White House while the ship of state floundered helplessly in the rough seas of fear and reaction. To the man on the street, Palmer was "running the administration," "a lion-hearted man [who] has brought order out of chaos," and "A Strong Man of Peace." Newspapers excitedly described him as "a tower of strength to his countrymen," and declared that his actions brought "thrills of joy to every American." [18]

The Senate which but a few weeks before had censured the attorney general for his lethargy, now complimented the Justice Department for its aggressiveness and on November 14, rapt attention was given to a letter from the attorney general which answered in detail the Senate's resolution of October 19. Accompanying this letter was a full report of what the Justice Department through its GID had since discovered concerning domestic radicalism. Both the report and the letter gave testimony to the vast extent of radical activity and propaganda in the United States and advocated that new peacetime sedition laws be passed. In this way, claimed the attorney general, not only radical aliens but also radical citizens could be apprehended through the raiding device.[19] This request did not fall on deaf ears and the Senate hurriedly renewed its consideration of suitable peacetime sedition legislation which, except for the brief period immediately following the June 2 bombings, had been allowed to lapse.

Meanwhile, radicals were appalled at this sudden turn of events. The November 7 raids and the suggestions for new antiradical

In the Nick of Time

(Cartoonist McCarthy in the New Orleans *Times-Picayune*)

legislation were denounced violently and a "Call to Arms" was issued by most radical organizations. Pamphlets of the American Anarchist Federated Commune warned that "no such horrible scene as on the bloody Friday of November 7th, 1919, should be repeated without bloody — yes, bloody — revenge." The Chicago *New Solidarity*, blasting the action of the government as the beginning of a "White Terror," cried, "Now is the time, all you Anarchists, Socialists, Communists, non-ists, all for the big drive! Let us hit the plutocrats and get rid of them!" The Chicago *Communist*, meanwhile, proclaimed that no matter what the government did it would avail nothing because suppression "will only breed blind fury" and in the long run, "the mass life will have its say." [20]

Among the nonradicals it was now widely hoped that the strong action of the attorney general would be a prelude to the ultimate expulsion of all alien radicals. In the ensuing weeks, therefore, the question of alien deportation became an important one. Under the influence of rising hysteria, general sentiment demanded that the nation be purged of all alien agitators and that wholesale deportations be started immediately.

However, the exact position of the government on the issue of radicalism still remained somewhat uncertain. There were many reasons for this. In the first place, there was no effective leadership at the top in either setting policy or giving unity to action. President Wilson was exercising very little control since both Dr. Grayson and Mrs. Wilson were seeing to it that the ailing Chief Executive was bothered as little as possible by governmental matters. If the coal strike was any indication, Wilson was paying scant heed to domestic affairs anyway. His one-track mind was fastened firmly on the League question and he was devoting what little strength he had almost exclusively to that problem. Indeed, from August 1919 to April 1920, no full discussion of any domestic matter was held with the President; he did not even call the Cabinet together. Voicing some concern over this, Secretary of State

Robert Lansing called a few such meetings on his own initiative up to February 1920, but when the President heard about it, he became highly indignant and informed him that the Cabinet was not to assemble without specific orders from the White House.[21] Such a situation abetted the charge that it was not the President but Mrs. Wilson who was actually making the important decisions. Remarked New Mexico's Senator Albert Fall caustically, "We have no President. We have a petticoat government." [22]

While there is little support for Fall's contention, no woman could have been more fickle or indefinite on the specific issue of radicalism than was the President. When he did find time to be bothered with this matter, he usually wound up in a complete quandary. Like most well-meaning liberals, his ideas on the subject ran in so many different directions that definite decisions on his part were virtually impossible. Of course, he was firmly wedded to the principles of freedom of speech and action and wanted to retain as much free play in those areas as possible. Yet, he was also sufficiently worried about the Bolshevik menace that he believed some restrictive safeguards were necessary. Just what form those should take he did not know.

At first Wilson seemed concerned only about the spread of bolshevism in Europe and vehemently addressed himself to that subject on numerous occasions.[23] But as time went on, he also perceived that the United States was not immune. Thereafter, he warned the American people to be wary of those who were trying to convert them to communism and more than once hinted that there were probably many Bolshevik agents at work in American society. In some instances, Wilson's feeling toward radicalism actually took the form of a mild hysteria. At a time when there was some pressure in his own Cabinet to release Debs from jail, President Wilson, backed by Palmer, stubbornly refused to consider it by saying simply, "No, I will not release him." [24] In late 1919, the Chief Executive ardently supported Palmer in his drive for the enactment of some form of peacetime sedition legislation, even requesting the passage of such a measure in his December 1919 annual message to Congress.[25] Moreover, Wilson himself showed that he was not above using the issue of radicalism to his own advantage when conditions warranted. During his western speaking tour, he consistently stated that the current domestic opposition to the League was fully compatible with the philosophy of bolshevism and, while he warned his listeners not to jump to the conclusion that his Republican opponents were Bolshevists, he strongly implied that they were indeed the unwitting dupes of Bolshevists in their nonsupport of the League.[26] Actually, by the time of his nervous breakdown, the President had come to think of the Bolshevists as being one of the most insidious pressure groups working against his ideas on world peace and hence he came to hate them bitterly for being not only a threat to the welfare of the United States, but traitors to all of civilization, to all mankind. This attitude, along with his forceful statements on the police and coal strikes, and his support of Coolidge in the Massachusetts gubernatorial election, indicated that Wilson, too, bore some responsibility for public hysteria in 1919.

President Wilson, however, also reflected that innate caution characteristic of most liberals on matters relating to a proper defense against radicalism. As he stated in his annual message of December 1919, he well recognized "the seed of revolution is repression" and therefore hoped that all restrictions on personal liberty necessary to combat radicalism would be administered with utmost care.[27] At the same time, he realized that the current intense feeling against radicalism was inimical to liberal progress of any kind and therefore was extremely dangerous. For this reason, the President warned his attorney general more than once, "Palmer, do not let this country see red." [28]

That Palmer did not heed such warnings was certainly not because the President stood alone in this underlying desire to exercise extreme caution. Certain other members of the official family were of like mind and looked askance at many of the attorney general's activities. Their objections, however, were considerably weakened by the fact that after September the President was missing from the scene. One can only speculate that had the President been able to attend Cabinet sessions between October 1919 and February 1920 some of the more onerous Red-baiting tactics of the attorney general might have been forestalled.

Secretaries Daniels (Navy), Lane (Interior), Houston (Agriculture), and William Wilson (Labor), in particular, were opposed to many of the Quaker's actions although none of them, except Secretary Wilson, ever displayed the courage to meet the attorney general head-on. These men registered disapproval of Palmer's objections to the release of Debs, claiming the Justice Department was encouraging the President to make a martyr out of the fiery Hoosier. They also deplored the manner in which Palmer, with the President's acquiescence, handled the coal strike. As secretary of labor and a former coal miner himself, William Wilson was particularly incensed at Palmer's coal strike action. Furthermore, these officials objected to Palmer's whole raiding policy and denounced his growing disregard for civil liberties. William Wilson more than once charged that Palmer's activities were creating Communists rather than eliminating them, and Secretary Lane stated that he, too, did not believe such tactics would ever wipe out radicalism. As Lane later complained to Frank Cobb of the New York *World*: "We are not going to destroy [radicalism] or prevent it . . . by refusing to answer it." [29]

On the other hand within the Cabinet and close to the President was that small, but powerful, element which favored strong action and influenced the Chief Executive in that direction. Palmer was unquestionably the primary figure in this cabal, but he was ably assisted by such individuals as Secretary of State Lansing, Postmaster General Burleson, and the presidential secretary, Tumulty. These men constantly strove for more aggressive action against domestic radicals and were inclined to allow their fears to run away with their better judgment. As early as July 1919, Lansing was confiding to his private diary that the radical situation in the United States was becoming so serious that the time for drastic action was near at hand. By September and the Boston police strike, he was convinced that the time to act had come and complained bitterly because other Cabinet officials such as Lane, Daniels, and Wilson did not agree with him. With the advent of the coal strike, Lansing enthusiastically endorsed Palmer's injunction move and greeted the Centralia episode with a prayerful entry in his diary that the deaths of the Legionnaires might at last force some real government action.[30]

Postmaster General Burleson reacted similarly to the passing parade of events. Even though the affable Texan knew in his heart that the avoidance of social wrongs and the creation of social justice and economic opportunity were the only sure preventives of radicalism, he vigorously championed a policy of suppression. Not only did he follow such a policy during the war with respect to antiwar publications, but he extended this attitude to anti-capitalist magazines and newspapers following the war. When, in February 1919, President Wilson wrote to Burleson that he thought it best for the postmaster general to ease off on this stringent policy, Burleson scrawled across the White House note that he would continue to suppress. Later, when President Wilson was toying with the idea of releasing some political prisoners put in jail during the war for their antiwar expressions of opinion, Burleson protested sharply and along with Palmer insisted on sticking by the original sentences.[31]

It was Tumulty, however, who was really the key man of the three, for he not only backed Palmer's various schemes but often pleaded the attorney general's case directly with the President. Palmer and Tumulty were close personal friends, Tumulty having been the one who first suggested the Pennsylvania Quaker's name to Wilson for the post of attorney general. Like Palmer, Tumulty was strongly opposed to bolshevism on both political and religious grounds, for the presidential secretary was both a firm believer in the democratic process and an ardent Catholic. Also like Palmer, Tumulty had become emotionally involved in his thinking on domestic radicalism and by late 1919 was experiencing real hysteria over the alleged menace. It was Tumulty who drafted the telegram from Wilson to Coolidge upon the latter's election victory in Massachusetts, and he also was responsible for the wording of the President's statement on the coal strike. In this connection, it was Tumulty who gave Palmer most of the arguments and verbal ammunition needed to convince the President that an injunction against the miners was the only feasible solution.[32]

With the President pulled first one way and then the other as the Cabinet itself remained badly divided over the radical menace, the ability of the government to withstand mounting public pressure rapidly weakened. Nowhere was this fact more apparent than in the matter of alien deportations. Under the law, deportations could not be ordered by the Justice Department but were handled as a function of the Department of Labor. Naturally, there was from the beginning the serious possibility that these two departments would not see eye to eye on deportation matters since not only Secretary Wilson but also Assistant Secretary Louis Post was evidencing a completely hostile attitude toward the attorney general's Red-hunting procedures. Moreover, both of these men were known to be thoroughly opposed to wholesale alien expulsions.

As this impasse threatened, however, two events occurred which increased the public clamor for deportation and strengthened Attorney General Palmer's position. The first involved the commissioner of immigration, Frederic C. Howe, and his administration of Ellis Island; the second was the discovery of a "bomb factory" in New York City.

The House Committee on Immigration began an investigation of Ellis Island on November 22 and found that from February 1917 to November 1919 more than 600 aliens had been arrested and detained by the federal government for preaching anarchy, but only sixty had actually been deported. Howe, who was primarily responsible for this situation and who was suspected of radical tendencies himself, resigned his position rather than be coerced into ordering deportations which he believed were unjust. His successor, Byron Uhl, immediately set about to rectify his leniency.[33]

The Ellis Island controversy acquired added significance when, on November 25, state and federal agents once again raided the Russian People's House and found a secret chamber in which reposed "material for 100 bombs." Newspapers from the Atlantic to the Pacific carried exaggerated accounts of the contents of the "50 or 60 small bottles" that were discovered and ran monstrous headlines declaring "RED BOMB LABORATORY FOUND" and "FIND REDS' BOMB SHOP." Inspector Owen Fagan of the Bureau of Combustibles was widely quoted as saying the room contained "the most deadly and most dangerous assortment of explosives and bomb ingredients . . . seen in many a year." [34]

Under such conditions, the public and the press shouted even more loudly for the deportation of all alien radicals. Why, they wanted to know, had so many Red dynamiters and bombers been allowed into the country, but so few let out? In this field, they concluded, our "imports" were certainly greater than our "exports." Congress, meanwhile, was deluged with petitions from Elks, Kiwanians, Rotarians, Legionnaires, and others declaring that the time "has arrived when Americans should assert themselves and drive from these shores all disloyal aliens." [35] Congressmen themselves succumbed to this mounting antialien passion. Numerous bills were proposed to relieve the Labor Department of the responsibility for deportation and give such power to the attorney general instead. Legislation was also advocated whereby a naturalized citizen might have his certificate canceled and be deported for espousing radical philosophies. Senator Kenneth D. McKellar of Tennessee even suggested that radical native-born Americans be expelled to a special penal colony on Guam, the nation thereby establishing its own Siberia! [36]

Such overwhelming public, press, and congressional sentiment ultimately forced the action desired. The Labor Department fell into line by proclaiming that membership in the Union of Russian Workers was indeed a deportable offense. Great speculation immediately arose as to when and how the first mass deportation would be carried out. Finally it was learned that a group would be shipped aboard the *Buford*, an Army transport, sometime before Christmas and the public press looked forward to its sailing with much enthusiasm.

As predicted, on December 21, 249 deportees, among them three women, set sail aboard the *Buford* from New York for an unknown destination (later found to be Hango, Finland, from whence the deportees were shipped by train into Soviet Russia). Christened by the press the "Soviet Ark," the vessel was stocked with sufficient provisions for a six weeks' voyage and, besides the crew, carried 250 soldiers to guard the 249 "guests." Of the passengers, 199 had been apprehended in the November raids and were members of the Union of Russian Workers; 43 were anarchists whose deportation had previously been directed; and the remaining 7 were public charges, criminals, or misfits.[37] Twelve of the men on board left behind wives and children, who earlier had attempted to break through the Ellis Island ferry gates in a vain attempt to join their fathers and husbands — an action which had been reported by the press with such ridiculous headlines as "REDS STORM FERRY GATES TO FREE PALS."[38]

Of the 249 who were deported, the vast majority had never participated in any terroristic action nor did they have any criminal record. Their belief in theoretical anarchism, rather than their actions, had made them subject to expulsion. However, a few of the deportees were notorious and the public labored under the delusion that all 249 were anarchist murderers and criminals of this sort. On board, for example, were Emma Goldman and Alex Berkman. Both had criminal records and both were well known for their violent anarchistic activities. Newspaper notoriety on Miss Goldman had begun in 1893 and in the following twenty-five years she had been arrested many times for making speeches "menacing to the public order." It had been claimed that she was actually the mentor of Leon Czolgosz, the assassin of McKinley, and as early as 1907 efforts were made to secure her deportation. Similarly, Berkman had come into prominence in 1892, when, during the Homestead strike, he attempted to murder Henry C. Frick.

Sentenced to twenty-one years, he served only fourteen before he was paroled. After his release, he made many violent speeches and insisted on "propaganda by deed." Nicknamed the "Red King" and the "Red Queen," both Alex Berkman and Emma Goldman left the United States defying and cursing the country, but, according to the press, loving and fondling the thousands of good old American dollars in their possession with which they hoped to gain a decided advantage over the rank and file of the Russian Bolshevists.[39] Said Emma Goldman upon leaving: "I do not consider it punishment to be sent back to Soviet Russia. I consider it an honor to be chosen as the first political agitator to be deported from the United States. . . ."[40]

The general press made the most of the whole deportation situation by announcing it with screaming headlines, while editorial columns bulged with favorable comment. Describing the group as "the unholiest cargo that ever left our shores," editors hailed the sailing of the *Buford* as "inaugurating a new policy in the treatment of convicted radicals." Most agreed that the departure of these men and women was "none too soon" and "timely and just." The New York *Evening Mail* declared that "Just as the sailing of the Ark that Noah built was a pledge for the preservation of the human race, so the sailing of·the Ark of the Soviet is a pledge for the preservation of America." The Boston *Evening Transcript* maintained the sailing was "as epoch-making as the immortal voyage of Columbus," while the *Saturday Evening Post* drew yet another nautical comparison by declaring, "The *Mayflower* brought the first of the builders to this country; the *Buford* has taken away the first destroyers." Quipped the New York *Tribune*, "The ultra-red faction is feeling a trifle ultra-marine."[41]

But in spite of this virtual unanimity of opinion, there were a few who remained either suspicious of the *Buford* venture or outright opposed to it. Such respectable newspapers as the Springfield *Republican* and the New York *Globe* warned against such excesses, while the Washington *Post* thought the deportation was "a serious mistake."[42] Liberal and radical sentiment was vehement.

The *New Republic, Nation,* and *Dial* agreed that the action marked the end of the United States as an asylum for the oppressed of all nations. Max Eastman in his *Liberator* charged that the American government had just proved itself "the most perfect bouncing system ever struck off by the hand of man." A cartoon in the latter magazine showed the smoke from the *Buford* as it steamed by the Statue of Liberty enveloping the head and torch, obliterating them completely.[43]

Nevertheless, to the vast majority of citizens the *Buford* remained the logical conclusion to the November raids. It proved that the government under the direction of A. Mitchell Palmer had at last awakened to the radical threat, and, like the New York Lusk Committee, was willing to undertake drastic measures to meet it. The government was finally fulfilling the demands for action which had been growing steadily since the Seattle strike of more than nine months before, and the general public was pleased. Indeed, burdened by its colossal fear, the public now demanded new forays and more action. "Let there be more deportations," cried the Philadelphia *Inquirer*. The Soviet Ark is "only a good begining," shouted the Portland *Oregonian*. "It is hoped and expected," said the Cleveland *Plain Dealer*, "that other vessels, larger, more commodious, carrying similar cargoes, will follow in her wake." [44]

13 ★ ★ ★ ★ ★ ★ ★ ★ ★ ★

The January Raids

Spurred on by the apparent success already achieved and mindful of the demand for more deportations, Attorney General Palmer now concentrated his attention on the recently formed Communist and Communist Labor parties. Considering these the backbone of the domestic revolutionary movement, he formulated plans whereby they might be eliminated, and, as in the case of the Union of Russian Workers, relied almost solely on the raiding device and the deportation statute of 1918 to achieve this goal.

The federal raid of November 7 had proved an excellent laboratory experiment. It had shown that if any raid was to be followed by deportations, close cooperation with the Department of Labor was absolutely essential because of its jurisdiction over deportation matters. Therefore, in laying plans for his new move, the attorney general attempted to bring Labor Department officials into closer harmony with his own views. In this attempt, he was aided by the fact that, at the moment, Secretary of Labor Wilson was ill and Assistant Secretary Post was otherwise occupied. This left John W. Abercrombie, solicitor of the Department of Labor, but in reality a member of the Justice Department, to function as acting labor secretary. Naturally, he proved most cooperative. Moreover, the Labor Department's top official on deportation affairs, Commissioner General of Immigration Anthony J. Caminetti, was currently evidencing as much hysteria over the Red menace as was the attorney general. Therefore he also fell easily into line.[1]

210

After consultation with these men, it was unanimously decided that alien members of both the Communist party and the Communist Labor party were subject to deportation under the 1918 Alien Act. On this basis, Acting Secretary of Labor Abercrombie signed on December 27 more than 3000 warrants for the arrest of known alien adherents to the two Communist organizations and gave such warrants to the Justice Department for execution. Four days later, on the advice of Commissioner Caminetti (who in turn was acting upon a suggestion made to him by one of Palmer's emissaries from the Justice Department), Abercrombie also made an important change in the rule governing the procedure of deportation arrest hearings. Prior to December 31 the rule had read: "At the beginning of the hearing under the warrant of arrest, the alien shall be allowed to inspect the warrant. . . and shall be apprised that he may be represented by counsel." [2] The rule, as changed, read as follows: "Preferably at the beginning of the hearing . . . or at any rate as soon as such hearing has proceeded sufficiently in the development of the facts to protect the Government's interests, the alien shall be allowed to inspect the warrant . . . and shall be apprised that thereafter he may be represented by counsel." [3]

It should be noted at this point that deportation involved no criminal proceeding since it was not regarded as punishment. There was no judge or jury and the case was handled administratively through the secretary of labor by immigration officials who heard the case and rendered the decision. The government was perfectly within its rights in changing the grounds and procedures for deportation hearings at any time, for deportable aliens obviously did not have the protection of the ex post facto clause in the Constitution.

But even though no criminal trial was involved and the whole matter was merely an administrative process, it was generally understood that the alien did have certain safeguards — namely those in the Sixth Amendment such as the "right to a . . . public trial . . . to be confronted with witnesses against him; to have compulsory process for obtaining witnesses in his favor and to have the Assistance of Counsel for his defense." The alien also had two possibilities for relief from an adverse administrative decision. The secretary of labor might personally review the record and reverse any deportation decision, or the alien might obtain a writ of habeas corpus which would bring his case before a federal judge, but only if it could be shown that the deportation proceedings had been manifestly unfair.[4]

[For these reasons it becomes obvious why Attorney General Palmer did not try to detect and prosecute actual crimes of radicals against the United States. This would have required an indictment and a trial by jury whether such crimes were committed by citizens or aliens. Rather, he relied on the administrative process for the apprehension and deportation of radical aliens and therefore circumvented most normal legal procedures. Moreover, by Abercrombie's change in the hearing rule, even under the administrative process the alien's opportunity for an able defense of his position was considerably weakened. Hence, through shrewd collusion with certain Labor Department and immigration officials, Palmer assured himself greater success in his drive on radicalism than if he had elected to arrest radical aliens as criminals and thus subject his whole anti-Red program to the vagaries of the courts of law.]

Confident now that all was in readiness and that large-scale deportations offered the best solution to the domestic radical problem, the attorney general set the night of January 2, 1920, as the time for his all-out drive on the two Communist parties. Seven days before, on December 27, Palmer sent specific orders to Bureau of Investigation district chiefs instructing them on exactly what to do. They were told to arrange with their undercover agents, some of whom had quietly slipped into radical ranks and had assumed the role of agitators of the wildest type, to have meetings of the two Communist organizations called for the night set if possible because such action would facilitate the making of arrests. Field agents were instructed to "obtain all documentary evidence possible," to secure "charters, meeting minutes, membership books, due books, membership correspondence, etc.," and to allow no person arrested to communicate with any outside person until permission was specifically granted. Such permission could only come from Flynn, Hoover, or Palmer. Further orders specified that if an individual claimed American citizenship "he must produce documentary evidence of same" and that upon arrest "aliens should be searched thoroughly; if found in groups in meeting rooms, line them up against the wall and there search them." [5]

Resultant action could not have been more stunning or more spectacular. On January 2, more than 4000 suspected radicals were rounded up in thirty-three major cities, covering twenty-three states. Virtually every local Communist organization in the nation was affected; practically every leader of the movement, national or local, was put under arrest. Often such arrests were made without the formality of warrants as bureau agents entered bowling alleys, pool halls, cafés, club rooms, and even homes, and seized everyone in sight. Families were separated; prisoners were held incommunicado and deprived of their right to legal counsel. According to the plan, those suspected radicals who were American citizens were not detained by federal agents, but were turned over to state officials for prosecution under state syndicalist laws. All aliens, of course, were incarcerated by the federal authorities and reserved for deportation hearings.

In the New England area, raids were conducted in such towns as Boston, Chelsea, Brockton, Nashua, Manchester, and Portsmouth. In all, about 800 persons were seized of whom approximately half were taken to the immigrant station in Boston and then shipped to Deer Island in Boston Harbor. In this shifting process, the prisoners were forced to march in chains from the immigrant station to the dock — a fact which newspapers played up as attesting to their dangerous, violent character. Upon arriving at Deer Island the prisoners found conditions deplorable; heat was lacking, sanitation was poor, and restrictions holding them incommunicado were rigidly enforced. One captive plunged five stories to his death, another went insane, and two others died of pneumonia. [6]

The remaining half of the 800 who were not sent to Deer Island were released after two or three days when it was determined they were in no way connected with the radical movement. For example, thirty-nine bakers in Lynn, Massachusetts, arrested on suspicion of holding a revolutionary caucus, were released when it was learned that they had come together on the evening of January 2 for the inoffensive purpose of establishing a cooperative bakery. In Boston, a woman named Minnie Federman, who was mistakenly arrested in her bedroom at 6 A.M. on January 3, was released without even an apology when it was discovered belatedly that she was an American citizen and had no interest whatsoever in revolution.[7]

In New York and Pennsylvania the pattern was the same. In New York City more than 400 individuals were arrested as the Communist party headquarters and the Rand School bore the brunt of the federal raid. Prisoners were rounded up and taken to 13 Park Row where they were questioned by GID agents before being sent on to Ellis Island or released. In these New York arrests it seems that brutality was practiced to an excessive degree. Prisoners in sworn affidavits later testified to the violent treatment they had received. One claimed he had been beaten by a Justice Department operative without any explanation; another maintained he was struck repeatedly on the head with a blackjack. Another alien asserted that his glasses had been knocked off by an agent, who then without the slightest provocation struck him in the face.[8] Still another testified: "I was struck on my head, and . . . was attacked by one detective, who knocked me down again, sat on my back, pressing me down to the floor with his knee and bending my body back until blood flowed out of my mouth and nose . . . after which . . . I was questioned and released."[9]

Meanwhile, in Philadelphia, more than 100 were arrested and the "third degree" was as shamefully practiced as in New York. In the Pittsburgh area, 115 individuals were seized although warrants had been issued for only twenty. Indeed, one Pittsburgh man was missed by his friends for almost a month before they discovered he was in jail, having been arrested without warrant and then held without explanation or bail.[10]

In New Jersey, such towns as Jersey City, Passaic, Newark, Hoboken, Paterson, and Trenton experienced similar Red roundups. Altogether, about 500 arrests were made, but the majority were finally released for insufficient evidence. Again many arrests were made without warrant. For instance, one man was arrested about 10 P.M. while walking along Newark's Charlton Street simply because he "looked like a radical." Another, much to his surprise, was seized when he stopped to inquire what all the commotion was about.[11] This zeal to ferret out dangerous radicals caused government agents not only to make many unjust arrests such as these, but also to jump to ridiculous conclusions. In New Brunswick, while a Socialist Club was being raided, the drawings of a phonograph invention were found and were immediately forwarded to demolition experts because the raiders thought they represented "the internal mechanism of various types of bombs." [12]

In the Midwest, the raids at Chicago and Detroit were particularly severe. In the Detroit raid about 800 persons were arrested and imprisoned from three to six days in a dark, windowless, narrow corridor in the city's antiquated Federal Building. The prisoners were forced to sleep on the bare floor and stand in long lines for access to the solitary toilet. Some, unable to wait, were forced to urinate in the corridor itself, and, as the custodian later testified, "Before many days . . . the stench was quite unbearable." It was later discovered that the prisoners were denied all food for the first twenty-four hours and thereafter were fed largely on what their families brought to them. Including among their number "citizens and aliens, college graduates and laborers, skilled mechanics making $15 a day and boys not yet out of short trousers," these 800 prisoners were closely questioned by bureau agents who finally released 300 by the end of the sixth day when it was proved that they had not even a cursory interest in the domestic radical movement.[13]

Meanwhile, about 140 of those remaining were transferred from the Federal Building to the Detroit Municipal Building. En route these individuals, who had been unable to shave or bathe for almost a week, served as excellent subjects for press photographers, and local Detroit newspapers ran their pictures as examples of the unkempt, dirty, filthy Bolshevik terrorists the government had netted in its raids.[14] Upon their arrival at the Municipal Building, the prisoners were placed in a room twenty-four feet by thirty feet which originally had been designed to hold offenders no longer than three to four hours. This "bull pen," as it was called, had only one window, a stone floor, and several wooden benches; yet the men remained here a whole week and were fed almost solely on food sent to them by their relatives. Indeed, conditions under which these prisoners lived were actually so wretched that even the Detroit press finally displayed some sympathy for them, and a citizens' committee was created to investigate their situation. This committee subsequently discovered that most of these "dangerous radicals" were but plain, ignorant foreigners who were completely unaware of why they were being so treated.[15]

In Chicago, a most peculiar set of circumstances arose. For five months, state and city officials had laid careful plans for their own drive on radicalism in the Chicago area, and had finally decided on January 1 as the date for such a move. Much to their dismay they then learned that the Justice Department had planned its foray for January 2. Cook County officials persisted in their desire to conduct a raid of their own, and, as a result, raids were held a day apart on radicals in that area.

The state raid of January 1 involved some seventy or more radical clubs or gatherings and netted between 150 and 200 prisoners. As a result of these incursions, some eighty-five Communists, among them "Big Bill" Haywood and Rose Pastor Stokes, were arraigned in Chicago on criminal anarchy charges.[16]

The federal raid which followed on January 2 was therefore somewhat anticlimactic. However, federal officials did nab 225 additional suspected radicals and after questioning held about 80 for deportation. One interesting sidelight on the Chicago raids was a riot which broke out in the municipal jail shortly after the various arrests were made. It seems that the jail's "patriotic" prisoners took violent exception to the fact that Reds were being thrown in the same cells with them. Remarked the Seattle *Times*, "There are some things at which even a Chicago crook draws the line." [17]

In the West and Far West, while raids were conducted, they were not especially significant. Most radicals of any importance, particularly in the Far West, had already been apprehended in the various state raids following the Centralia massacre. Hence, the present forays were carried out only in a cursory manner and arrests were few in number. In Los Angeles, one was arrested; in Portland, twenty; Denver, eight; and Des Moines, sixteen. Only in Kansas City was there much activity and there 100 were taken and 35 held.[18]

The January raids dazzled the public. The mass of Americans cheered the hunters from the sidelines while Attorney General Palmer once again was hailed as the savior of the nation. In view of the obvious abridgement of civil liberties which the raids entailed, such support can only be explained on the basis that the public mind was under the influence of a tremendous social delirium — a colossal fear which condoned monstrous procedures and acts. Against a background of the three major fall strikes, the Centralia murders, and exaggerated press and official claims, that fear seemed so real it was positively overpowering. Said the Washington *Evening Star*, "This is no mere scare, no phantom of heated imagination — it is a cold, hard, plain fact." [19] As far as the deleterious effect on civil liberties was concerned, the Washington *Post* exclaimed, "There is no time to waste on hairsplitting over infringement of liberty. . . ." [20]

Agreeing therefore that the raids were a cause for satisfaction and willing to overlook the many dangers and injustices involved, most journals were now quick to counsel a rapid follow-through. The immediate deportation of the prisoners, variously described as "the kind of cranks that murder Presidents" or "send bombs through the mails to statesmen," was forcefully demanded. In fact, such action was regarded "as necessary as cauterizing a wound to prevent gangrene." Under such headlines as "ALL ABOARD FOR THE NEXT SOVIET ARK," the press advocated that "ships be made ready quickly and the passengers put aboard." [21]

However, there was still the feeling in some quarters that the government was going too far and that its action gave rise to more dangers than it allayed. Not only did certain Cabinet officers remain opposed, but a few courageous voices both in labor and in industry also spoke out against the raids and excoriated Palmer for his activities. The Chicago Federation of Labor adopted resolutions of protest denouncing federal agents for using "Czaristic methods" and "terroristic tactics." Certain industrialists such as Charles M. Schwab stanchly maintained that the raids would make more Bolshevists than they would destroy and hence the government's action was itself dangerous. Even within Palmer's own department there was some disaffection. On January 12, Francis F. Kane, United States attorney for the Eastern District of Pennsylvania, submitted his resignation to President Wilson because he felt "out of sympathy with the anti-radical policies of Mr. Palmer and his method of carrying them out." [22]

A small segment of the general press also evidenced uneasiness by counseling moderation and warned that the continuance of the anti-Red craze might eventually destroy traditional American liberties. Such papers as the New York *World*, Richmond *Times-Union*, Newark *News*, and St. Louis *Globe-Democrat* claimed that the rigid repression of freedom of speech and action which the January raids portended signified weakness rather than strength and that indications of domestic radical activity were not sufficient to justify such action. The Baltimore *Sun* concluded: "Let us hope that the net effect of this pretentious movement against the so-called 'reds' will not turn out to be merely a huge advertizement of them and their cause and a consequent increase in their membership." [23]

As usual, the strongest denunciations were voiced by the liberal, Socialist, and radical presses. The New York *Call* pooh-poohed the possibility of a radical-inspired revolution and claimed that the primary intent of the government raids was not to stamp out radicalism but to put Palmer in the White House. The *New Republic* and the *Nation* maintained that Palmer was "improving on the Czar," and that his justification of the raids on the basis of imminent revolution was so utterly silly that even Palmer could not believe it. The Chicago *New Solidarity* and the various proclamations of the two Communist parties asserted the government action was merely symptomatic of the hysterical attempt of American business to stave off the inevitable collapse of capitalism. Quipped the *Liberator*:

> Who is it worries all the Feds,
> And fills the *Times* with scarey heads,
> And murders people in their beds?
> The Reds.[24]

In spite of this opposition, however, both the attorney general and the vast majority of the public remained convinced that such action had been necessary. Palmer declared information secured in the raids proved beyond doubt that the radical alien element dominated the domestic radical movement and therefore constituted an imminent threat to the peace and security of the nation. Moreover, he asserted, this alien group was controlled by Moscow and received its orders directly from Lenin and Trotsky. "Each and every adherent of this movement," continued the attorney general, "is a potential murderer or a potential thief." In describing the prisoners caught in the raids, Palmer allowed his imagination to run rampant: "Out of the sly and crafty eyes of many of them leap cupidity, cruelty, insanity, and crime; from their lopsided faces, sloping brows, and misshapen features may be recognized the unmistakable criminal type."[25]

As to the success of the raids, Palmer and the Bureau of Investigation spoke in glowing terms. The attorney general claimed the raids "halted the advance of 'red radicalism' in the United States," while Flynn maintained they marked the beginning of the end of organized revolutionaries in this country.[26]

As a matter of fact, the raids did have a devastating effect on the domestic radical movement. James Cannon later maintained that the movement disintegrated for the time being. Benjamin Gitlow testified the raids struck terror into the hearts of alien members of the two Communist parties and hurt membership tremendously.[27] It was true that for many weeks after the government action the radical press ceased its activities and meetings of the Communist organizations were suspended. Perhaps the best indication of the effect of the raids can be seen in a report made in February 1920 by the American delegate to the Amsterdam meeting of the Bureau of Propaganda of the Third International. He claimed at that time that the January raids had so wrecked the Communist movement in the United States that it could not be counted on to exert any influence whatsoever.[28]

While satisfied up to this point with the success of his antiradical program, Attorney General Palmer now allowed no lag to develop. With the aid of Flynn and Hoover, he intensified the department's propaganda campaign until it reached its height in late January 1920. Large numbers of antiradical articles and cartoons were sent to the nation's newspapers and magazines without charge, the postage being prepaid by the Department of Justice itself. A sample cartoon, secured by the Justice Department from the New York *Tribune* and used with its permission, depicted Uncle Sam as a farmer weeding up thistles, each one of which had a Bolshevik head, while in the background a woman named "America" was replacing the thistles with pure "American" grass seed. "Give the American Bluegrass a Show," it said.[29]

At the same time, Palmer vigorously continued his drive to secure some kind of peacetime sedition legislation in order to give the federal government the power necessary to deal with citizen radicals effectively. Shortly after the January raids, he again appealed to Congress for such legislation, underlining the potential danger which such citizens presented to the country.

Palmer also promised the nation more action to rid the country of all alien agitators. He declared there would be more raids and

Give the American Bluegrass a Show
(Cartoonist Ding in the New York *Tribune*)

that on the basis of what already had been done there would be at least 2720 deportations. Like a barker in charge of a colossal sideshow, the attorney general promised New Yorkers, in particular, the exhilarating spectacle of "a second, third, and fourth Soviet Ark sailing down their beautiful harbor in the near future." [30]

14 ★ ★ ★ ★ ★ ★ ★ ★ ★ ★

Race between Governments

WHILE the Palmer raids and the *Buford* deportation represented the most spectacular manifestation of government hysteria in 1919-20, there were many other indications as both the state and federal governments rushed to meet the radical challenge. Indeed, beginning in November 1919, it appeared as if the various governments were trying to outstrip one another in the fury of their drive on both the Communist doctrine and nonconformity of all types. Extremely sensitive to mounting public feeling, government officials at all levels and in all stages of responsibility geared their actions to what they thought the public wanted and hence sponsored many unorthodox and dangerous procedures on the ground that such were necessary to save the nation. This was true whether it involved merely the passage of restrictive legislation or the outright denial of constitutional privileges and guarantees.

But, as with the Palmer raids, most of these endeavors proved to be ill-advised and in the long run aided in the apprehension of relatively few subversives. Generally, only the innocent or the eccentric suffered, and their suffering did little to advance the democratic cause. In the main, such action, whether by the federal or state governments, produced an undesirable effect on the exercise of civil liberties and clearly demonstrated that during the Scare period the basic principles of free speech, press, and representative government were in jeopardy, not because of radical activity, but because of the impractical manner in which the public and its officials attempted to protect them.

Through the activities of Attorney General Palmer, the executive branch of the federal government was the first to display a sustained irrational antipathy to domestic radicalism and a willingness to employ drastic measures to wipe it out. Soon, however, both the judicial and the legislative branches also became involved and by their actions demonstrated that they, too, were rapidly succumbing to popular pressures and irrational fears.

Normally, the courts are regarded as the nation's chief guardians of civil liberties and bastions of sane thinking on this subject even when public opinion may be somewhat awry. Unfortunately, this was not the case in 1919–20. In general, the courts drew such a restricted interpretation of civil liberties that the protection necessary to their maintenance was virtually lacking. In this respect, the attitude of the Supreme Court was especially significant. Although the high tribunal was not asked to take a specific stand on the suppression of the Red menace as such, in the one case which did come before it involving radicalism to a degree — the Abrams case — the Court showed its inability to withstand popular hysteria.

Unlike the earlier Schenck case which was prosecuted on the basis of the Espionage Law, the Abrams case rested on the Sedition Act and did not involve pro-German or pacifist utterances but an attack on the government's policy of intervention in Russia in the summer of 1918. At that time, six men and one woman (the oldest being Jacob Abrams) were apprehended for printing and distributing 5000 leaflets which called on American laborers to begin a general strike in order to prevent American participation in intervention. One of the seven defendants died before the trial began and another received an indefinite postponement of the hearing. As a result, four men and the woman, all Russian aliens, were left to face prosecution. In October 1918, these five were found guilty of conspiracy to violate the Sedition Act and received sentences ranging from three to twenty years.[1]

In deciding the appeal of these individuals on November 10, 1919 (just three days after the first Palmer raids), Justice John H. Clarke rendered the majority opinion of the Supreme Court by declaring the defendants were guilty of printing and publishing disloyal and scurrilous language about the United States government and of attempting to incite disloyalty in the nation's armed forces. The decision of the lower courts were thereupon affirmed.

Justices Holmes and Brandeis dissented, maintaining that the leaflets issued by these individuals did not constitute a clear and present danger. Wrote Holmes: "Prosecution for the expression of opinions seems to me perfectly logical. If you have no doubt of your premises or your power and want a certain result with all your heart you naturally express your wishes in law and sweep away all opposition. . . . But when men have realized that time has upset many fighting faiths, they may come to believe even more than they believe the very foundations of their own conduct that the ultimate good desired is better reached by free trade in ideas — that the best test of truth is the power of the thought to get itself accepted in the competition of the market, and that truth is the only ground upon which their wishes can be safely carried out. . . . we should be eternally vigilant against attempts to check the expression of opinions that we loathe and believe to be fraught with death, unless they so imminently threaten immediate interference with the lawful and pressing purposes of the law that an immediate check is required to save the country." [2]

Both the majority and minority opinions of the Court demonstrated that Holmes's clear and present danger principle did not constitute a sure-fire safeguard of civil liberties when a period of hysteria existed. Where to draw the line as to what constituted a clear and present danger proved as difficult for the justices as it did for the general public, and the majority of the Court, swayed by current popular emotions, showed that freedom of speech in times of crisis is largely in the custody of legislative majorities, juries, and the public, not judges. In short, despite all the legal double talk, the Court was merely reflecting the widespread sentiment that "Too many persons in this country are enjoying the right of free speech." [3]

The legislative branch, meanwhile, mirrored this sentiment to an even greater degree. By late 1919 and early 1920, more and more congressmen were following the lead of their constituents and were developing a highly emotional approach to the radical problem. Influenced both by events and by some of their more articulate colleagues, many congressmen were preparing to throw caution to the winds in their desire to strike at the alleged Bolshevik menace. Surprisingly enough, partisanship was rarely involved in all this since Republicans and Democrats alike found themselves united on the radical issue.

Perhaps the best case in point concerned Victor Berger. Berger, it will be remembered, was the Socialist who had been elected to Congress from the Fifth Wisconsin District in November 1918, at a time when he was already under indictment for violation of the Espionage Act because of his antiwar utterances. Although subsequently found guilty and sentenced to twenty years by Judge Landis, Berger had filed an appeal and while this was pending presented himself to Congress in April 1919 to be sworn in.

The House was indignant. A majority of the members falsely believed Berger was "a German at heart" and that his type of pacifistic socialism was "off the same cloth as Russian Bolshevism." Hence, on May 19, Representative Frederick W. Dallinger of Massachusetts offered a resolution which called for the appointment of a special House committee to review his qualifications. The resolution further provided that Berger should not be sworn in as a member until the investigation was completed. [4]

Two days later, Representative Dallinger was himself appointed chairman of the special committee and the investigation was begun. Never was the decision in doubt. Although Berger's testimony sounded very much like later revisionist historians' ideas concerning the causes for World War I, the committee labeled all such assertions as "traitorous" and "Bolshevistic," and in late October

1919 voted 8 to 1 to recommend his permanent exclusion. The report of the committee concluded, "It is not only the right but the constitutional duty of the House to exclude him." [5]

On November 10, the same day the Abrams case was decided in the Supreme Court, the House debated the report of the special committee and, amid cries of "un-American," "Hun," "Dutchman," "Bolshevik," and "traitor," passed a resolution "that under the facts and circumstances of this case Victor L. Berger is not entitled to take the oath of office as a Representative in this House . . . or to hold a seat therein as such Representative." Only one lone vote was cast against this measure. [6]

The general press strongly backed the House action. Newspapers, which had followed the case closely, applauded both the special committee's recommendation and the final vote. The Washington *Post* contended the House could not have given a "finer or more impressive demonstration of Americanism," and the Toledo *Blade* claimed that by refusing Berger a seat the representatives had kept "their self respect" and reflected the opinion of the entire country. The Baltimore *Sun*, however, expressed indignation that even one vote had been cast in Berger's favor. [7]

According to law, the governor of Wisconsin now ordered a special election in the Fifth Wisconsin District (which embraced the city of Milwaukee) in order to fill the vacancy created by Berger's exclusion. Berger was defiantly renominated by the Socialist party, while the Democrats and Republicans ran a fusion candidate in order to ensure his defeat. The nation's newspapers maintained the coming election was a definite "Challenge to Loyalty" and called upon all voters in the Milwaukee area to cast their ballots against the alien influence which Berger represented. But much to everyone's surprise, on election day, December 19, the excluded Socialist received 25,802 votes while his opponent received only 19,800. On hearing this, Berger told the Fifth District voters "Well done," while his disgruntled opponent charged that Berger had beaten him with the aid of "foreign agitators and Bolshevist adherents." [8]

This latter charge was unadulterated nonsense since it is clear neither bolshevism nor socialism re-elected Berger. He was against prohibition and was strongly backed by the "wets." He had labor's backing and made a strong appeal to all those who were dissatisfied with the high cost of living. Then, too, according to Hearst's *Wisconsin-News*, there were some who, although opposed to Berger politically, voted for him as a protest against the House's arbitrary action in refusing him his seat.

Nevertheless, the nation's press described Berger's re-election as an "Amazing Victory" and spread the fiction that the 25,000 who voted for him were "deluded, unthinking fools" who were "opposed to American institutions." The *Outlook* maintained the election marked "Milwaukee's Secession." The Buffalo *Evening News* felt that "Milwaukee needs sympathy." The Boston *Evening Transcript* was so enraged that it claimed "The sooner Berger and his sympathizers follow Emma Goldman and Berkman out of the United States, the sooner the United States will be a better place to live in." On the other hand, a few journals were delighted at the unexpected outcome. Punned the *Liberator*, "As time goes on the Fifth Wisconsin district seems to get Berger and Berger." [9]

It was a foregone conclusion that a second attempt would be made to exclude Berger when he presented himself to Congress at the opening of the new session in January. In fact, the day after Berger's re-election, Representative Dallinger declared he would again object to the seating of Berger in the House just as he had done previously. On January 10, 1920, Dallinger formally challenged Berger's right to a seat and offered a new resolution again barring him from the House. Dallinger's resolution stressed Berger's conviction under the Espionage Act and declared his exclusion was necessary for the safety of the nation. [10]

This time, however, there developed some slight opposition to excluding him. Although opposed to Berger's Socialist views, several representatives felt the principle of representative government was now clearly at stake and believed that since the people of Wisconsin had re-elected him he should be seated. Representative Isaac R. Sherwood of Ohio even went so far as to claim the Dallinger resolution sprang from a hysterical and unfounded fear of radicalism and that Socialists, such as Berger, constituted no real danger to the Republic. Representative Edward Voigt of Wisconsin, who was the only one to vote for Berger the first time, again strongly opposed the Dallinger resolution.

But these were all too few. When Voigt called Berger a "high-minded and honorable gentleman," the House rocked with laughter and immediately proceeded to vote overwhelmingly for his exclusion. The count was 330 to 6.[11]

The nation's press applauded the second exclusion no less vigorously than it had the first. At the same time, the Socialist party in Wisconsin declared, "We will continue nominating Berger until Hades freezes over if that un-American aggregation called Congress continues to exclude him." [12] However, the Wisconsin governor wisely decided against holding another special election and it was not until the regular November election of 1920 that the Socialists had the opportunity to run Berger again. This time he was defeated and thus the problem of seating him was automatically laid to rest.

The Berger case remained clearly indicative of the extent to which emotional sentiment against nonconformity had carried the federal legislature by the close of 1919. Berger's inability to take his seat was unquestionably a grave injustice to the voters of the Fifth Wisconsin District and a clear abrogation of the basic principles of representative government. Because of the exclusion, these Wisconsin voters remained unrepresented in Congress for over a year and a half. At the same time, it became increasingly obvious that Berger was excluded, not so much because of his conviction under the Espionage Act (since that question was still undecided by the higher courts), but because of his earlier political opposition to the war — a position which, by late 1919, had in most minds become identified with bolshevism. Of course, it was sheer folly to connect Berger with the Bolshevists in any way, since he was one of their bitterest opponents and the most conservative of all Socialists.

While the Berger case remained the most notorious example, there were other indications that the federal legislature was prepared to take dangerous steps to curb the suspected radical threat. Of particular importance was its continued consideration of peacetime sedition legislation. Except for the Alien and Sedition laws of 1798, the United States Congress had never attempted to establish national peacetime restriction of opinions, and it had been generally agreed that only the gravest national emergency would lead to the re-enactment of such legislation. To an increasing number of congressmen, the Red menace now seemed to be such an emergency.

Smitten badly by his own exaggerated fear of radicalism, Attorney General Palmer led the drive for peacetime sedition legislation and, because of his incessant urging together with rising popular hysteria, some seventy sedition bills were proposed in Congress in the late fall and winter of 1919–20. Beginning in October, such representatives as Thomas L. Blanton (Texas), James F. Byrnes (South Carolina), Martin L. Davey (Ohio), John W. Summers (Washington), and Isaac Siegel (New York) flooded the House with proposals for strict postal censorship and long prison terms for those advocating forceful changes in the American form of government. Finally, on January 5, 1920, Representative George S. Graham of Pennsylvania combined all such sedition measures into the so-called Graham Bill which imposed a $10,000 fine or twenty years' imprisonment, or both, on any person who sought to overthrow or destroy the government, or prevent or delay the execution of federal law, or harm or terrorize any officer or employee of the United States government.[13]

Meanwhile, in the upper house, many senators proposed bills which called for stricter control of the press through the suspension of mailing privileges and the levying of heavy fines (some as high as $50,000), as well as long jail sentences, for personal seditious utterances. On January 10, all such proposals were incorporated into the Sterling Bill, which was much like the Graham Bill. It was quickly passed and sent on to the House.[14]

Upon receipt of the Sterling Bill, the House ordered a review of its own Graham Bill and on January 14 the House Judiciary Committee amalgamated the two measures into the Graham-Sterling Bill. There began then a series of hearings on the combined measure. Attorney General Palmer, for one, expressed relief that Congress was at last taking some definite action and maintained that public opinion endorsed such restrictive legislation.[15]

As events later proved, the attorney general was rather far from the truth, for neither the Graham-Sterling Bill nor any other peacetime sedition measure would be passed. However, by even considering the idea of restricting freedom of opinion, Congress betrayed the hysterical condition of many congressional minds in the winter of 1919–20.

In spite of the fact that all branches of the federal government ultimately became involved in one way or another in antiradical activity, the situation in the states was even worse. In fact, the states far surpassed the federal government in the actual suppression, or threats of suppression, of all forms of nonconformity and illustrated more clearly than the federal government the extent of hysteria in the nation in late 1919 and early 1920. This was natural since their legislative bodies were more directly affected by popular opinion and their actions were based more concretely on how far the public was willing to go in striking at the Red threat. Moreover, untrammeled by the indecision and bureaucratic crosscurrents which so often hampered the national government, the states, within their own local areas, were able to deal with nonconformity much more effectively, and, although their procedures were far less spectacular than, say, the Palmer raids, they were much more deadly.

Criminal anarchy, syndicalist, Red flag, and sedition laws were the states' major weapons. Before 1919, a few states already had some of this legislation on their statute books. As early as 1902, for example, New York had instituted a criminal anarchy law to deal with anarchists of the type who assassinated McKinley. Later, in

1917–18, several western and midwestern states such as Idaho, Minnesota, Montana, South Dakota, and Nebraska enacted similar legislation to facilitate the prosecution of the IWW. In all such laws, criminal anarchy, or sedition, was defined as "the doctrine that organized government should be overthrown by force or violence, or by assassination . . . or by any unlawful means," and any person who either by speech or writing sought to teach such a doctrine was usually subject to a fine of $5000 or ten years in jail, or both.[16]

In 1919, the enactment of such laws became an epidemic. Because of the growing fear of domestic radicalism and the incessant prodding of various super-patriots and politicians, no fewer than twenty state legislatures enacted laws of this nature. Some states adopted such measures upon the direct suggestion of Attorney General Palmer who, during the height of the Scare, spoke before several state assemblies and urged the enactment of syndicalist and sedition laws as the best means available to local governments to stop radicalism. Also of importance in influencing many states along this line were Senators Miles Poindexter (Washington), William King (Utah), and Atlee Pomerene (Ohio). These men, both in their many speeches on the floor of the Senate and in their various addresses elsewhere in the nation, recommended the passage of local restrictive laws as the only sure way to save the nation.[17]

With local public feeling against radicalism at a high pitch anyway, the recommendations by these national figures were in most instances superfluous as many state legislatures whooped through syndicalist and sedition legislation without a single dissenting vote.[18] Although such laws varied slightly from state to state, the effect was generally the same. Opinions were labeled as objectionable and punished for their own sake without any consideration of the probability of criminal acts; severe penalties were imposed for the advocacy of small offenses; and a practical censorship of speech and press was established ex post facto.

An excellent case in point was the Ohio criminal syndicalist law of 1919. Defining criminal syndicalism as "the doctrine which advocates crime, sabotage . . . violence, or unlawful methods of terrorism as a means of accomplishing industrial or political reform," the law provided that any person who by word of mouth or writing advocated such a doctrine was "guilty of a felony and punishable in the state penitentiary for not more than ten years, or by a fine of not more than five thousand dollars, or both." The law further stated that ". . . the owner, agent, superintendent, janitor, caretaker, or occupant of any place, building or room, who wilfully and knowingly permits therein any assemblage or persons [prohibited by the Act] . . . is guilty of a misdemeanor and punishable by imprisonment in the county jail for not more than one year or by a fine of not more than five hundred dollars, or both." [19]

The enthusiasm for such legislation continued into 1920 and several other states added their names to the list. Also, by 1920, many of the states had supplemented their existing syndicalist legislation with rigid sedition laws. States such as Indiana, New Hampshire, New Mexico, Arkansas, Colorado, Illinois, Pennsylvania, and West Virginia made the speaking or printing of abusive language against public officials or the republican form of government a major offense. By the year 1921, there were thirty-five states plus two territories (Alaska and Hawaii) which had in force either peacetime sedition legislation or criminal syndicalist laws, or both. [20]

The other major type of restrictive law employed by the states was Red flag legislation. Since the Red flag had always represented the rebellious discontent of the rabble and was, itself, a symbol of revolution, some public resentment had risen against it and such states as Pennsylvania, Massachusetts, and Rhode Island had long since outlawed its use. However, never before had prejudice against the Red banner become sufficiently intense to promote the general feeling that the Red flag would have to go if democracy was to survive. As one newspaper put it, "Time to flag the red flag." [21]

As a result, twenty-four states passed Red flag laws in 1919, and eight others acted similarly in 1920. At the same time, numerous cities such as New York, Los Angeles, and New Haven enacted Red flag ordinances. All these statutes were similar in nature and were designed to prevent Red flag demonstrations like those that had occurred on May Day 1919.

Even a cursory examination of these laws quickly reveals their intent. The Wisconsin law forbade the display of a Red flag or any flag which symbolized "a purpose to overthrow, by force or violence" the government of the United States or of the state of Wisconsin. The Oklahoma law forbade the display of banners "indicating disloyalty or a belief in anarchy or other political doctrines." The New York statute made it a misdemeanor to display the Red banner "in any public assembly or parade as a symbol or emblem of any organization or association, or in furtherance of any political, social, or economic principle, doctrine or propaganda." [22]

In none of these states, however, was the violation of such legislation made as serious an offense as sedition or criminal anarchy. Usually, a Red flag misdemeanor involved a fine of not more than $500 with a jail sentence of not longer than six months, subject to the discretion of the local courts.

The numerous convictions secured by the states on the basis of their sedition, syndicalist, and Red flag legislation attested to its general effectiveness. Beginning in the last two months of 1919, state courts were called upon to implement the action of the state legislatures by upholding such legislation and interpreting it in a broad manner. In the meantime, business interests as well as conservative labor leaders joined with super-patriots in vigorously supporting the activities of state law enforcement officers. It has been estimated that in 1919–20 no fewer than 1400 persons, both citizens and aliens, were arrested under this state legislation and of this number about 300 were ultimately convicted and sent to prison. [23]

[Prosecution on the basis of these laws was unusually rigorous in the three states of Illinois, New York, and California.] On January

21, 1920, William Lloyd and thirty-seven other members of the Communist Labor party were indicted in Chicago on grounds of criminal anarchy and Lloyd, along with nineteen others, was found guilty, receiving a $3000 fine and from one to five years in jail. Two days later, Rose Pastor Stokes, "Big Bill" Haywood, and eighty-three other Communists, all garnered in the January 1 Illinois raid, were indicted by the Cook County grand jury and later received sentences of from five to ten years in the state penitentiary.[24]

In New York, such radical leaders as Charles Ruthenberg, I. E. Ferguson, James Larkin, Harry Winitsky, and Benjamin Gitlow were arrested and convicted on the basis of the state's criminal anarchy law and each received the maximum penalty of from five to ten years in prison. For his stalwart defense of communism during his trial, Benjamin Gitlow was subsequently made an honorary member of the Moscow Soviet — even in making his last plea before the jury, Gitlow fearlessly denounced the United States government as a capitalistic dictatorship and called for its immediate overthrow.[25]

In California, a state which had criminal syndicalist, sedition, and Red flag laws, an estimated 500 persons were arrested and 264 were ultimately convicted during the years 1919–21. In fact, even after the crest of hysteria had passed nationally and such restrictive legislation had become a dead letter in other states, California was still pressing hers to the limit. Probably the most famous conviction involving California law was that of Mrs. Anita Whitney. A graduate of Wellesley, social worker, suffragist, Socialist, and finally a member of the Communist Labor party, she was arrested on November 29, 1919, and after a four weeks' trial was convicted in February 1920 for violation of the state's syndicalist legislation. She was sentenced to from one to fourteen years in San Quentin.[26]

[Of all the actions taken by the states against radicalism during the Scare period, none were so notorious as the continued antics of the New York Lusk Committee and the expulsion of the Socialists from the New York State Legislature.]

235

While most states, despite the looseness of their restrictive laws, directed their action mainly against bona fide radicals who were known agitators, New York did not. Here, hysteria seemed to exist to a much greater degree, and although the Lusk Committee brought a few radical leaders like Gitlow within the net of the law, its over-all activities were so emotionally directed at all nonconformity that an amazing amount of intolerance was displayed.

This fact was most glaringly illustrated in the case of the New York Socialists. To find Socialist members in the New York State Legislature was not novel. In fact, in the spring of 1918, while the war was still on, ten of them had sat in that body. However, under the influence of the Red Scare and particularly the hysterical propaganda of the Lusk Committee, the idea had grown that socialism was merely bolshevism with a shave, and there was some talk of barring Socialists on the grounds of disloyalty and radicalism.

On January 7, 1920, just three days before the second congressional exclusion of Berger and with the newspapers still full of Palmer's raids, a new session of the legislature began. For two hours the assembly busied itself with organizational matters. Then, suddenly, Speaker Thaddeus C. Sweet called the five Socialist members of the new assembly before the bar and read the following statement, "You, whom I have summoned before the bar of the house . . . have been elected on a platform that is absolutely inimical to the best interests of the State of New York and of the United States." Simon Adler, majority floor leader, thereupon arose and presented a resolution which had been drawn up in advance by Attorney General Newton in his capacity as counsel for the Lusk Committee. This resolution provided that the five Socialist members "be, and they hereby are, denied seats in the Assembly, pending the determination of their qualifications and eligibility to their respective seats." The vote was 140 to 6.[27]

Two of the disbarred Socialists were from Manhattan; two others were from the Bronx; and one was from Kings County. The Socialist party was a legally recognized party under New York election laws, and four of these five had previously served in the assembly. In disbarring them the assembly clearly committed an illegal act, for unlike Berger who at least had been convicted of crime these men were barred from their seats without any provocation. The net result was that some 60,000 voters of New York City were unrepresented and disfranchised.

The assembly justified its action by maintaining that the Socialist party was revolutionary, unpatriotic, and disloyal, that it owed allegiance to the Third International, and that it wanted a Soviet type regime established in the United States. Specifically, the five Socialists were charged with disloyal opposition to the war and with giving aid and comfort to the nation's enemies. One assemblyman was reportedly so carried away by these charges of treason against the five Socialists that he suggested they ought to be shot instead of barred.[28]

Two weeks after their disbarment, an investigation of their qualifications was begun by the assembly's Judiciary Committee. As a result of its probing, the committee agreed that the Socialist party, of which these five assemblymen were members, was a "revolutionary party" interested only in destroying American institutions. Holding the five members personally responsible for the party's "crimes," the committee therefore recommended that they be permanently expelled.

On April 1, 1920, after an all-night debate, the New York assembly voted upon the recommendation of the committee, but not before some opposition arose. Young Theodore Roosevelt bitterly denounced the committee's recommendation and claimed expulsion would completely negate the principle of representative government. However, such opposition did not go far. Speaker Sweet openly rebuked Roosevelt Junior by reading aloud to the assembly passages from Roosevelt Senior so that the "Americanism" of the father might "painfully" be contrasted with the "un-Americanism" of the son.[29] Finally, amid cries of "Little Lenins," "little Trotskys," and "representatives of the Russian Soviet Government," a vote of 116 to 28 was delivered against three of the Socialists and 104 to 40 against the remaining two.[30]

The concluding chapter to this unsavory episode occurred six months later after much of the Red Scare had died down. On September 16, the five expelled Socialists were overwhelmingly re-elected by their districts in spite of the combined opposition of the two major parties. Four days later they presented themselves once again before the assembly to be sworn in. The Judiciary Committee again recommended their expulsion and, after a seven-hour debate, the assembly voted to expel three, but seat the remaining two. Quite naturally the two refused to be a party to such action and resigned rather than take the oath of office without their three colleagues.[31]

In the meantime, the Lusk Committee was not completely satisfied with its work and, believing additional safeguards were necessary to protect New York citizens from such "radicalism," proposed to the assembly a series of five antiradical bills. These measures were passed by the legislature in April 1920, shortly after the expulsion of the Socialists. Two of these bills were directed against the Socialist party, making it an illegal organization and barring its candidates from the state ballot. Two others represented a direct attack on the freedom of the state's educational system by requiring a blanket loyalty oath from all teachers and giving the Board of Regents power to license all private schools, except those of religious sects or denominations. The fifth law provided for the appropriation of $100,000 for establishing a State Bureau of Investigation in the attorney general's office to ferret out and prosecute all types of sedition, disloyalty, and criminal anarchy.[32] Although Governor Alfred E. Smith vetoed this legislation by declaring that it struck a blow at "the fundamental right of the people to enjoy full liberty in the domain of idea and speech," the measures were re-passed and in the following year, 1921, were signed into law by Smith's successor, Governor Nathan L. Miller.[33]

15 ★ ★ ★ ★ ★ ★ ★ ★ ★ ★

Ebbing Tide

THE month of January 1920 marked the height of the Great Red Scare.

Since the Seattle general strike of almost a year before, public fear of domestic radicalism had been piling up to this peak of intensity. Through the complicated interaction of economic instability, personal ambition, group pressure, deep-seated prejudice, suspicious events, and some radical activity, that fear had been nurtured carefully — and with what disastrous results. The principle of representative government was being cast aside, free speech was rapidly becoming little more than a shibboleth, and even free press was in danger. With the opening of the new decade, national insanity ruled; most of the nation's thought and energy was being devoted to stopping an exaggerated Red menace by any means as government officials, congressmen, state legislators, private citizens, and the public press concentrated their major attention on the problem of domestic radicalism.

Then, suddenly, the crest of hysteria passed. Thereafter public fear was never again as intense. Surprisingly enough, during the following months of 1920 anti-Red hysteria subsided almost as quickly as it had developed and, although the scars of the Scare remained, the nation rather rapidly regained its composure. By the fall of 1920, the public pulse had become considerably calmer and hair-raising warnings of impending revolutions were largely missing from the scene. Except for a few areas such as New York and California, bolshevism was no longer the key to public interest and most newspapers, government officials, and politicians ceased wasting their time on the problem of domestic radicalism. In fact, by the fall of 1920 the nation as a whole was tiring of chasing Bolshevists and was turning its attention to other things.

What then killed hysteria and caused this rapid demise of the Red Scare? There were a variety of factors, most of them as complicated and difficult to assess as those which had given it birth. [There was the dawning realization, for one thing, that there never had been any real cause for alarm and that, despite some fire behind all the smoke, the number of Bolshevists in the country had been badly exaggerated.] As we will presently see, domestic events in the spring and summer of 1920 underscored this fact, and a growing number of citizens, among them certain prominent and respected public figures, became increasingly disgusted with the excesses of the Scare hysteria and worked actively to bring about a halt. For another thing, [there was the localization of bolshevism in Europe.] By the middle of 1920, as Germany, Italy, and France failed to be engulfed by communism, it seemed less and less likely that the doctrine would sweep across the Atlantic and overwhelm the United States. Moreover, many domestic radicals had been so scared by the aggressive action of those like Palmer that they had lapsed into a sort of pinkishness which made them less conspicuous to a Red-conscious public. By mid-1920, many college professors, public school teachers, clerics, and social reformers had abandoned what seemed to be a hopeless fight, canceled their subscriptions to liberal magazines and newspapers, and either maintained a stony silence or leaned over backwards to appear as conservative as Judge Gary. This, especially, was soothing to the public mind.

[But of even greater importance was the fact that at last the temper of war was giving way to the temper of peace. The aftermath of war with its irritability and restlessness was passing and the nation was again learning how to amuse itself and relax.] Simultaneously, it found itself bedazzled by a host of wonderful new fads, fashions, and gadgets on which it could more interestingly spend its time and energy. The radio, along with Prohibition, soon supplanted communism as the chief topic of conversation, and by the fall of 1920 the average citizen seemed less concerned about the Bolsheviki than about how he could afford one of those new Lexington touring cars, an Overland sedan, or a Paige Light Six.

At the same time, newspapers, especially the new tabloids, began to view American life not so much as a political and economic struggle but as a hilarious merry-go-round of sport, crime, and sex, interspersing their reporting with increasing dosages of advertising. More and more newspaper space was devoted to testimonials for Lux ("Safe for the daintiest things"), Pear's Soap ("Creates a matchless complexion"), Grape Nuts ("When you feel dumpy and out of sorts . . ."), and Camel cigarettes ("In a class by themselves") and less to a discussion of domestic and foreign matters. Meanwhile, men had already started to ogle women's hemlines as they reached all of nine inches above the ground by the fall of 1920, and observed with equal fascination the appearance of rouge and the rolled sock. Little wonder that it was difficult for the radical to command attention!

A growing public interest in postwar sports also helped take the nation's mind off bolshevism as attention shifted from the antics of Lusk and Palmer to those of Jack Dempsey and Babe Ruth. Sports-hungry fans swarmed into professional baseball and college football stadiums in the summer and fall of 1920 and spent their evenings devouring columns of batting averages or dopesters' gossip about the relative merits of such teams as Pittsburgh, Harvard, and Penn State.

For those who did not like their entertainment either so demanding or so rough, the era of the bathing beauty, Mah Jong, and bathtub gin was just beginning; for those who still wanted to worry about menaces, there was the emerging revolt of the "flaming youth" generation.

But whatever were the precise reasons or their exact interaction on each other, there was no doubt that by the fall of 1920 the Great Red Scare was dying. Hysteria, as such, had all but disappeared before spring had passed. As one contemporary writer described the domestic scene in May 1920, "From a state of hysteria the average American citizen has relaxed into a more or less comfortable contemplation of the annual income-tax ordeal, the lure of the seed catalogues and the sporting chances of presidential candidates." [1]

[Aside from the general factors mentioned above, the decline of the Red Scare really begins with the disbarment of the New York Socialists. No other incident during the Scare called forth so much opposition or resentment.]According to the *Literary Digest*, "Emphatic protest and almost universal condemnation [were] launched by Republican, Democratic, and Socialist newspapers alike at the unprecedented action of the New York Assembly." [2] Indeed, some strange bedfellows were suddenly and miraculously created. Conservative journals such as the New York *Tribune, Christian Science Monitor*, and Chicago *Tribune* joined with the *Nation, New Republic*, and New York *Call* in upbraiding the New York legislators first for the January disbarment and then for the April exclusion. Except for the liberal press such protests started mainly as minor murmurings of displeasure despite the *Literary Digest*'s claim; but it is true that shortly thereafter they did burst into loud shouts of anger as the Empire State's assembly continued its high-handed procedures.

Of course, this sentiment did not result from any growing sympathy for radicalism. Rather, it sprang from a resurgent belief that such activity abridged the American principle of representative government. By the time of the assembly's exclusion action in April, many journals were in agreement that not all the Bolshevists in Russia could strike such a blow at the heart of American democratic institutions as that aimed by the members of the New York State Legislature. Others began to wonder where it all might end and asked, "Shall we sometime see Republicans excluding Democrats and Democrats excluding Republicans from our lawmaking bodies, on the ground that the other party's principles are 'inimical to the best interests' of the United States?" Such mounting concern was perhaps best portrayed in a cartoon appearing in the New Orleans *Times-Picayune* which compared the assembly's action with burning down a house to get rid of the rats. Thus, although some papers such as the New York *Times* continued to claim that exclusion was necessary to protect the nation, most newspapers agreed that in the light of traditional American practice, the action was "a shocking blunder," "politically unwise," "dangerous," "legally unjust," and "an evidence of acute hysteria." [8]

The general press was by no means alone in its objections. Numerous prominent individuals soon came to the Socialists' defense. Senator Warren G. Harding and Dean Roscoe Pound joined sentiments in denouncing the New York assembly, and even A. Mitchell Palmer admitted it was wrong to treat Socialists as if they belonged in the same category as Communists. William Allen White, the "barometer" of the prairies, labeled the New York action "preposterous" and claimed the refusal of the majority of the New York assembly to seat the Socialists "merely martyrizes the advocates of a stupid cause." Former Senator Albert J. Beveridge of Indiana agreed by stating that "attempts to smother thought by force only make converts to the very doctrines thus sought to be destroyed" and concluded, "Denial of lawful free speech is the noxious culture in which crazy radicalism is propagated most rapidly." Fiorello H. LaGuardia, president of the Board of New York Aldermen, maintained that "if we keep on at this rate, we shall build up a radical party in this country," and Governor Smith asserted that "To discard the methods of representative government leads to the misdeeds of the very extremists we denounce, and serves to increase the enemies of orderly free government." [4]

Perhaps the most vigorous expression of such adverse sentiment appeared in a letter submitted to the New York assembly by Charles Evans Hughes, representing the New York Bar Association. The former Republican presidential candidate denounced the assembly's action as a "serious mistake," warned of the danger of denying seats to legally elected representatives, and offered the

New York Bar's services to defend the excluded assemblymen. The New York assembly subsequently expressed profound shock that such a stalwart "conservative" as Hughes should take this "extreme" position and proceeded to denounce him as "pro-German," "disloyal," and a "fourflusher"! [5]

With the second expulsion of the Socialists in September, responsible persons now seemed prepared to write off the Empire State's assembly as lost. Even some of the nation's most conservative newspapers expressed embarrassment over the incident and decried the second expulsion as "a worse blunder than the first." "A nauseous and high-handed violation of the principle of political liberty," was the general verdict, while Hughes branded it as another act of "incredible folly." [6]

If any one incident can be credited directly with breaking the thin thread of public hysteria, this certainly was it. Individual and press comment on the New York situation marked a spectacular and sudden contrast with the frenzied anti-Red activity of the past. For the first time during the Scare period there was a serious attempt to concentrate on the basic principle involved and not to be emotionally swayed by hysterical assertions or grim warnings. The action of the New York assembly more than any other event underscored for the entire nation the dangerous effect of continued hysterical fear, and the grotesque spectacle of New York solons being frightened by five mild Socialists made many Americans laugh. Citizens could now see their own exaggerated fears mirrored in those of the New York legislators and the reflection appeared ridiculous. Under the impact of the assembly's blundering stand, many Americans began to feel that it was perhaps time for the nation's preoccupation with the alleged radical menace to end.

Contemporaneously with this unexpected turn of events, opposition also grew both inside and outside of Congress to any further consideration of peacetime sedition legislation. As a result, despite much pressure to the contrary, Congress delayed action and, finally, so many congressmen proved sufficiently skeptical of the need for such legislation that none was passed.

Admittedly, the expulsion of the New York Socialists made many congressmen all the more cautious, but adverse press and individual sentiment affected them even more. Beginning almost exactly on the same date as the Socialists' disbarment in January, the general press began to devote much space to discussions of the Graham and Sterling bills and was overwhelming in its opposition. Because such laws offered at least an indirect threat to the principle of free press, many conservative newspapers and magazines suddenly found themselves speaking in the same terms as the *Nation* and the *New Republic* when they labeled all such proposals "vicious and absurd," "reactionary," and "hysterical." In fact, many journals now agreed that in the haste to avoid bolshevism, the nation was backing into reaction and the institutions most in danger were not those attacked by revolutionists but the basic rights of free speech, free press, and free assemblage. Even the New York *Times* threw its weight against peacetime sedition measures because it feared their adverse effect on the freedom of the press would go far beyond the limit of constitutional definition. Attorney General Palmer, meanwhile, was assailed for his insistence upon such legislation and was even charged with trying to "Prussianize the United States." [7]

Opinion quickly crystallized outside the journalistic world. Justice Holmes indirectly condemned the proposed sedition bills by stating that "with effervescing opinions, as with the not yet forgotten champagnes, the quickest way to let them get flat is to let them get exposed to the air." Samuel Gompers declared such measures would only manufacture lawbreakers and not apprehend them. Twenty-two American clergymen signed an appeal to the Christian churches condemning all such sedition legislation and urging Christian people to use their influence "for the return to the old faith in the fundamental principles of our civil liberty." [8]

Thus, although American Legion posts, the National Civic Federation, the American Defense Society, the Lusk Committee, and other super-patriotic organizations continued to call for sedition laws, the tide of battle was turning. During the House hearings on the Graham-Sterling Bill in late January and early February, such vigorous opposition was voiced by outstanding lawyers like Zechariah Chafee, Jr., that even Attorney General Palmer was forced to admit the measures under consideration were perhaps too strict and simpler legislation ought to be written. As a result, the House Rules Committee subsequently reported unfavorably on both bills and no action was taken. Immediately, the general press expressed a sigh of relief. Said the Kansas City *Star*: ". . . it is so difficult to [enact sedition legislation] without invading the field of opinion and making possible the intimidation of people who are within their traditional rights of American citizenship that perhaps it had best not be attempted. Additional legislation is more dangerous than soap-box oratory or foolish publications." [9]

Even though a few die-hards still attempted to secure passage of some kind of sedition legislation, by the close of February 1920 all hope for passage was gone. Continued energetic opposition from prominent lawyers, the AFL, the liberal press, and many general newspapers and periodicals doomed all such measures to defeat. In this respect, it was encouraging to see the "Americans," as contrasted with the "Bill Haywoods," fight sedition proposals to a standstill and reach the conclusion that there was no profit in destroying their liberties in order to preserve them.

With these strides having already been made toward a return to sanity, there remained the thorny problem of alien deportations, left as a legacy of the federal and state raids that had been held in January 1920.

The manner in which this problem was settled also led to a decline in hysteria, although for a time public and press opinion ran directly counter to the restoration of stability. General opinion still called for immediate and wholesale deportations on the *Buford* pattern. In this instance, it was not the public or the press, but a few officials in the Labor Department who, through a tangled mass of court decisions and deportation hearings, stemmed the tide of injudicious actions.

No sooner were the January raids completed than many newspapers expressed fears that Secretary of Labor Wilson and Assistant Secretary Post might undo the work already done by Attorney General Palmer. Such fears were somewhat allayed when on January 25 Secretary Wilson decided in the deportation case of a certain Englebert Preis that membership in or affiliation with the Communist party was a deportable offense under the 1918 Alien Law.[10] The press immediately hailed this decision by declaring that Wilson's action "gives assurance that in the near future other 'soviet arks' will sail."[11]

But despite the Preis decision, there were other straws in the wind which signified that deportations would not proceed as quickly or as easily as many had hoped. On January 26, Justice Holmes in the case of the *Silverthorne Lumber Company v. U.S.* established the principle that information gathered on the basis of the illegal seizure of papers and files could not thereafter be used to incriminate a defendant.[12] Two weeks later, Judge G. M. Bourquin of the District Court of Montana applied this dictum in the case of deportee John Jackson and issued a writ of habeas corpus because the evidence used against him had been illegally secured.[13] In the meantime, on January 27, Secretary Wilson revoked Solicitor Abercrombie's earlier change in the rule governing deportation hearings and restored it to its former wording.[14]

The spotlight now turned on Assistant Secretary Post. Acting as final departmental arbiter in deportation cases, and being a firm believer in freedom of speech and assemblage, he applied Judge Bourquin's decision and the reinstated rule vigorously. He believed that many arrested aliens had not been allowed to secure proper counsel and that information against them had been illegally secured. He was also convinced that many of the aliens did not know the basic philosophy of the Communist parties, having been drawn into them as a result of holding membership in elements which were amalgamated with the Communist factions after their inception. Moreover, he refused to throw all anarchists, whether terroristic or pacifistic, into the same pile or apply the label

"Communist" to IWW's or others not technically members of the Communist organizations.[15]

Unable in most cases to find any concrete basis for deportation and shocked by the infringements of civil liberty which his review of the deportation hearings revealed, Post ordered wholesale cancellations of warrants and by April had released almost half of those apprehended in the January raids. Post justified his action by claiming most of the aliens were, in his own words, "wage workers, useful in industry, good natured in their dispositions, unconscious of having given offense." "Very few, if any," added the assistant secretary, "were the kind of aliens that Congress could in all reasonable probability have intended to comprehend in its anti-alien legislation." [16]

Press and congressional opinion was vehement. Post was immediately charged with "coddling the Reds" and with being a "moon-struck parlor radical" himself. His handling of the deportation situation was derisively called "the calm after the storm," and it was widely rumored that the Labor Department was "so honeycombed with Bolshevism" that it was unfit to handle the cases of persons classed as undesirable.[17]

As a result of such furor, sentiment grew to have Post impeached and finally, on April 15, Representative Homer Hoch of Kansas offered a resolution which directed an investigation of Post's administration and subsequent impeachment if the facts warranted. Although a few liberal journals denounced this resolution, the majority of the press hailed its adoption and believed Post would have "a good deal to explain" because he was "more guilty than the men he sets free to stir up revolution." [18]

On April 27, the House Committee on Rules began a series of hearings on the advisability of impeachment. In the course of the hearings, the assistant secretary's deportation decisions were brought under careful scrutiny. Yet, despite the introduction of much prejudicial evidence against Post, the House Committee could find no clear-cut reason to impeach him and, on May 1, decided merely to offer a resolution censuring him for his leniency.[19]

Post, meanwhile, was indignant and demanded that he be allowed to appear in his own behalf. To satisfy him, the hearings were held over until May 7, at which time the assistant secretary testified. He proceeded to outline in detail the injustices resulting from the government raids of November and January, and contended that the Justice Department, spurred on by the general press and super-patriots, had manufactured a revolution which simply was not there. He pointed to the fact that in the raids of January 2 only three pistols capable of being fired were found and of these, two were of only .22 caliber. Post then defended the 1293 cancellations of warrants which he had already ordered and concluded his remarks by roundly assailing the Department of Justice for its high-handed procedures and illegal actions.[20]

All in all, the assistant secretary was so sure in his testimony, so eloquent in his defense, and mustered so much evidence in his own behalf that he completely confounded his accusers. Few engaged in the hearings, including those who originally advocated his impeachment, knew much concerning the actual procedure of deportation or understood the complicated political and economic philosophies sometimes involved. Few, except Post, could have explained the differences among Marx, Tolstoy, Proudhon, and Sorel.

Struck by his forthrightness, wit, and intelligence, the Committee on Rules suspended all further consideration of the matter. Surprisingly enough, most newspapers were also sufficiently impressed by Post's testimony that they agreed the Rules Committee ought to make a "graceful withdrawal." Indeed, the committee did look very much like a person who had picked up a hot poker and was trying to find a place to put it.

Meanwhile, the decline in deportable cases continued. On May 5, two days before Post made his able defense, Secretary Wilson in the case of a certain Carl Miller declared that membership in or affiliation with the Communist Labor party was not a deportable offense under the 1918 Act.[21] Actually, there was such a slight difference between the Communist party and the Communist

Labor party that it is difficult to see even from the wording of the decision how such a distinction could have been made. Perhaps a partial explanation lies in the fact the Preis decision concerning the Communist party had occurred in January at a time when hysteria was still high, while this Miller decision was delivered as hysteria was definitely on the wane.

Indeed, although Justice Department officials and some newspapers denounced the Miller decision, most agents of public expression greeted it by merely regretting the existence of such basic differences of opinion between the Labor and Justice departments. Congress, however, was not so impassive and on June 5 voiced its hostility to the Miller verdict by amending the deportation provisions of the 1918 Law to include not only all revolutionary aliens, but also all aliens convicted under the wartime Espionage and Sedition statutes. The law was further amended to read that the giving or lending of money to a proscribed revolutionary organization was to be regarded as proof of advocacy or membership.[22] Congress still was unwilling to let the radical menace die.

In spite of this congressional action, a final blow was struck on June 23 against arbitrary and wholesale alien deportations when Judge George W. Anderson of the Massachusetts District Court declared in the case of *Colyer et al. v. Skeffington* that even membership in the Communist party did not necessarily subject an alien to deportation. In reaching this conclusion, Judge Anderson sharply denounced the ruthless action of many Bureau of Investigation agents and bitterly assailed the Justice Department for its use of undercover spies, for making arrests without proper warrants, and for generally violating constitutional rights. Maintaining that the whole raiding procedure of the government had been based on a theory of "hang first and try afterwards," he released seventeen prospective Communist deportees on writs.[23]

Even the Labor Department was at first shocked by the Colyer decision, but proceeded to apply it in the remaining deportation review hearings. And while the liberal press naturally acclaimed the verdict, the conservative press also reluctantly came to the conclusion that in view of the slipshod methods used by the Justice Department in the November and January raids the decision was probably wise. Said the *Christian Science Monitor*, "In the light of what is now known, it seems clear that what appeared to be an excess of radicalism on the one hand was certainly met with something like an excess of suppression." The paper added that the Colyer decision allowed Americans to take a second look at what had been done and claimed it was "a matter for general satisfaction [that] sentiment has become noticeably calmer." [24]

This return to sanity was sharply reflected in the status of deportation cases in June 1920. From November 1919 to January 1920, about 5000 arrest warrants had been issued of which 3000 had been used. Of these latter, 2202 were subsequently canceled by Assistant Secretary Post as a result of his review of deportation hearings and only 556 of the remainder were upheld and the persons involved ordered deported. To these must be added 35 deportees who had been left over from the *Buford* deportation, which meant a total of only 591 aliens who were awaiting deportation in June 1920. During the rest of 1920 and 1921, these were sent in small groups aboard American ships to their native lands. [25]

Surely this represented a far cry from the 2720 deportations which the attorney general had prophesied earlier and from the "second, third, and fourth" Soviet arks which had been promised.

As hysteria continued to wane in the spring and summer of 1920, Attorney General Palmer found himself in a ticklish situation. Partially because of his continuing fear of radicalism, but now more especially because of his desire to gain the presidency, he attempted to keep public emotion at fever pitch through persistent anti-Red propaganda and warnings of yet unborn revolutions. [26] But, as the domestic scene became increasingly calmer, his anti-radical activities elicited less and less response and not only did he succeed in losing a considerable measure of the immense support he once enjoyed, but he even found himself having to explain his actions to several congressional investigating committees. Those who would emulate Mr. Palmer in their own Red-baiting campaigns should take heed.

Although Palmer had already compromised his position in some quarters because of his continual insistence on peacetime sedition legislation, it was not until May Day 1920 that he finally overreached himself. For some weeks before May 1, the General Intelligence Division on orders from the attorney general released elaborate warnings to citizens to be on guard against a recurrence of May 1, 1919. Newspapers reprinted such warnings and speculated on the turbulence that might actually arise. As May 1 drew nearer, speculation increased as the GID stepped up its warnings of impending terror by declaring that another nation-wide plot to kill high government officials was in the offing and that a general strike and the blowing up of government buildings were also planned. All this, the division claimed, was part of a scheme to overthrow the American government and force recognition of Soviet Russia. The division assured the public, however, that every available federal agent would be thrown into the breach to thwart such an attempt and urged local law enforcement officers to augment their own forces in order to forestall the approaching holocaust.[27]

The whole situation was highly reminiscent of the July 4 scare of 1919. Overpowered by the claims of the attorney general, the press suddenly broke out in a rash of sensational headlines and for the moment the Red Scare was again in full flower. Local police officers immediately alerted their forces to be in a state of complete readiness. Public buildings, churches, and the homes of prominent citizens were placed under guard. State militias were called up in certain states in order to thwart any riots which might occur. In New York City, the entire police force of 11,000 men was put on twenty-four-hour duty and the public library, Pennsylvania Station, and the general post office were heavily guarded. In Boston, trucks with mounted machine guns were parked at various strategic locations while special protection was provided for the state house and the city jail. In Pittsburgh, the bomb squad was placed on a twenty-four-hour alert; in Washington, all public buildings and the homes of certain federal officials were protected; in Chicago, 360 suspected radicals were put under lock and key for the day "just in case." [28]

As with the earlier July 4 scare, not a single disturbance occurred in the entire nation. The few radical meetings that were held were quiet and devoid of even the usual inflammatory speeches. The press evidenced some surprise at this, but quickly attributed it to the fact that no real menace had actually existed. Even some of the most rabidly antiradical journalists were beginning to see things again in their proper perspective and agreed that domestic radicalism was about as important and dangerous as indicated in cartoonist McCarthy's May 1 cartoon for the New Orleans *Times-Picayune* which showed a huge figure of a public leaning over trying to hear the rantings of a little pip-squeak radical. "What Did You Say?" the caption read.[29]

Of course, the Justice Department immediately claimed that its timely warnings had headed off an impending revolution and the country had been saved. But this time the nation was not fooled and, torn between laughter and rage, heaped coals of fire on the attorney general's head. Except for a very few newspapers, the press, whether radical, liberal, or conservative, agreed that the scare had been a "mare's nest hatched in the Attorney General's brain" and denounced him as "full of hot air," "a national menace," and "Little Red Riding Hood with a cry of 'Wolf.'" Most newspapers now begged the attorney general, despite his political ambitions, to leave the Red menace alone. "We can never get to work," remarked the *Rocky Mountain News*, "if we keep jumping sideways in fear of the bewiskered Bolshevik." [30]

The May Day fiasco truly marked the beginning of Palmer's downfall since even Congress was so infuriated that a concerted drive was begun to bring the activities of the attorney general under congressional scrutiny. On May 11, the House Rules Committee, which was just then completing the impeachment investigation of Assistant Secretary Post, "invited" Palmer to appear

What Did You Say?

(Cartoonist McCarthy in the New Orleans *Times-Picayune*)

before it and defend himself and his department against all the various charges being made. Palmer accepted the invitation and agreed to testify on June 1.[31]

In the meantime, criticism of the attorney general grew, and on May 28, the National Popular Government League issued a pamphlet entitled *Report upon the Illegal Practices of the United States Department of Justice*. This was the most authoritative denunciation of the anti-Red activities of the Justice Department yet made. It was skillfully written by twelve of the nation's most prominent lawyers, among them Zechariah Chafee, Jr., Felix Frankfurter, Ernst Freund, Roscoe Pound, and Frank P. Walsh. Among other things, these twelve lawyers charged that the wholesale arrests of both aliens and citizens during the Department's various raids had been made without justification, that the prisoners had been illegally held incommunicado, that homes had been entered and property seized without proper warrant, that aliens had been illegally treated while incarcerated, and that agent provocateurs had purposely enticed many innocent persons into a trap. All this, contended the authors, had been done at the expense of the United States government and was wholly outside the scope of the attorney general's normal duties.[32]

On June 1 when Attorney General Palmer appeared before the Rules Committee, he denied first of all the charges made earlier by Assistant Secretary Post. Then, backed by affidavits from his field agents, he denied the assertions of the twelve lawyers. He maintained that as many warrants had been supplied as possible, but admitted that under the press of expediency it had been necessary to make some arrests without them. He denounced the furor over the department's use of undercover informants by claiming this had been essential to ferret out underground radical units. The attorney general then concluded that although the department's methods might have appeared arbitrary and hasty, they were undertaken to alleviate a very real and awful danger, and, in that respect, the department's actions had proved successful. They would have been even more successful, added Palmer, if it had not been for Louis Post and certain others who because of their "tender solicitude for social revolution and perverted sympathy for the criminal anarchists of the country . . . set at large among the people the very public enemies whom it was the desire and intention of the Congress to be rid of." [33]

Faced with this defense of his position, the House delved no further into the Palmer controversy. The nation's newspapers factually reported the charges against Palmer and the testimony as it occurred, but displayed no great emotion one way or the other. Although a few newspapers such as the New York *Times* sided with the attorney general, most seemed to feel the incident was indicative of how "rudderless" the Wilson administration had become.

Certain elements, however, were not content to allow Palmer to slip off the hook and after the presidential race, in which Palmer's fortunes fared badly, Senator Thomas J. Walsh of Montana secured Senate passage of a resolution which authorized the Senate Judiciary Committee to investigate the activities of the Justice Department. In these hearings, held from January 19 to March 3, 1921, the attorney general reiterated his statements made before the House Rules Committee six months earlier. He declared that at the height of the Red Scare he was "shouted at from every editorial sanctum in America from sea to sea . . . to do something," and concluded: "I apologize for nothing that the Department of Justice has done in this matter. I glory in it. I point with pride and enthusiasm to the results of that work; and if, as I said before, some of my agents out in the field . . . were a little rough and unkind, or short and curt, with these alien agitators, whom they observed seeking to destroy their homes, their religion and their country, I think it might be well overlooked in the general good to the country which has come from it. That is all I have to say." [34]

The final report of these hearings carried no recommendation and the Senate took no action. Once again public opinion was apathetic. Except from the extreme right and the extreme left, neither condemnation nor praise for Palmer's position was forthcoming. Sentiment was confused, for although many had become skeptical of the attorney general's earlier activities, they were still willing to accept the possibility that his 1919 anti-Red campaign had had some basis in fact.

However, anti-Palmerites continued their relentless pursuit, and, as late as February 1923 (almost two years after Palmer had left office), Senator Walsh again tried to force the matter on the attention of the Senate. On February 5, 1923, that body evidenced its antipathy to such overtures by voting to release the Judiciary Committee from all further consideration of Palmer's Red Scare activities. Thereupon, Senator Walsh submitted a minority report which roundly condemned the actions of the former attorney general as marking a period when "justice 'for a season bade the world farewell'," and then he, too, allowed the matter to drop.[35]

There remained yet two other major indications that the tide of fear had indeed ebbed by the close of 1920. The first was the Wall Street bombing of September 1920, and the second was the presidential campaign. Of the two, the presidential campaign was perhaps more significant, but the Wall Street bombing was certainly more spectacular.

Had the Wall Street bombing occurred one year earlier it would have been interpreted as part of a concerted plan to overthrow the American government. However, transpiring as it did in September 1920, this sensational event aroused no great fears of impending crisis. Instead it filled the nation with the resolute desire not to become again either ridiculous or panic-stricken. Certainly the sane way in which newspapers and periodicals greeted the event marked a decided contrast with their earlier hysterical activities.

The corner of Broad and Wall streets in New York City had long been regarded as the very center of American capitalism. On the north side of Wall Street stood the Sub-Treasury Building; next to it was the United States Assay Office; directly opposite on the southeast corner was the home of J. P. Morgan and Company; and just around the corner on Broad Street was the Stock Exchange.

Almost at this exact spot on September 16, just as the workers of the neighborhood were preparing to go to lunch, there was a blinding flash followed by a crashing roar — a huge bomb had gone off directly in front of the Assay Office, opposite the House of Morgan. Twenty-nine persons were killed outright, four more succumbed as a result of their injuries, and over two hundred others were hospitalized. So intense was the heat from the explosion that people near open windows six stories above the street were badly burned. If, however, the explosion was designed to wipe out the great barons of capitalism, it was certainly a dismal fizzle. None of the victims were Wall Street's financial tycoons (Morgan was abroad), but ordinary runners, clerks, and stenographers. Property damage was assessed from $1,500,000 to $2,500,000. The interior of the Morgan Building was wrecked, windows were smashed for blocks around, and the walls of the Equitable Building up to the 20th floor were charred by pieces of the explosion.[36]

While major cities such as Chicago and Boston immediately surrounded their own financial districts with police reserves in order to prevent a similar catastrophe, New York City police and federal agents began an investigation to determine the exact cause of the explosion. Various theories were advanced, but the most probable arose from the fact that the carcass of a horse and bits of steel, wood, and canvas were found at the spot of the disaster. These pitiful remains suggested that a TNT bomb had gone off in a horse-drawn wagon, presumably while its driver left the scene. Several witnesses later testified that such a wagon had been seen in front of the Assay Office shortly before the explosion, but there was no unanimity of opinion concerning the nature of the driver. He was variously described as swarthy and fair, tall and short, heavy and slight, foreign and American. Rewards were offered for information leading to the apprehension of the man in question and police attempted to trace parts of the wagon, the shoes of the horse, and even the lead slugs used in the bomb.[37]

In the meantime, bureau chief Flynn and Attorney General Palmer, both of whom had gone to New York City to lead the investigation, proclaimed in their typically hysterical fashion that the Wall Street bombing was part of a gigantic plot to overthrow capitalism and establish a new soviet order in the United States. The public and the press, however, remained unconvinced and followed the stages of the investigation with interest but certainly not hysteria. Most Americans were beginning to see that no such insane plot could ever command the support of more than a few persons and most discussion centered on the probability that a small group of dedicated, crazed anarchists had committed the crime.[38]

As a result, Palmer and Flynn were ridiculed for their hysterical assertions, particularly since they failed to uncover any real evidence which might lead to the perpetrators of the crime. The *Rocky Mountain News* declared that the Justice Department "is subservient to bureaucracy. A great big secret-service army, composed largely of politicians, is employed. The usual pinch of salt must be used." And during the ensuing weeks as police officers entered a series of blind alleys in their efforts to trace down what few clues they had, most newspapers continued to maintain that this latest bomb outrage "defeats its own purpose. . . . It fails to terrorize or frighten." Said the Cleveland *Plain Dealer*: ". . . Capitalism is untouched. The federal government is not shaken in the slightest degree. The public is merely shocked, not terrorized, much less converted to the merits of anarchism. Business and life as usual. Society, government, industry functioning precisely as if nothing had happened."[39]

The presidential election campaign of 1920 which was just then getting under way helps to explain, to a large degree, this attitude. Actually, the campaign might be looked upon as the capstone of declining hysteria since intense interest over the pending election and the choosing of candidates temporarily relegated almost everything else to the background. Caught up in the swirl of election-year pageantry, the nation found little time to waste on fears of domestic revolutions and it was especially significant that neither political party, at their nominating conventions in June or later, evidenced any great desire to use domestic radicalism as a campaign issue.

The radical issue might have played a more important role had it not been for the singular political failure of Attorney General Palmer. As early as March 1920, he announced his candidacy for the presidency and during the following months built up an organization to further his cause. In the meantime, the "Fighting Quaker" concentrated heavily on keeping the Red Scare alive since it was obvious his popular support depended directly on the extent to which the public felt he was saving the nation from radicalism. However, such glaring blunders as the May Day fiasco lost him so much popular prestige that ten days before the Democratic convention President Wilson reportedly told Carter Glass that Palmer would make a "weak" candidate. Even Palmer's good friend and accomplice, Joe Tumulty, regarded him as poor presidential timber because of his Red Scare excesses and his unpopularity with organized labor. Others were somewhat less kind and simply wrote him off as the "Quaking Fighter," "Faking Fighter," and "Quaking Quitter." [40]

Nevertheless, the attorney general made a strong opening bid at the convention and was one of the leading contenders for the nomination along with Governor James M. Cox of Ohio and President Wilson's son-in-law, William Gibbs McAdoo. Finally perceiving that the tide was running against him, Palmer freed his delegates and Governor Cox was subsequently nominated. Then, in the endeavor to make the election a "great and solemn referendum" on the League, as Wilson wanted, the party as a whole minimized domestic problems and the issue of radicalism completely.

Oddly enough, it was in the Republican convention that the only incident occurred which indicated the emotional days of the Red Scare were not entirely forgotten. Just as the same Senate group which was primarily responsible for Warren Harding's nomination prepared to force Senator Lenroot's name through the convention as the Ohioan's running mate, a delegate from Oregon "with a foghorn voice" mounted a chair and nominated "for vice-president Calvin Coolidge, a one-hundred-per-cent American." To the immediate cries of "We want Coolidge," he was accepted unanimously, mainly because of his fame as the savior of Boston during the police strike. Never, according to Chauncey Depew, had a vice-presidential nominee received such a spontaneous and enthusiastic tribute as that given by the convention to Coolidge.[41]

In the ensuing campaign, the Republicans stressed the radical issue no more than did the Democrats. Rather, the tendency was to assure the nation that nothing was amiss. As early as May 1920, Senator Harding keynoted his campaign by declaring, "America's present need is not heroics but healing; not nostrums but normalcy . . . not surgery but serenity." Somewhat later, he re-emphasized this fact by urging the nation to return to the ordinary business of living and forget past fears and problems. As far as radicalism was concerned, he persistently contended that the number of domestic radicals had been greatly magnified and that "too much has been said about Bolshevism in America."[42]

While McAdoo maintained that Harding's speeches left the impression "of an army of pompous phrases moving over the landscape in search of an idea," the Republican candidate's words struck a responsive chord in the breasts of most citizens and he was swept into office as the champion of a placid conservatism based on America First. Harding proved himself the high priest of the American people's intense desire for tranquility which thus far had eluded them in the postwar era. Now, the reaction of the right, with "normalcy" as its slogan, finally conquered, but not by usurpation or hysteria. It ruled by a franchise from the public which sprang from a growing indifference.

It was this indifference which unquestionably was the real key to the rapid decline in Red Scare hysteria. Americans had at last clearly demonstrated that they wished to be less concerned with weighty and compelling foreign and domestic problems and more with radios, sports contests, Mah Jong, and homemade gin recipes. And, as these latter interests gradually occupied a more important place in the public mind, they constituted a formidable deterrent to either the continuation or the recurrence of anti-Red hysteria. At the same time, the Red Scare itself indirectly helped heighten public interest in these other matters, for as the public tired of the Scare it eagerly seized upon any new fad or gadget to provide a new emotional charge or thrill. Under such conditions there was of course a growing preoccupation with the "business of everyday living," as Harding called it, and a complete unwillingness to assume responsibility for anyone except oneself. At least this was an elemental kind of "normalcy" that almost everyone could agree on.

Thus, Harding's simple assurances of tranquillity, the nonemphasis on the radical issue during the campaign, and the outcome of the election with all of its many ramifications marked significant steps in the return of public stability. And even though Eugene Debs, presidential candidate of the Socialist party and still a prisoner in the Atlanta penitentiary, received 915,302 votes, most journals calmly agreed that when compared with Harding's sixteen million and Cox's nine million, his figure represented "a very long distance . . . between unrest and revolution, or. anything that distantly approaches revolution." [43]

16 ★ ★ ★ ★ ★ ★ ★ ★ ★ ★

Pebbles on the Beach

THE decline of anti-Red hysteria and the return of public stability by late 1920 technically marked the end of the Great Red Scare. Gone were the bombings, the government raids, the mass deportations, the shocking displays of mob violence.

[However, the underlying fear of radicalism and the proclivity for intolerance which the Red Scare had engendered remained long after these various events were forgotten and hysteria had passed from the scene. In fact, the antiradical emotionalism emanating from the Scare affected both governmental and private thinking for almost a decade to come and left its unmistakable imprint upon many phases of American life. Continued insistence upon ideological conformity, suspicion of organized labor, public intolerance toward aliens, and a hatred for Soviet Russia were but a few of the more important legacies left by the Red Scare. Moreover, the decline in liberal thought, the general apathy toward reform, and the intense spirit of nationalism which so characterized the 1920s were, partially at least, outgrowths of the Scare period.]

A more detailed analysis than is possible here would probably show that the Red Scare was a much more vital conditioning factor for the "Roaring Twenties" than has generally been supposed. True, it is common knowledge that the Red Scare ushered in the twenties and served as a sort of bridge between war and peace. But its influence did not stop there. Even a cursory examination of the Scare's ramifications reveals that while the phenomenon did not basically change the pattern of modern American history, it did greatly affect certain subsequent developments, and, indeed, to some extent even colors public opinion today. If for no other reason than the latter, the Red Scare has a timely significance which is worthy of considerable attention.

The aftermath period following the Red Scare hysteria has no well-defined limits nor does it lend itself easily to critical or accurate examination. Generally speaking, there was a high degree of Scare-inspired psychology at work on public opinion down to 1924–25. In the broader view, the whole pattern of thought and action common to the 1920s was in part at least traceable to the Red Scare.

Here, however, we are most interested in those developments which related most directly to the Scare phenomenon, for the receding tide of anti-Red hysteria did cast up some distinctive pebbles on the beach of normalcy. The first was the continuing crusade for 100 per cent Americanism.

Still rooted in the belief that true patriotism could be instilled by slogans and parades, this campaign mushroomed as a result of the Red Scare. For example, the American Defense Society, National Security League, and National Civic Federation were soon joined by other such agencies as the Better America Federation (1920), Allied Patriotic Societies (1923), National Patriotic Council (1924), and United States Patriotic Society (1925). Using the Red Scare as their point of departure, these organizations, amply aided by the American Legion and the Ku Klux Klan, persisted in distributing much antiradical literature during the entire decade and as late as 1928 maintained the nation was still riddled with bolshevism. They claimed the churches, schools, colleges, and labor unions were all badly infected, and they kept such prominent individuals as Rev. S. Parkes Cadman, Clarence Darrow, and Dean Roscoe Pound in the parlor Red category.[1] Such irresponsible charges served to sustain a degree of public intolerance by retaining the word "Bolshevik" as a scare word and the easiest means of eliminating all opposition. As before, wise schoolteachers, college professors, and clergymen remained clear of controversial subjects; a whispered "He's a Bolshevist" was still an effective weapon to use against a man in 1929.

During the twenties these patriotic societies kept alive some public intolerance not only by the means cited above, but also by supplying anti-Red speakers, often dressed as Uncle Sam, to fraternal meetings, business luncheons, women's clubs, schools, and the like. At the same time, they lobbied for the enactment of peacetime sedition legislation, anti-strike laws, and other sorts of repressive measures. In particular, the American Legion and the Ku Klux Klan, the latter having an estimated membership of 4,500,000 in 1924, propagandized the need for the "Americanization" of school texts, loyalty oaths for teachers, and more stringent immigration legislation.[2]

This problem of immigration legislation and the public attitude toward aliens in general reflected the most obvious effect of the continuing patriotic crusade. Through it, the belief was perpetuated that most aliens were susceptible to radical philosophies and therefore represented an element which particularly endangered the nation. As a result the AFL, the general press, and a host of other institutions, agencies, and prominent citizens had long since joined the patriotic societies in demanding more stringent immigration laws for this as well as for other reasons. As far as the specific factor of radicalism was concerned, General Leonard Wood, of Gary strike fame, summed up opinion fairly well when he exclaimed, "We do not want to be a dumping ground for radicals, agitators, Reds, who do not understand our ideals."[3]

Such constant agitation was not lost on Congress and with the opening of the decade new immigration measures were rapidly taken under consideration. While an analysis of the congressional debates shows that most congressmen emphasized that unrestricted immigration would increase domestic unemployment, depress native labor standards, and destroy traditional blood lines,

the argument that American institutions had to be protected somehow from immigrant "Reds" and all others who were likely to be
unsympathetic to the existing order was not ignored.[4] Such a belief
ultimately found expression in both the Emergency Immigration
Act of 1921 and the permanent statute of 1924 which discriminated
especially against prospective immigrants from southern and
southeastern Europe, the origin of the newer, more radical, less
educated, and less assimilable groups. The National Origins Quota
System which followed was but a further expression and adapta-
tion of this discriminatory attitude toward "unorthodox" aliens.[5]

Even more directly expressive of this continued anti-alien feeling was the case of Nicola Sacco and Bartolomeo Vanzetti, the
cause célèbre of the 1920s. These men, both Italian aliens and
avowed anarchists, were arrested in May 1920 for the robbery and
murder of a shoe company paymaster in South Braintree, Massachusetts. Although at their trial the state was unable to prove con-
clusively that the two Italians were responsible for the crime, they
were found guilty under what appeared to be highly prejudicial
circumstances and were sentenced to death in July 1921 by Judge
Webster Thayer of Worcester.

The execution date, however, was continually postponed as a
result of widespread protests both at home and abroad concerning
the validity of the decision. For six years Sacco and Vanzetti remained in prison awaiting death while bitter controversy raged
over their trial. Meanwhile, such eminent figures as Anatole France,
George Bernard Shaw, H. G. Wells, John Galsworthy, and Albert
Einstein appealed for a complete review of their case. Simultaneously, radical elements throughout the world seized upon their
plight and made "Sacco and Vanzetti" a rallying cry against American capitalism, claiming the two men were being railroaded to
their deaths merely because they were radical aliens and not because of any crime.

But, in the long run, Massachusetts's justice was not to be denied.
After a series of refusals for a rehearing and the investigation of
an advisory committee appointed by Governor Alvan T. Fuller,

the execution date was finally set for August 22, 1927. As this date approached and clamor throughout the world increased, the American press, which itself up to this point had been divided on the issue, now sharply reverted to an intense nationalism and stanchly defended the decision in the belief that the whole fabric of American law and justice was undergoing a radical foreign attack.

Sacco and Vanzetti went to their deaths with "This is our career, and our triumph" being the last words they gave to the world. Quite naturally, they were regarded as martyrs by their many sympathizers. These latter continued to claim that the word "anarchist" rather than any criminal act had sent them to the electric chair, and the whole incident was denounced as a prime example of American disdain for justice and prejudice against the foreigner. Feeling ran so high in some areas of the world that upon receipt of the news of their execution, American embassies were stoned, diplomatic officials were assaulted, and the American flag was defamed. Indeed, in most parts of the world, the prestige of American justice dropped so sharply that the damage done to the reputation of American freedom was a long time repairing. It was a costly price to pay for the lives of two men.

Such was the legacy of Sacco and Vanzetti — and of the Red Scare.[6]

The deteriorating position of organized labor and the extensive antiunion activities of American business in the years immediately following the Red Scare indicate another important contribution of the Scare to life in the 1920s.

Public suspicion of organized labor lingered on as open-shop adherents continued to draw heavily on Scare-inspired fears and prejudices to hamper the labor movement. Intensifying its operation from 1920 to 1923, the open-shop crusade ultimately reached into every community where there was an employment relationship worthy of the name. During this period there were open-shop groups in no fewer than 240 cities of forty-four states. Also

267

espousing the open-shop principle and spreading information in its behalf were the 1400 member organizations of the United States Chamber of Commerce; the 6000 corporate and individual members of the NAM; the 540 affiliated bodies of the National Founders Association; the Bankers Association, representing 53,000 members; and the National Grange, spokesman for some one million farmers. Locally, such organizations as the Detroit Employers Association, the Southwestern Open Shop Association, the Industrial Association of San Francisco, the Citizens' Alliance of Minneapolis, and the Associated Industries of Tacoma, to mention just a few, were carrying forward the antiradical propaganda of the open-shop campaign. It was estimated that in the year 1920 the Associated Employers of Indianapolis, alone, distributed 1,500,000 pieces of open-shop literature.[7]

The open shop, or "American Plan" as it was now popularly called, was declared to be *the* major bulwark against radicalism and the "subversive foreign concept" of unionism. And although Samuel Gompers and other leaders of the AFL declared war on the movement, they were virtually helpless before the onslaught. Under the direct guidance of the National Association of Manufacturers, the National Founders Association, and other such employer groups, the "American Plan" increased its popular support and through its continued charges of labor "radicalism" had a devastating effect on organized labor. It was obvious the police strike, the steel strike, and the coal strike were not yet forgotten.[8]

In desperation, labor leaders during these years valiantly attempted to shake off the label of radicalism by intensifying their own Red-baiting activities, while at the same time trying to appear as conservative as possible on most social, economic, and political matters. John L. Lewis, Samuel Gompers, and the *American Federationist* constantly lambasted radicalism of all types, and at the various AFL conventions the Bolshevik philosophy received its full share of condemnation both in resolutions from the floor and in speeches from the platform.[9] In fact, as late as 1928, the annual AFL convention passed a resolution branding the Russian Soviet regime "the most unscrupulous, most anti-social, most menacing institution in the world today." [10]

Yet the AFL was completely unable to regain any great measure of public confidence or garner any sympathy from either the government or the courts. Within the several years following the Red Scare the government evidenced its hostility by sponsoring some of the most sweeping strike injunctions in labor history, and the courts in a series of famous decisions upheld the validity of yellow-dog contracts, invalidated minimum wage laws, and struck down the supposed labor safeguards in the Clayton Act. [11]

As far as the effect of all this on union membership was concerned, the figures prove more eloquent than words. By 1923 the organized labor movement numbered only 3,780,000, marking a loss of more than a million members in two years — and this staggering loss was not recouped until after the crash of 1929. [12]

Perhaps the most disheartening effect of the Red Scare upon American life was its impact on civil liberties, particularly freedom of expression. Subsequent state legislation concerning teacher loyalty oaths and the movement to purge school textbooks of "un-Americanism" during the twenties were largely an extension of the earlier trend toward absolute ideological conformity which the Scare had promoted. As might be expected, back of this crusade was continuous and unstinting agitation by certain newspapers, fraternal organizations, and patriotic societies. These pressure groups considered the schools the "main line of defense" against radicalism and therefore urged that only "patriotic instruction" be given in the classroom. At the same time they also demanded that the personal political and economic convictions of teachers be above reproach.

The main device used to enforce such educational conformity was the teacher loyalty oath. It was not entirely new to the American educational scene since five states had already enacted such laws by 1919–20. However, it was not until after the Red Scare that the oath gained widespread acceptance. The device received its greatest publicity by being incorporated in the New York Lusk legislation of 1920, and, in 1921, four other states followed suit. In the following years of the 1920s, fifteen additional states enacted such legislation.[13]

As far as is known, however, teacher loyalty oaths did not prevent a single Communist from occupying a teaching position during the period of enforcement. At best, these laws only offended those sincere and patriotic educators who believed in the essential rightness and efficacy of academic freedom in a democratic society. Indeed, not one Communist teacher stepped forward to challenge the loyalty oaths. Evidently they simply signed and went on about their proselytizing business.

The purging of textbooks occurred simultaneously with this drive for loyalty oath legislation. As a result of pressure from the Hearst papers, bar associations, the American Legion, Ku Klux Klan, and Sons and Daughters of the American Revolution, history texts in particular were carefully scrutinized for "unpatriotic" statements. Whether such statements were truly unpatriotic or merely "pro-British," they were similarly regarded as too dangerous to pass on to America's youth. Those who wanted to wield the red pencils claimed consistently that the basic desire still was to tell the American story "truthfully," but it was felt that under no circumstances should historical investigation be allowed to lessen the greatness of the nation or its leaders. So serious was this whole matter regarded in some areas that more than one state enacted legislation providing for the "purification" of all its schools' history and civics texts! [14]

The same narrow and dangerous conception of freedom of expression which underlay the loyalty oaths and textbook purging was also evidenced by the courts in the years immediately following the Red Scare. Of the major free speech cases reaching the Supreme Court during the 1920s, only a few decisions toward the very end of the decade could be construed as favorable to civil liberty. It seemed that the closer to the actual Scare period a case was decided, the more unfavorable was the decision of the Court.

In the two years following the Scare, four major cases involving the wartime sedition legislation of both the state and federal governments — *Pierce et al. v. U.S., Schaefer v. U.S., Gilbert v. Minnesota,* and *Milwaukee Social Democratic Publishing Co. v. Burleson* — came before the Supreme Court. In each of these cases the decision followed the pattern already established in the Schenck and Abrams cases of a few years earlier; nonconformist ideas were held to be dangerous whether any overt act followed from the advocacy of such ideas or not. In each instance the decisions of the lower courts were affirmed, the sedition statutes involved were held to be constitutional, and the resultant abridgement of freedom of speech or press was declared justifiable on the basis of the clear and present danger principle.[15]

Since none of these cases dealt with incidents arising from the Red Scare itself, they remain merely indicative of what probably would have been the situation had court review been called for. However, by 1925 a few cases involving actual Red Scare activity did appear before the Supreme Court the first and most famous being *Gitlow v. New York.* This case revolved around Benjamin Gitlow's earlier arrest and conviction under the New York criminal anarchy law. The defendant claimed that the New York statute was unconstitutional because of its abridgement of personal liberty under the implied guarantees of the due process clause of the Fourteenth Amendment.

In delivering the majority opinion of the Court, Justice Edward T. Sanford, although agreeing that freedom of speech was indeed implicit in the due process clause and therefore protected from impairment by the states, asserted that the state through its police power might punish those who abuse this freedom when their utterances are so inimical to the general welfare that they must be stopped. In so doing, added the justice, the state need not wait for any overt act or breach of the peace. Hence, the decisions of the lower courts against Gitlow were affirmed.[16]

The decision in the Gitlow case was reiterated two years later in 1927 in two similar syndicalist cases. The first, *Whitney v. Califor-*

nia, involved the validity of Mrs. Whitney's conviction for revolutionary activities under the California criminal syndicalist act of 1919. In making the decision on the appeal, the majority of the Supreme Court held that the California law was constitutional, that it did not unduly abridge personal liberty under the due process clause of the Fourteenth Amendment, and that Mrs. Whitney, by advocating the doctrines of the Communist Labor party, had contravened the statute.[17]

The second case, *Burns v. U.S.,* also involved the California law. Burns, an IWW organizer, had been convicted under the measure for belonging to an organization which advocated sabotage and unlawful methods for bringing about reforms. Justice Pierce Butler, speaking for the Court, once again upheld the California statute and declared that as applied in the Burns case it had not illegally infringed upon the defendant's personal liberty.[18]

The continuing effect of the Red Scare on such decisions is fairly obvious. The Court, usually over the protests of Justices Holmes and Brandeis, could not refrain from holding that ideological nonconformity, even though no criminal act was involved, constituted in itself a clear and present danger. Fortunately, however, the Whitney and Burns decisions of 1927 represented the high-water mark of such a strict interpretation and after that date the Court evidenced a growing liberal attitude. In the next several years, it began to whittle away at hastily drawn state sedition, syndicalist, and Red flag legislation, and drew an ever broader definition of personal liberty. The emphasis was gradually shifting to the overt and specific acts of the individual involved and away from the theoretical tenets of the organizations to which he belonged.[19]

In connection with these judicial activities, it must be stated that during the seven years following the Red Scare it was not the judiciary, but the executive branch of government which acted as the champion of civil liberty and proved itself most free from the continuing effects of the earlier anti-Red hysteria. And it is particularly interesting to note that the first steps taken in this direction were not by Woodrow Wilson, the liberal, but by Warren Harding, the conservative. While to the end of his term Wilson remained un-sympathetic to pleas for the release of political prisoners, Harding early displayed a lenient attitude. On Christmas Day 1921, he ordered the release of twenty-seven political prisoners, among them Eugene Debs. Other executive pardons rapidly followed, and after Harding's death Coolidge continued in the same vein. As a result, by Christmas 1923, very few federal prisoners were left in jail.[20]

Within the states the trend was much the same. The governor, rather than the courts, remained the last outpost of hope for many convicted radicals. This was particularly true in New York and California where syndicalist legislation was still being vigorously enforced. For example, Governor Smith of New York pardoned Gitlow even after the Supreme Court had upheld his conviction, and Governor Clement C. Young of California ordered the release of Mrs. Whitney following her defeat at the hands of the same tribunal. In fact, the use of the executive pardon was so widespread that by the close of the twenties not a single Communist or Social-ist was in jail for his political views. Of the few score who still remained in custody, all were members of the IWW. For these, pardons did not come until 1933 and the advent of Franklin Delano Roosevelt.[21]

Not only did certain facets of the domestic scene during the 1920s illustrate the continuing significance of the Red Scare; for-eign policy as well was affected by the experience. Certainly our whole attitude of diplomatic aloofness was partially the result of the fear and distrust we harbored for everything foreign, and the rampant nationalism which we displayed was promoted to some degree by the Red Scare.

Especially was this true with respect to subsequent relations with Soviet Russia. Although by April 1920 the United States ceased its participation in intervention (not so much because of the decline of anti-Red hysteria as because of the emergence of a strong isolationist feeling), the Red Scare had so prejudiced

Americans against cordial relations with Russia that continued nonrecognition was almost inevitable. The belief persisted that the Russian Bolsheviki did not represent the Russian people at all and that they were holding their position only by murder and violence. Hence, neither the American government nor the American people displayed any desire to associate with that power. Had we done so, modern history might read somewhat differently.

In this connection, the case of L. C. A. K. Martens is particularly significant since it presaged the developing trend in American-Soviet relations. Martens, it will be remembered, was the self-styled Bolshevik ambassador to the United States who earlier had run afoul of the New York Lusk Committee, which not only had raided his offices but also had laid plans to rid the country of him altogether. This committee subsequently had subpoenaed Martens for questioning, afterwards charging that the investigation showed his errand here was "not diplomatic in any sense." For this reason, in connection with the January 2 raids, a warrant was issued for his arrest by Solicitor Abercrombie upon the direct request of both Attorney General Palmer and the Lusk Committee.

Martens, however, was not arrested on January 2 because he fled surreptitiously to Washington, D.C., where he placed himself in the custody of the Senate Foreign Relations Committee which, on December 20, 1919, had been instructed by the Senate to inquire into Martens's status. The arrangement was convenient for both parties since Martens escaped arrest through the immunity given him by the Senate committee and the committee in turn was now assured he would appear at its hearings.

In spite of Martens's continual insistence at these hearings that he was in the country for the express purpose of restoring American-Russian relations and was not giving any aid whatsoever to the domestic Communist movement, the findings of the Senate committee were unfavorable. It contended that Martens's mission was not of a diplomatic quality and recommended his immediate deportation as an undesirable alien. At the close of the hearings Martens was dumped in the lap of the Labor Department which, after its own investigation, ordered him deported. A directive was immediately forthcoming from Foreign Commissar Chicherin ordering Martens to return to Russia of his own accord. Therefore, on January 22, 1921, he was permitted to leave the country, according to Chicherin's instructions, under his own power and without the ignominy of deportation.[22]

This incident was typical of subsequent dealings with Russia. Although the Soviet regime soon wiped out the last vestiges of counterrevolution and demonstrated that the Communist order in Russia would stand, the United States still vainly hoped that the Bolsheviki would somehow lose control or that Russia could be cured by the "absent treatment." The State Department throughout the decade acted on the premise that "we cannot recognize . . . a Government which is determined and bound to conspire against our institutions; whose diplomats will be the agitators of dangerous revolt. . . ."[23] In the meantime, the patriotic societies as well as the general press kept alive the Russian Bolshevik bogy and maximized the ideological barrier existing between the two countries.

One can find no clearer indication of the complete bankruptcy of our Russian policy than this. If we were convinced that the Russian Communists represented a real danger to world stability and peace, which they did, then we should have acted upon our convictions and pursued the intervention policy to the limit. On the other hand, if we wished to cut our losses in the Russian situation, we should have accepted the challenge of trying to work through the Russian Communists to the possible benefit, not only of the Russian people, but also of ourselves. Instead, while the press growled and grumbled, the State Department simply pretended they were not there. In the light of present circumstances, it would seem that neither alternative outlined above would have produced as many long-run disasters.

As far as recognition itself was concerned, the inevitable desirability and indeed necessity of trade relations overshadowed other considerations and finally, in 1933, recognition was granted.

Even so, primarily because of the Red Scare and the events which grew out of it, the United States had the distinction of being the last major power to recognize her.

But of all the effects of the Red Scare on life in the 1920s, probably none was more striking that the impact on the domestic radical movement itself. As a result of the Scare hysteria, the two Communist factions were driven completely underground where they found it increasingly difficult to publicize the Communist movement. Although they did produce some above-ground offshoots such as lecture forums and study clubs, what few radical publications remained had to be printed in secret with no indication where they were published or by whom.

Membership in the Communist parties dropped sharply in 1920 from an estimated 70,000 to 16,000, only the most resolute, fanatic, and zealous Communists remaining in the ranks. These, temporarily at least, seemed to enjoy their *sub rosa* existence, likening their position to that of the Russian Bolsheviki under the Czar. They even began to call each other by the same assumed names used by the Russian Bolsheviki in their underground days. In spite of this flair for the dramatic, the fact remains that the Red Scare had broken the back of the Communist movement for the time being. Even the Chicago *Communist* later admitted that by February 1920 the two thriving parties of October 1919 had vanished.[24]

In the meantime, both the Socialist party and the IWW broke with the Communists altogether since neither the Socialists nor the Wobblies cared to follow the Communists' insistence on the Moscow program of world revolution. Eugene Debs, who heretofore had evidenced some sympathy for the Communist cause, now began to attack them bitterly and continued doing so until his death in 1926. Similarly, except for "Big Bill" Haywood and other IWW leaders, the Wobblies rapidly lost their zeal for the Communist program and began denouncing it in such violent terms that according to the Communists their tirades could only be matched by the "Debsian Socialists." Like the Socialist party, the Wobbly organization appeared to be moving farther toward the right under the pressures generated by the Red Scare and gradually even lost its emphasis on violence to accomplish industrial and economic reform. However, while such anti-Communist activity saved the Socialist party, it did not stave off the collapse of the IWW. With most of its leaders in jail, and many of its members lost to the Communists, the IWW virtually ceased to be a factor in the domestic radical movement by 1924.[25]

Thus, the underground Communist movement continued its way alone. Split itself, for a time, by factionalism and bitter dissension, it finally achieved a measure of unity and, as the domestic scene became quieter, emerged once again into the light in 1923. Organized thereafter into a single organization known as the Communist party, its followers soon forgot most of their absurdities, dropped their ridiculous Russian titles, and dispensed with their wild revolutionary tirades. The Communists now began to adjust their propaganda more carefully than before to the particular conditions in America and concentrated more directly on immediate gains. Their emphasis was no longer so much on revolution as on "questions of bread and butter, on housing, on labor organizations, wages and hours." [26]

But, despite the new subtlety of the movement, there was no increased desire on the part of Americans to join it. The word "Communist" continued to repel most citizens. This was amply illustrated in the election of 1924 when William Z. Foster and Benjamin Gitlow, Communist party presidential and vice-presidential nominees respectively, received only 36,000 votes. Such a dire situation caused Gregory Zinoviev, general secretary of the Third International, to wail, "Probably there are fewer than 5,000 Communists in America upon whom we can really depend." [27]

Zinoviev was almost right. In 1927 the Communist party had only 8000 members.[28] When compared with the 70,000 which the movement supposedly had in 1919, this figure certainly shows what a tremendous role Scare-inspired anti-Communist sentiment played in the movement's rapid decline. But whether 70,000 or 8000, the inescapable conclusion remains that at no time either before, during, or after the Red Scare did the radical movement in this country ever approach anything remotely near revolutionary proportions.

The Great Red Scare of 1919–20 belongs to past history. Yet, it is the not too distant past that we deal with here. That past still belongs to contemporary America because it embraces an era in which many living Americans took an active part — that carefree era of the Model A, the talkie movie, the crossword puzzle, the Dayton "Monkey" Trial, the Harding scandals, the hip flask, and Lindy's Atlantic hop.

Still, occurring more than thirty years ago, the Red Scare with its hysteria and its many sensational events is presently unknown to millions of Americans. Indeed, even those other millions who actually lived through the hectic Scare days probably remember it only with a vagueness that is natural to memories held for a long time in the recesses of the human mind. Of course, its strikes, riots, and bombs still reside on the pages of history books where they are referred to from time to time by college freshmen, graduate students, or experienced scholars. Even so, only casual notice is taken of the Palmer raids or the *Buford* deportation, and it is highly doubtful if many readers are deeply moved by the sensational Centralia murders.

Even though the facts and the details of the Great Red Scare may be dead and largely forgotten, the underlying hysterical spirit of American anti-bolshevism, which the Red Scare so clearly represented, lives on. As a nation we are still hagridden by the specter of domestic bolshevism and jump instinctively when the word is mentioned. Our present reaction to the Communist philosophy in large measure still reflects the first impressions we received during the years 1917–20, which indicates that in thirty years we have made little headway in adjusting ourselves either politically or psychologically to living in the same world with this doctrine.

The indications of similarity between the antiradicalism of the years immediately following World War I and the present are certainly striking. Charges and countercharges are made daily concerning the degree of radicalism in organized labor. Violent discussions arise on all sides with respect to communism in the schools and in government. Intense public interest is focused on sensational congressional investigations which have done much investigating but thus far have turned up relatively few dangerous radicals. Spy trials and spy hunts fill the newspapers to a degree completely out of proportion to their relative success or importance. Loyalty oaths are being more widely applied than ever before. Even a new word, "McCarthyism," has been added to our vocabulary which makes the old "Palmerism" fade into insignificance.

Thus, although many years have passed and the precise factors which produced hysteria in 1919 will never repeat themselves in detail, it is obvious to even the most casual observer that the ingredients necessary for a new Red Scare are still present in American life and with sufficient prompting possibly could be made to produce one.

Admittedly, the present intense anti-Red feeling is in some respects more valid today than it was in 1919. But this is not because there are known Communists active in the ranks of organized labor, or because there are subversives at work in the church, the academic profession, or the government. The major reason lies in the fact Soviet Russia is presently in an entirely different position than she was in 1919. No longer is she under serious attack from counterrevolutionaries within or, regardless of Communist claims, in danger of attack from without. Today she is strong and militant, and, unlike her situation in 1919, can and does give effective aid, both morally and militarily, to those who look to her for guidance. Her expanding hold on the minds and souls of people the world over has been spectacular and alarming. Because of this, on the chessboard of international diplomacy and power politics international communism represents an infinitely greater menace today than that faced by Americans in 1919.

This does not negate the fact that from the strictly domestic point of view there remains the danger, as in 1919, of totally exaggerating domestic Communist activity and its effect on American life. Perhaps this danger is even greater since Americans have but recently learned from experience what Communist "fifth columns" can do to weak and unsuspecting countries. The Communist threat is potentially serious to any nation, but the natural American fear and hatred for the Communist doctrine is still prone to permit the creation of too much fantasy and underwrite a pattern of domestic repressive action which is both unnecessary and unwise.

Our Red Scare experience of 1919–20 illustrates clearly that communism cannot be fought effectively by hysteria, or by restrictive legislation, or by mob violence. In the long run we do far more damage to ourselves than to the enemy. Neither raids, nor bloodshed, nor name-calling can possibly hope to bring the menace to its knees. Instead, by retaining our national sanity and by removing the turmoil, the tension, the race prejudice, and the poverty which communism exploits, we stand a much better chance of rendering the doctrine impotent. The real key to fighting communism is not spy hunts, congressional investigations, or loyalty oaths; it rests instead in combating those very problems which bring the issue of communism to the fore — low living standards, sickness and disease, illiteracy, racial intolerance, unequal opportunity, and war. These problems can be solved only by the exercise of sane thinking and the use of greater freedom, not less; by the maintenance of individual liberties, not their repression or destruction. Under these conditions if there are still those who adhere to communism, they will surely represent only the lunatic fringe and thus constitute merely a nuisance, not a dangerous threat.

It must be recognized that a nation which is afraid in the face of an opposing ideology is a nation without faith; and a nation without faith makes an easy mark. Indeed, if a nation becomes so fearful of its life that in order to live it destroys those liberties which gave it birth, then it deserves to die. Faith in the integrity of the individual, in freedom of action, in freedom of worship, and in freedom of speech is essential in defeating any and all dangerous doctrines. If a nation and its people retain these freedoms and have faith in their application, there need be no worry that doom is imminent. Indeed, this faith and these freedoms will sustain and protect a nation when all else fails.

Of course, this does not deny that there are some radicals at work in American society who seek only to destroy, nor does it deny that at times such persons may represent a real danger. But it has always been thus, for such is not an abnormal condition of human affairs but rather is to be expected. It is assumed that the democratic state, acting for the majority, must protect itself from these wreckers; even freedom has a limit to its exercise and cannot be absolute. However, regardless of the dangers sometimes involved, the basic strength of any government still lies in the measure of liberty which it sustains for its various citizens, and the true democrat cannot help but believe that a well-defined line between state authority and personal liberty must be maintained. Thus, individual liberty, particularly for minorities, must be sustained up to the very point where the majority has to act to maintain order. Where that precise point is provides the crucial issue. Generally, during times of crisis, it is a little beyond where the majority thinks it ought to be.

If there is any one lesson to be gleaned from the Red Scare experience of 1919 it is a perception of the incalculable injustice and intolerance that can result from defining the limits of liberty too narrowly. Since it would appear from the current trend of events that many of the same problems and fears which plagued the American public of 1919 still bother us today, it seemed of particular value to return to that almost forgotten scene. Unfortunately, as in 1919, our present-day solutions must be the product of some facts, some exaggeration, some misinformation, and some personal prejudice. And yet, the important fact remains that the nature of our response to these problems and fears will determine in large measure whether we will forestall or, like the public of 1919, succumb to a much greater, more intense, and more disastrous Red Scare that can come. . . .

Note on Sources

No ATTEMPT is made here to exhaust the available literature relating to the Red Scare or to describe all the various materials used or consulted in the preparation of this book. Rather, this note is appended merely to indicate those sources which proved particularly valuable. For specific references concerning all the materials used the footnotes should be utilized. They were designed to supply such detailed information and make unnecessary an elaborate bibliography.

Manuscript Sources

While a number of manuscript collections were investigated and proved helpful in a limited way, there were several collections that were particularly valuable to this study.

The first was the Burleson Collection (Library of Congress), including both the Papers of Albert S. Burleson and his sundry scrapbook materials. Of the 31 bound volumes and 7 boxes of subsidiary material which comprise the collection, volumes 22–25 (covering the period October 1918 to May 1920) and boxes 4 and 6 were immensely instructive in clarifying Burleson's role in the Scare as well as shedding some light on the position of other major figures.

Also of importance were the Papers of A. Mitchell Palmer, which are to be found in box 47 of the Woodrow Wilson Collection (Library of Congress). This box contains letters and other communications addressed to A. Mitchell Palmer by Woodrow Wilson during the years 1910–23. It also contains a few letters written by the attorney general to the President. These were especially valuable in re-creating the relationship between Wilson and Palmer. I only wished that there were more such letters available since this collection is really quite small and spotty and leaves much to be desired on the period from November 1919 to January 1920, when Palmer was most active in his antiradical crusade.

Of much greater importance to this study were the Robert Lansing Papers (Library of Congress), including Lansing's Desk Diaries and his Private Memoranda. There are two boxes containing 12 volumes of the secretary of state's Private Memoranda covering the years 1915–22 and one box containing 5 volumes of desk diaries dating from 1916 to 1920. Both of these sources are rich in information concerning the Red Scare since they not only reflect Lansing's own feelings about the phenomenon but contain many references to the feelings of other prominent officials as well. In ascertaining the position of Cabinet members, the Lansing material was absolutely indispensable.

Other manuscript collections of more than routine interest were the Papers of Senator William E. Borah (Library of Congress), covering the years 1917–21, and boxes 1–10 of tray 23 of the Papers of George W. Norris (Library of Congress). Both of these collections were mainly significant in indicating the personal antipathy of these two famous senators to Red Scare hysteria and especially to Palmerism. The Norris papers, in particular, were useful in reconstructing the mood and behind-the-scene activity during the Senate's investigation of the Justice Department in the spring of 1921.

Published Sources

FEDERAL AND STATE PUBLICATIONS

In large measure, this present study rests on the voluminous federal publications relating to the Red Scare or special phases of it. Of value were the annual reports of the attorney general, the secretary of labor, and the commissioner general of immigration for the years 1918, 1919, and 1920. Also of importance were the many Senate and House reports of the results of investigations and hearings relative to the Red Scare. But of transcendant significance were the transcripts of the many investigations and hearings themselves. Each of these proved to be of inestimable value whether the topic at issue happened to be Bolshevik propaganda, Communist and anarchist deportations, the activities of the Ku Klux Klan, the right of Victor Berger to his seat, the administration of Louis Post, or the illegal practices of the Justice Department. For specific citations the footnotes should be consulted.

In general, state publications proved far less significant except for the published report of the New York Lusk Committee, entitled *Revolutionary Radicalism: Its History, Purpose and Tactics*, 4 vols. (J. B. Lyon Company, Albany, 1920). Without question, these four volumes represent the most complete and detailed published repository of radical literature and information available. Indeed, no one conducting research in the field of modern American radicalism can afford to ignore the Lusk reports. At the same time, caution must be exercised in their use since the conclusions reached by the Lusk Committee and published in conjunction with this compilation of radical information are almost completely invalid.

Certain other state publications were useful where they related to a specific Red Scare phase or event. Reference to the various published consolidated laws and annotated codes of states was necessary in evaluating state syndicalist, Red flag, and sedition legislation. The *Massachusetts Reports*, CCXXXV (Little, Brown and Company, Boston, 1921) contains vital information regarding the May Day riots in Boston, and the *Washington Reports*, CXV (Bancroft-Whitney Company, Seattle, 1922) proved extremely useful in reconstructing the Centralia Massacre.

MEMOIRS, WRITINGS, AND AUTOBIOGRAPHIES

At no stage in the course of this study would I have been able to proceed without the memoirs, writings, and autobiographies of the major participants involved. For example, of importance in assessing the roles and attitudes of the various members of Wilson's official family were Anne W. Lane and Louise H. Wall, eds., *The Letters of Franklin K. Lane, Personal and Political* (Houghton Mifflin Company, Boston, 1922); Josephus Daniels, *The Wilson Era; Years of War and After, 1917–1923* (University of North Carolina Press, Chapel Hill, 1946); David F. Houston, *Eight Years with Wilson's Cabinet, 1913 to 1920*, 2 vols. (Doubleday, Page and Company, New York, 1926); and Frederic C. Howe, *The Confessions of a Reformer* (Charles Scribner's Sons, New York, 1926). President Wilson's attitude was largely pieced together from speeches and other writings recorded in such standard works as Ray S. Baker, *Woodrow Wilson; Life and Letters*, 8 vols. (Doubleday, Page and Company, New York, 1927–39); Ray S. Baker and William E. Dodd, eds., *War and Peace* (in *The Public Papers of Woodrow Wilson*, VI–VII, Harper and Brothers, New York, 1925–27); Donald Day, ed., *Woodrow Wilson's Own Story* (Little,

Brown and Company, Boston, 1952); and Albert Shaw, ed., *The Messages and Papers of Woodrow Wilson*, 2 vols. (George H. Doran Company, New York, 1924). Also important not only in determining Wilson's role in the Red Scare but also in establishing their own positions were Joseph P. Tumulty, *Woodrow Wilson as I Know Him* (Doubleday, Page and Company, New York, 1921) and Edith B. Wilson, *My Memoir* (Bobbs-Merrill Company, New York, 1938).

Calvin Coolidge's *The Autobiography of Calvin Coolidge* (Cosmopolitan Book Corporation, New York, 1929) provided interesting material on the Boston police strike and his connection with it. Likewise, Samuel Gompers's *Seventy Years of Life and Labor; An Autobiography*, 2 vols. (E. P. Dutton and Company, New York, 1925) was indispensable in determining both his own and the AFL's position during the Red Scare period. Other memoirs or collected writings which shed some, although definitely limited, light on various personages or aspects of the Red Scare era include Evan J. David, comp., *Leonard Wood on National Issues* (Doubleday, Page and Company, New York, 1920), on Wood's views concerning immigrants, organized labor, strikes, and bolshevism; Chauncey M. Depew, *My Memoirs of Eighty Years* (Charles Scribner's Sons, New York, 1922), excellent for its sometimes witty and biting comments on contemporary figures; Helen O. Mahin, ed., *The Editor and His People: Editorials by William Allen White* (Macmillan Company, New York, 1924) and William Allen White, *The Autobiography of William Allen White* (Macmillan Company, New York, 1946), valuable mainly for White's personal attitude toward bolshevism, although in a limited way also indicating midwestern opinion; and Oswald G. Villard, *Fighting Years; Memoirs of a Liberal Editor* (Harcourt, Brace and Company, New York, 1939), extremely good on liberal opinion during the Red Scare and public intolerance toward such opinion.

The memoirs and writings of famous radicals operating during the Scare era I used liberally. William Z. Foster has published several semi-autobiographical books which pertain both to the rise of communism in the United States and to his connection with that movement. In particular, his *Pages from a Worker's Life* (International Publishers, New York, 1939) and his *From Bryan to Stalin* (International Publishers, New York, 1937), although both are misleading as to emphasis, contain valuable information on Foster himself. Likewise, William D. Haywood's *Bill Haywood's*

Book; The Autobiography of William D. Haywood (International Publishers, New York, 1929) provides much color concerning this spectacular labor leader and presents his own personal account of the IWW and of his deflection to the Communists. One should keep in mind that the latter part of this book was written, probably by a Russian Communist ghost writer, while Haywood lay dying in the Kremlin hospital. Benjamin Gitlow and Ralph Chaplin, both famous Red Scare radicals, have recently published books which fill in important gaps in the rise of American Communism. Chaplin's *Wobbly; The Rough-and-Tumble Story of an American Radical* (University of Chicago Press, Chicago, 1948) is a fascinating story of his connection with the IWW, and Gitlow's *I Confess; The Truth about American Communism* (E. P. Dutton and Company, New York, 1940) is a well-written autobiographical exposé of the trials, tribulations, and successes of the American Communist party.

Other radical writings, each important for an understanding of both the person and the period include Victor L. Berger, *Voice and Pen of Victor L. Berger; Congressional Speeches and Editorials* (The Milwaukee Leader, Milwaukee, 1929); Charles E. Ruthenberg, *Speeches and Writings of Charles E. Ruthenberg* (in *Voices of Revolt*, X, International Publishers, New York, 1928); and Stephen M. Reynolds, ed., *Debs: His Life, Writings and Speeches* (The Appeal to Reason, Girard, Kansas, 1908).

PAMPHLETS, PROCEEDINGS OF CONVENTIONS, AND SPECIAL REPORTS

Among the printed sources necessary to this study were a variety of pamphlets, proceedings of conventions, and special reports. The pamphlet material was truly voluminous. Available were the many antiradical and super-patriotic pamphlets of such organizations as the American Defense Society, the National Security League, the National Association of Manufacturers, and the Ku Klux Klan. For specific references the footnotes should be consulted. Fortunately for the researcher, many of the radical pamphlets of the period have been gathered together into bound volumes by the Library of Congress. Of particular importance among these were the *Collected Pamphlets Issued by or Relating to the Communist International*, *IWW Leaflets*, and *Pamphlets on Socialism, Communism and Bolshevism*.

Of the many reports surveyed, the annual reports of the Na-

tional Civil Liberties Bureau and the American Civil Lil
Union for the years 1918 to 1923 were helpful in untangling
many instances of public intolerance and mob violence. Seve...ा
special reports proved especially valuable on the steel strike situation. The best over-all account of the steel struggle is the report of
the Commission of Inquiry of the Interchurch World Movement
entitled *Report on the Steel Strike of 1919* (Harcourt, Brace and
Howe, New York, 1920). Likewise, the Interchurch World Movement's *Public Opinion and the Steel Strike* (Harcourt, Brace and
Company, New York, 1921) is particularly good in pinpointing
public attitudes during that conflict. For a factual exposé of the
malpractices of the steel trust, *The Twelve Hour Day in the
Steel Industry* (Research Department of the Federal Council of
Churches of Christ in America, New York, 1923) is certainly one
of the best. One of the most important and interesting accounts of
the Seattle strike incident, although written from a biased point of
view, is the *History of the General Strike* (Seattle Union-Record
Publishing Company, 1919), representing the "official" history of
the event by the History Committee of the Seattle General Strike
Committee. For a description of the miners' position on the coal
strike, *The Case of the Bituminous Coal Mine Workers* (United
Mine Workers of America, Indianapolis, 1920) is most useful if for
no other reason than that it represents the official attitude of the
United Mine Workers Union. Without a doubt, the ablest attack
made on the Justice Department for its infringement on civil liberties during the Scare period appears in a special report of the
National Popular Government League entitled *Report upon the
Illegal Practices of the United States Department of Justice by
Twelve Lawyers* (National Popular Government League, Washington, D.C., 1920).

In determining the official position of certain pressure groups
during the Scare era, I consulted the proceedings of their conventions wherever possible. Of particular value in this respect were
the *Report of the Proceedings of the Thirty-Ninth Annual Convention of the American Federation of Labor* (Law Reporter Printing
Company, Washington, D.C., 1919); *Report of the Proceedings of
the Fortieth Annual Convention of the American Federation of
Labor* (Law Reporter Printing Company, Washington, D.C.,
1920); *Caucus of the American Legion, Proceedings and Committees at St. Louis, Missouri, 1919* (Evening Post Job Printing
Office, New York, 1919); and United Mine Workers of America,

Proceedings of the Twenty-Seventh Annual Convention (Book-walter-Ball Printing Company, Indianapolis, 1919).

NEWSPAPERS AND PERIODICALS

It is immediately obvious to the reader that much of this study rests on information and attitudes expressed by newspapers and periodicals during the Scare period. Since much of the Scare was in reality a mental condition, these sources were invaluable to an adequate appraisal of public opinion.

I made a serious attempt to cover all the major periodicals of the day and to take samplings from all ranges of opinion. For trade union opinion the American Federationist (Washington, D.C.), Railway Carmen's Journal (Kansas City), and United Mine Workers' Journal (Indianapolis) were used. Super-patriotic thinking was found in abundance in the American Legion Weekly (Washington, D.C.), National Civic Federation Review (New York), and Open Shop Review (Chicago). Liberal attitudes were most clearly stated in the Dial (New York), Nation (New York), New Republic (New York), Public (New York), and Survey (New York). Church opinion, ranging from conservative to liberal, was found in such religious periodicals as the Catholic World (New York), Christian Century (Chicago), Christian Observer (Louisville), Christian Register (Boston), Congregationalist and Advance (Boston), United Presbyterian (Pittsburgh), and Watchmen-Examiner (New York). The most important radical periodicals used were the Communist International (Petrograd, Russia), Liberator (New York), and Socialist Review (New York). General periodicals surveyed include Atlantic Monthly (Boston), Century (New York), Current Opinion (New York), Everybody's Magazine (New York), Independent (New York), Living Age (Boston), Outlook (New York), Saturday Evening Post (Philadelphia), Scribner's Magazine (New York), and World's Work (New York).

Of course, special mention must be made of the Literary Digest (New York). As a repository of information concerning public attitudes on various national events, it is unsurpassed. No coverage of the Red Scare period would be possible without liberal use of this magazine.

With respect to newspapers, the attempt was again made to cover as much ground as possible from the extreme left to the extreme right. Radical newspapers which proved particularly useful were the Chicago Communist (official organ of the Communist party, Chicago), *New Majority* (official organ of the Labor Party of Illinois, Chicago), *New Solidarity* (official organ of the IWW, Chicago), New York *Call* (official organ of the Socialist party, New York), *Revolutionary Age* (official organ of the Socialist Left Wing, Boston), *Socialist News* (Cleveland), and *Voice of Labor* (official organ of the Communist Labor party, New York). General newspapers, ranging in opinion and editorial policy from conservative to liberal, include the *Wall Street Journal* (New York), New York *Sun*, Chicago *Tribune*, Baltimore *Sun*, Los Angeles *Times*, New York *Evening Post*, New York *Times*, Atlanta *Constitution*, New York *Tribune*, *Christian Science Monitor* (Boston), Boston *Evening Transcript*, Cincinnati *Enquirer*, Cleveland *Plain Dealer*, Columbus (Ohio) *Citizen*, Seattle *Times*, Seattle *Post-Intelligencer*, Washington *Evening Star*, Washington *Post*, San Francisco *Examiner*, Pittsburgh *Post*, *Ohio State Journal* (Columbus, Ohio), Philadelphia *Inquirer*, New York *World*, Portland *Oregonian*, Detroit *News*, Kansas City *Star*, New Orleans *Times-Picayune*, Milwaukee *Sentinel*, *Rocky Mountain News* (Denver), and St. Louis *Post-Dispatch*. I selected these papers not only because of their range of opinion but also because they represented every geographic area of the country.

Secondary Sources

BIOGRAPHIES

Biographies were employed where possible to supplement existing manuscript and published source material concerning the major figures in the Red Scare story. With great disappointment, however, I found that for some of the key actors in the Scare drama there are no biographies, while for others there are only out-of-date or largely worthless biographical sketches. For example, there is no biography of A. Mitchell Palmer, the central figure of the whole Red Scare phenomenon.

The best volume on Warren Harding and hence of some value to this study is Samuel H. Adams, *Incredible Era; The Life and Times of Warren Gamaliel Harding* (Houghton Mifflin Company, Boston, 1939). Much important background material was gained from Claude G. Bowers, *Beveridge and the Progressive Era* (Houghton Mifflin Company, Boston, 1932). John M. Blum's recently published *Joe Tumulty and the Wilson Era* (Houghton Mifflin Company, Boston, 1951) is the result of a very careful examination of the Tumulty papers and therefore was of considerable value in assessing Tumulty's role in the Scare incident. The two biographies of Eugene Debs which were useful are McAllister Coleman, *Eugene V. Debs, A Man Unafraid* (Greenberg, New York, 1930) and the more recent Ray Ginger, *The Bending Cross: A Biography of Eugene Victor Debs* (Rutgers University Press, Rutgers, New Jersey, 1949). Likewise, there are two biographies of Calvin Coolidge which deserve mention: Claude M. Fuess, *Calvin Coolidge, The Man from Vermont* (Little, Brown and Company, Boston, 1940) and William A. White, *A Puritan in Babylon, The Story of Calvin Coolidge* (Macmillan Company, New York, 1938). Of the two, the former is by far the best.

While not as impartial as one might like, Granville Hicks's *John Reed; The Making of a Revolutionary* (Macmillan Company, New York, 1936) is important because it blazes a biographical trail among the lesser known, but in some respects more significant, radicals in modern American history. Rowland H. Harvey's *Samuel Gompers, Champion of the Toiling Masses* (Stanford University Press, Stanford University, California, 1935) and Louis S. Reed's *The Labor Philosophy of Samuel Gompers* (in *Studies in History, Economics and Public Law*, CCCXXVII, Columbia University Press, New York, 1930) are little more than routine, yet they do throw some light on the 1919–20 activities of the AFL's chief. Also useful in a limited way were Bruce Minton and John Stuart, *Men Who Lead Labor* (Modern Age Books, Inc., New York, 1937); C. L. Sulzberger, *Sit Down with John L. Lewis* (Random House, New York, 1937); and James A. Wechsler, *Labor Baron, A Portrait of John L. Lewis* (William Morrow and Company, New York, 1944). Important for an understanding of both Judge Gary's personality and management's side of the steel strike was Ida M. Tarbell, *The Life of Elbert H. Gary; The Story of Steel* (D. Appleton and Company, New York, 1925).

SPECIAL MONOGRAPHS AND HISTORIES

If there was a paucity of good biographical material, there was no such lack with respect to monographs or general histories. Only a limited number can possibly be mentioned here.

For an analysis of organized labor's position and activities, I found the standard works are still the best: Selig Perlman and Philip Taft, eds., *Labor Movements* (in *History of Labour in the United States 1896–1932*, IV, edited by John R. Commons, Macmillan Company, New York, 1935); Lewis L. Lorwin, *The Ameri-*

can *Federation of Labor: History, Policies, and Prospects* (The Brookings Institution, Washington, D.C., 1933); Herbert Harris, *American Labor* (Yale University Press, New Haven, 1938); and Samuel Yellen, *American Labor Struggles* (Harcourt, Brace and Company, New York, 1936). Also of value were Foster R. Dulles's more recent *Labor in America, A History* (T. Y. Crowell Company, New York, 1949), which is a more popular and readable account than those mentioned heretofore; John R. Commons, ed., *Trade Unionism and Labor Problems* (Ginn and Company, Boston, 1921), which more specifically concentrates attention on certain of the labor problems confronted in this study; and Jerome L. Toner, *The Closed Shop in the American Labor Movement* (Catholic University Press, Washington, D.C., 1941), the best account of the closed-shop versus the open-shop issue in this period of labor history.

Monographs on foreign policy matters which proved particularly useful were Thomas A. Bailey's *Woodrow Wilson and the Great Betrayal* (Macmillan Company, New York, 1945) for an excellent coverage of the League question and its relationship to the period of which the Red Scare was a part; Foster R. Dulles's little book *Road to Teheran; The Story of Russia and America 1781–1943* (Princeton University Press, Princeton, New Jersey, 1945), not only because of the excellent summary of the Red Scare which it contains but also because it ably connects the Scare with Soviet-American relations from 1919 to 1933; William S. Graves, *America's Siberian Adventure, 1918–1920* (Jonathan Cape and Harrison Smith, New York, 1931), a straightforward account of American intervention in Siberia by the commander of the American forces; Sophia R. Pelzel, *American Intervention in Siberia 1918–1920* (University of Pennsylvania, Philadelphia, 1946), which along with Graves's book ranks as the best on this subject; and Leonid I. Strakhovsky, *The Origins of American Intervention in North Russia* (Princeton University Press, Princeton, New Jersey, 1937), which does for American intervention in North Russia what Graves and Pelzel do for Siberia.

There are a number of secondary works on the American radical movement or certain phases of it which deserve special mention. Perhaps the most definitive book on radical groups during the time period indicated by its title is Nathan Fine, *Labor and Farmer Parties in the United States 1828–1928* (Rand School of Social Science, New York, 1928). Best in the matter of analyzing radical literature and tracing it to its source is Robert E. Park, *The Immigrant Press and Its Control* (Harper and Brothers, New York, 1922). Of primary importance in determining the effect of the Bolshevik Revolution on the domestic radical movement is Paul H. Anderson, *The Attitude of the American Leftist Leaders toward the Russian Revolution 1917–1923* (University of Notre Dame Press, Notre Dame, Indiana, 1942). The two authoritative works on the IWW are Paul F. Brissenden, *The IWW: A Study of American Syndicalism* (in *Studies in History, Economics and Public Law*, LXXXIII, Columbia University Press, New York, 1919), and John S. Gambs, *The Decline of the IWW* (in *Studies in History, Economics and Public Law*, CCCLXI, Columbia University Press, New York, 1932).

William Z. Foster's various monographic writings were of no less importance to this study than his autobiographical ones. His *History of the Communist Party of the United States* (International Publishers, New York, 1952) proved to be an amazingly accurate account although his interpretations and his general approach to his subject are naturally communistically inclined. His *The Great Steel Strike and Its Lessons* (B. W. Huebsch, Inc., New York, 1920) describes that struggle from his (and he claims, the worker's) point of view; even so, it contains much valuable general information on that incident. Of less importance is his *Toward Soviet America* (Coward-McCann, Inc., New York, 1932), which is little more than a potboiler arguing the merits of communism for the United States. Along with Foster's works, the writings of Benjamin Gitlow proved valuable if used judiciously. In particular, his *The Whole of Their Lives: Communism in America* (Charles Scribner's Sons, New York, 1948) is an able account of the machinations of American Communists and the rise of that movement in the United States. One wonders, however, if Gitlow, being an ex-Communist when he wrote it, did not somewhat exaggerate the importance of the movement in relation to the total American scene.

Without a doubt, the most useful and uncluttered account of American communism is James Oneal and G. A. Werner, *American Communism*, rev. ed. (E. P. Dutton and Company, New York, 1947).

The best discussion of socialism in the period under study is contained in three books written by one of the more conservative members of the movement, Morris Hillquit: *History of Socialism in the United States* (Funk and Wagnalls Company, New York,

1910), *Present-Day Socialism* (Rand School of Social Science, New York, 1920), and *Socialism on Trial* (B. W. Huebsch, Inc., New York, 1920). The most useful work on radical unions and their activities is David J. Saposs, *Left Wing Unionism; A Study of Radical Policies and Tactics* (International Publishers, New York, 1936), although I wished for more information bearing directly on the period under survey. While extremely biased, Ralph Chaplin's *The Centralia Conspiracy,* 3rd rev. ed. (General Defense Committee, Chicago, 1924) remains one of the most exciting accounts of the Centralia Massacre.

I found a number of significant secondary sources which dealt with Palmer's 1919–20 Red Scare excesses. The more important ones follow. An extremely able narration of the Palmer raids is Robert W. Dunn, ed., *The Palmer Raids* (International Publishers, New York, 1948). Of even greater significance is Constantine M. Panunzio's *The Deportation Cases of 1919–1920* (Federal Council of Churches of Christ in America, New York, 1921). A Methodist minister, Panunzio has written here the most accurate and definitive account of the Palmer raids and the deportations growing out of them. Less detailed, but in some ways more valuable since he was one of the persons most directly involved, is Louis F. Post's *The Deportations Delirium of Nineteen-Twenty* (Charles H. Kerr and Company, Chicago, 1923). For the most recent discussion of the illegal activities of the Justice Department during the Red Scare era I used Max Lowenthal, *The Federal Bureau of Investigation* (William Sloane Associates, Inc., New York, 1950).

On matters relating to free speech I utilized the standard works, particularly Zechariah Chafee, Jr.'s *Freedom of Speech* (Harcourt, Brace and Howe, New York, 1920), which was written just at the time of the Red Scare, and his *Free Speech in the United States* (Harvard University Press, Cambridge, Massachusetts, 1941), which was written much later and is broader in scope. The most definitive and useful study of state syndicalist legislation and its effect on free speech and free press during the years 1919–35 is Elbridge F. Dowell, *A History of Criminal Syndicalist Legislation in the United States* (in *Johns Hopkins University Studies in Historical and Political Science,* series LVII, No. 1, Johns Hopkins Press, Baltimore, Maryland, 1939). The relationship of the Supreme Court to civil liberties and especially to free speech is interestingly handled in Osmond K. Fraenkel's *The Supreme Court and Civil Liberties* (American Civil Liberties Union, New York, 1937).

However, for a more level-headed and judicious account I consulted Carl B. Swisher's general text, *American Constitutional Development* (Houghton Mifflin Company, Boston, 1943). Although sometimes biased, the most exciting presentation of famous modern trials involving free speech or civil liberties appears in Arthur G. Hays, *Trial by Prejudice* (Covici Friede Publishers, New York, 1933). The two sources I used most on the trial of Sacco and Vanzetti were Felix Frankfurter, *The Case of Sacco and Vanzetti* (Little, Brown and Company, Boston, 1927), and George L. Joughin and Edmund M. Morgan, *The Legacy of Sacco and Vanzetti* (Harcourt, Brace and Company, New York, 1948).

Unfortunately, there are only a relatively few works existing in the important field of public opinion. Those that I found of particular value follow: Meno Lovenstein, *American Opinion of Soviet Russia* (American Council on Public Affairs, Washington, D.C., 1941), extremely good on the period 1917–33; James R. Mock and Cedric Larson, *Words That Won the War; The Story of the Committee on Public Information, 1917–1919* (Princeton University Press, Princeton, New Jersey, 1939), useful in tracing the roots of both wartime and postwar hysteria; George Creel, *How We Advertized America* (Harper and Brothers, New York, 1920), an account by the man who was most responsible for establishing the pattern of public opinion prior to 1919; and Bessie L. Pierce, *Public Opinion and the Teaching of History in the United States* (Alfred A. Knopf, New York, 1926), most enlightening on the subject of textbook purging during the years 1919–25.

Much to my surprise I discovered that good secondary source material is almost totally lacking on the Ku Klux Klan and its operation during the Red Scare period. Emerson H. Loucks, *The Ku Klux Klan in Pennsylvania; A Study in Nativism* (Telegraph Press, New York, 1936) is excellent for the area it covers, but it is too restricted in scope to be of great value here. John M. Mecklin, *The Ku Klux Klan: A Study of the American Mind* (Harcourt, Brace and Company, New York, 1924) is now somewhat out of date and needs to be rewritten in the light of recent historical research. Stanley Frost's *The Challenge of the Klan* (Bobbs-Merrill Company, Indianapolis, 1924) is too much like a propaganda treatise to command scholarly attention.

A brief note must be injected here on certain works dealing with a variety of subjects which the reader will find cited in the footnotes but which were used only with considerable caution. These books proved valuable to this study only because of the extreme bias which they represented or because of certain quotations or incidental material which could not be found elsewhere. Prospective researchers in the field of modern American radicalism must be especially careful of these sources of information. Louis Adamic's *Dynamite: The Story of Class Violence in America* (Viking Press, New York, 1931) is a colorful, but overdrawn, picture of American labor injustices; likewise, Stanley Frost's *Labor and Revolt* (E. P. Dutton and Company, New York, 1920) is too highly seasoned for reliable use. Blair Coan's *The Red Web* (Northwest Publishing Company, Chicago, 1925) is a very much exaggerated account of the Communist menace in the United States; Elizabeth Dilling's *The Red Network* (Published by the author, Chicago, 1934) is even worse than Coan; Ole Hanson, *Americanism versus Bolshevism* (Doubleday, Page and Company, New York, 1920) also represents a hopelessly biased account of the activities of domestic radicals by the emotionally upset mayor of Seattle; Norman Hapgood, ed., *Professional Patriots* (Albert and Charles Boni, New York, 1927) contains much valuable information on the patriotic defense against bolshevism, but it is always couched in militantly biased terms; George Seldes's *Witch Hunt; The Technique and Profits of Red-Baiting* (Modern Age Books, New York, 1940) is even more sensationally slanted than that of Hapgood. Other works which I subjected to more than routine scrutiny were William J. Ghent, *The Reds Bring Reaction* (Princeton University Press, Princeton, New Jersey, 1923); William H. Irwin, *How Red Is America* (J. H. Sears and Company, New York, 1927); and Richard M. Whitney, *Reds in America* (Beckwith Press, New York, 1924).

In closing, some mention should be made of the debt I owe to the many fine bibliographical aids and indexes which facilitated the gathering of material for this study. And more than passing attention must be given to those many general histories which helped place the Red Scare in its proper context and led to a better understanding of the entire environment. Of particular value in this regard were Frederick L. Allen's *Only Yesterday; An Informal History of the Nineteen-Twenties* (Harper and Brothers, New York, 1931), still, in my estimation, the best and most readable general account of life in the 1920s; George Soule, *Prosperity Decade; From War to Depression 1917–1929* (Rinehart and Company, Inc., New York, 1947), for the best general description of postwar economic problems and development; Merle E. Curti, *The Growth of American Thought* (Harper and Brothers, New York, 1943), for pertinent and useful insights into the public mind of the period; and finally, Mark Sullivan's *Our Times; The United States, 1900–1925*, VI (Charles Scribner's Sons, New York, 1935), for an excellent, almost day-to-day account of a fascinating era.

Footnotes

Chapter 1

[1] James R. Mock and Evangeline Thurber, *Report on Demobilization* (Norman, Oklahoma, 1944), 202–7; Frederick L. Paxson, "The Great Demobilization," *American Historical Review*, XLIV (January 1939), 243–47.

[2] George Soule, *Prosperity Decade; From War to Depression 1917–1929* (New York, 1947), 83–84.

[3] *Ibid.*, 82–83.

[4] *Bulletin of the United States Bureau of Labor Statistics*, CCCLVII (May 1924), 466.

[5] Ray S. Baker, *Woodrow Wilson; Life and Letters*, 8 vols. (New York, 1927–39), VI, 506, footnote 2.

[6] Soule, *Prosperity Decade*, 188.

[7] Merle Curti, *The Growth of American Thought* (New York, 1943), 686; Frederick L. Allen, *Only Yesterday; An Informal History of the Nineteen-Twenties* (New York, 1931), 45.

[8] See Thomas A. Bailey, *Woodrow Wilson and the Great Betrayal* (New York, 1945), 90–122, 123–34. The most vivid description of Wilson's illness is found in Edith B. Wilson, *My Memoir* (New York, 1938).

[9] George Creel, *How We Advertized America* (New York, 1920), 168; *Cong. Record*, 65 Cong., 3 Sess., 103; *House Reports* A, No. 1173 (Washington, D.C., 1919), 16.

[10] *Complete Report of the Chairman of the Committee on Public Information, 1917, 1918, 1919* (Washington, D.C., 1920), 2–5.

[11] Frank Cobb, "The Press and Public Opinion," *New Republic*, XXI (December 31, 1919), 144.

[12] National Civil Liberties Bureau, *Wartime Persecutions and Mob Violence* (New York, 1919), 5–11; *Cong. Record*, 66 Cong., 2 Sess., 1055, 8113.

[13] *Statutes at Large*, XL, 219.

[14] *Ibid.*, 553.

[15] *Ibid.*, 1012.

[16] A. C. Gardiner, *Portraits and Portents* (New York, 1926), 13.

Chapter 2

[1] Morris Hillquit, *History of Socialism in the United States* (New York, 1910); Nathan Fine, *Labor and Farmer Parties in the United States 1828–1928*

297

(New York, 1928), 184–215; McAllister Coleman, *Eugene V. Debs* (New York, 1930), 162–214; Paul Brissenden, *The IWW: A Study of American Syndicalism* (New York, 1919), 46–47; James Oneal and G. A. Werner, *American Communism*, rev. ed. (New York, 1947), 33–34.

² Lusk Committee, *Revolutionary Radicalism: Its History, Purpose and Tactics*, 4 vols. (Albany, New York, 1920), I, 613, 617, hereafter cited as *Lusk Reports*; Morris Hillquit, *Socialism on Trial* (New York, 1920), 15; New York *Call*, August 27, 1917, p. 1; *Speeches and Writings of Charles E. Ruthenberg*, in *Voices of Revolt* (New York, 1928), X, 41.

³ *Cong. Record*, 66 Cong., 1 Sess., 8220; *Annual Report of the Attorney General, 1918* (Washington, D.C., 1918), 49–50; *The Trial of Scott Nearing and the American Socialist Society* (New York, 1919), 7, 249.

⁴ For examples of Berger's opinions see Victor L. Berger, *Voice and Pen of Victor L. Berger; Congressional Speeches and Editorials* (Milwaukee, 1929). Also see Coleman, *Eugene V. Debs*, 257, and Zechariah Chafee, Jr., *Freedom of Speech* (New York, 1920), 315.

⁵ Coleman, *Eugene V. Debs*, 283.

⁶ *Victor L. Berger*, Hearings before a Special Committee of the House, 2 vols. (Washington, D.C., 1919), I, 53. Hereafter this is cited as *Berger Hearings*.

⁷ *Ibid.*, 52, 144, 681.

⁸ *Ibid.*, II, 56, 61, 697.

⁹ 249 *U.S.* 47–52.

¹⁰ Ralph Chaplin, *Wobbly* (Chicago, 1948), 343.

¹¹ Coleman, *Eugene V. Debs*, 284–87.

¹² Quoted in the *Christian Science Monitor*, March 13, 1919, p. 16; for examples of earlier speeches see Stephen M. Reynolds, ed., *Debs: His Life, Writings and Speeches* (Girard, Kansas, 1908), 401–66.

¹³ 249 *U.S.* 217.

¹⁴ *Christian Science Monitor*, March 13, 1919, p. 16; Atlanta *Constitution*, March 14, 1919, p. 8; Coleman, *Eugene V. Debs*, 298, quoting Cleveland *Plain Dealer*.

¹⁵ *World Almanac, 1920* (New York, 1920), 717–20.

¹⁶ The two outstanding works on the IWW are Brissenden, *IWW*, and John S. Gambs, *The Decline of the IWW* (New York, 1932). For Haywood's own account of his life see William D. Haywood, *Bill Haywood's Book* (New York, 1929).

¹⁷ See Reynolds, ed., *Debs: His Life, Writings and Speeches*, 401–25, 445–66; Brissenden, *IWW*, 279; *Bolshevik Propaganda*, Hearings before a Subcommittee of the Committee on the Judiciary (Washington, D.C., 1919), 15.

¹⁸ Brissenden, *IWW*, 281, 331, 357; Chaplin, *Wobbly*, 135.

¹⁹ *Cong. Record*, 65 Cong., 2 Sess., 4945, 6093, quoting IWW pamphlets and posters; Chaplin, *Wobbly*, 209.

²⁰ Robert E. Park, *The Immigrant Press and Its Control* (New York, 1922), 215, quoting *L'Era Nuova*, an anarchist newspaper.

²¹ *Lusk Reports*, I, 844, 855; *Investigation Activities of the Department of Justice*, Sen. Doc. 153, 66 Cong., 1 Sess. (Washington, D.C., 1919), 137–44, Exhibit No. 7.

²² See Lewis A. Browne, "Bolshevism in America," *Forum*, LXI (June 1919), 711; John B. Mitchell, "Reds in New York Slums," *Forum*, LXI (April 1919),

455; Ole Hanson, *Americanism versus Bolshevism* (New York, 1920) 231–32.

²³ Los Angeles *Times*, December 9, 1917; *Cong. Record*, 66 Cong., 1 Sess., 5949, 6104; Brissenden, *IWW*, 9; Gambs, *Decline of the IWW*, 44.

²⁴ Examples of public intolerance are found in Chaplin, *Wobbly*, 211; Gambs, *Decline of the IWW*, 30; *Cong. Record*, 65 Cong., 2 Sess., 8066; Haywood, *Bill Haywood's Book*, 301, 399.

²⁵ For accounts of the raids see Chaplin, *Wobbly*, 221, and Haywood, *Bill Haywood's Book*, 302. For the trial see *Annual Report of the Attorney General, 1918*, 53. Senator Kenyon's statement appears in *Cong. Record*, 65 Cong., 3 Sess., 2950.

Chapter 3

¹ Meno Lovenstein, *American Opinion of Soviet Russia* (Washington, D.C., 1941), 9–16, 50, gives examples of labor, business, and church opinion on Russian bolshevism. See also Johan W. Prins, "The Siberian Chaos," *Scribner's*, LXIV (November 1918), 629; *Cong. Record*, 65 Cong., 3 Sess., 4022–23.

² Lovenstein, *American Opinion of Soviet Russia*, 33, quoting *Saturday Evening Post*; "Liberty through the Guillotine," *Literary Digest*, LVII (May 11, 1918), 18; *Cong. Record*, 65 Cong., 2 Sess., 8064.

³ "Red Russia as Our Foe," *Literary Digest*, LVIII (September 21, 1918), 10, reprints various cartoons; the specific cartoon is found in the New York *World*, September 3, 1918, p. 10.

⁴ "Why the Russian Revolution Failed," *Literary Digest*, LVIII (August 3, 1918), 27.

⁵ Morris Hillquit, *Present-Day Socialism* (New York, 1920), 84; Coleman, *Eugene V. Debs*, 281.

⁶ *Cong. Record*, 65 Cong., 2 Sess., 9185; *Lusk Reports*, II, 1238.

⁷ For a discussion of leftist opinions on bolshevism see Paul H. Anderson, *The Attitude of the American Leftist Leaders toward the Russian Revolution* (Notre Dame, Indiana, 1942). For a discussion and list of the various Socialist federations see Fine, *Labor and Farmer Parties in the United States*, 324–28.

⁸ *Lusk Reports*, II, 1322.

⁹ Park, *The Immigrant Press and Its Control*, 219, 235–36.

¹⁰ *Cong. Record*, 65 Cong., 2 Sess., 8066.

¹¹ Park, *The Immigrant Press and Its Control*, 217, 230–31, 236, *Bolshevik Propaganda*, 20, 29, quoting radical journals.

¹² Brissenden, *IWW*, 373, quoting the Wobbly song.

¹³ *Foreign Relations of the United States, 1918*, (Washington, D.C., 1919), II, 643, and III, 207, quoting Ambassador Francis and Consul DeWitt Poole.

¹⁴ See Foster R. Dulles, *Road to Teheran* (Princeton, New Jersey, 1945), 131–33. Leonid I. Strakhovsky, *The Origins of American Intervention in North Russia* (Princeton, New Jersey, 1937) offers the most careful analysis of intervention in this area.

¹⁵ Examples of public opinion are found in Lovenstein, *American Opinion of Soviet Russia*, 8, 13, 44; "The Problem of Intervention in Russia," *Literary Digest*, LVII (June 29, 1918), 20–21; "Fiddling While Russia Burns," *ibid.*, LVIII (August 10, 1918), 14. For an account of the intervention in Siberia by one of the participants see William S. Graves, *America's Siberian Adventure 1918–1920* (New York, 1931).

[16] Quoted in *Cong. Record*, 65 Cong., 3 Sess., 344.

[17] Some interesting light is shed on this indecision by sentiments expressed in the *Cong. Record*, 65 Cong., 2 Sess., pt. 11 (consult index), and Anne W. Lane and Louise H. Wall, eds., *The Letters of Franklin K. Lane* (Boston, 1922), 298.

[18] Atlanta *Constitution*, issues February 6–19, 1919; San Francisco *Examiner*, February 6, 1919.

[19] Dulles, *Road to Teheran*, 144.

[20] New York *Times*, January 17, 1919, p. 1.

[21] *Lusk Reports*, I, 418, 467; Michael T. Florinsky, *World Revolution and the USSR* (New York, 1933), 13, 41. The complete Third International Program and Manifesto are found in *Revolutionary Age*, issues May 10, 17, 1919.

[22] New York *Times*, June 14, 1919, p. 12.

[23] *Ibid.*, September 16, 1919, p. 19, quoting Secretary of War Baker.

[24] 250 *U.S.* 623.

[25] *Bolshevik Propaganda*, 564–66, 603, 630; Granville Hicks, *John Reed* (New York, 1936), 295; *Lusk Reports*, I, 205.

[26] Examples of Third International material are found in *Charges of the Illegal Practices of the Department of Justice*, Hearings before a Subcommittee of the Senate Committee on the Judiciary (Washington, D.C., 1921), 613, hereafter cited as *Charges of Illegal Practices*; Communist International *Collected Pamphlets Issued by or Relating to the Communist International* (compiled by the Library of Congress, Washington, D.C.); *Lusk Reports*, I, 657–75; *Communist International* (Petrograd, Russia), Nos. 1–2 (May–June 1919).

[27] *Lusk Reports*, I, 639.

[28] *Ibid.*, 646.

[29] See *Pamphlets on Socialism, Communism and Bolshevism* (compiled by the Library of Congress, Washington, D.C.), VII; *Communist International*, No. 2 (June 1, 1919), 271.

[30] *Revolutionary Age* (Boston), February 1, 1919, p. 4, quoting the *Novy Mir*; *Red Radicalism, as Described by Its Own Leaders*, Exhibits Collected by A. Mitchell Palmer (Washington, D.C., 1920), 9, hereafter cited as *Red Radicalism*.

[31] New York *Call*, June 10, 1919, p. 1.

[32] *Revolutionary Age*, July 5, 1919, p. 1, full text.

[33] Benjamin Gitlow, *I Confess* (New York, 1940), 33–34, 37, 57. The figures used by Gitlow are generally accepted as being the most accurate.

[34] For an interesting contemporary account of the Chicago conventions see Max Eastman, "The Chicago Conventions," *Liberator*, II (October 1919), 7.

[35] Quoted in the New York *Times*, August 31, 1919, p. 5.

[36] *Lusk Reports*, I, 801.

[37] See the *Communist* (Chicago), September 27, 1919, pp. 4–8; *Cong. Record*, 66 Cong., 2 Sess., 2204, reprint of the Manifesto; *Lusk Reports*, I, 755–56.

[38] The membership figures are from Fine, *Labor and Farmer Parties in the United States*, 326. See also Gitlow, *I Confess*, 57, and William Z. Foster, *History of the Communist Party of the United States* (New York, 1952), 169. Foster gives the figures as 104,822 and 26,766.

[39] Coleman, *Eugene V. Debs*, 315–16.

⁴⁰ Gambs, *Decline of the IWW*, 89.

⁴¹ Haywood, *Bill Haywood's Book*, 360.

⁴² Comparative figures are from *Charges of Illegal Practices*, 616; *Red Radicalism*, 13; and Benjamin Gitlow, *The Whole of Their Lives* (New York, 1948), 53.

⁴³ *Annual Report of the Attorney General, 1920* (Washington, D.C., 1920), 179; Park, *The Immigrant Press and Its Control*, 442.

⁴⁴ *Investigation Activities of the Department of Justice*, 11–12. See *Lusk Reports*, II, 1145–50, for examples.

⁴⁵ Peter W. Collins, "Bolshevism in America," *Current Opinion*, LXVIII, 324; John Spargo, "The Psychology of the Parlor Bolshevik," *World's Work*, CXXVII, 127–29.

⁴⁶ *Ibid.*, 131; *Bolshevik Propaganda*, 592.

⁴⁷ Gitlow, *The Whole of Their Lives*, 53.

Chapter 4

¹ "The Truth about Soviet Russia and Bolshevism," *American Federationist*, XXVII, pt. 1 (February 1919), 167.

² See *Cong. Record*, 65 Cong., 3 Sess., 2151. For the best account of IWW activities in the Pacific Northwest see Robert L. Tyler, "Rebels of the Woods," *Oregon Historical Quarterly*, LV, No. 1 (March 1954), 3–44.

³ Hanson, *Americanism versus Bolshevism*, 12, 90–91; Gambs, *Decline of the IWW*, 134. James A. Duncan should not be confused with James Duncan, first vice-president of the AFL.

⁴ History Committee of the General Strike Committee, *History of the General Strike* (Seattle, 1919), 12–13, 18.

⁵ *Ibid.*, 47; Portland *Oregonian*, February 6, 1919, p. 1.

⁶ *History of the General Strike*, 6.

⁷ Seattle *Star*, February 4, 1919, p. 1.

⁸ Seattle *Post-Intelligencer*, February 6, 1919, p. 1.

⁹ *History of the General Strike*, 3, 21, 24–25; Gambs, *Decline of the IWW*, 134; "Meaning of the Western Strikes," *Literary Digest*, LX (March 1, 1919), 15. Robert Tyler claims in his "Rebels of the Woods" (see footnote 2 above), p. 35, that the Wobblies did play a significant role in the strike although for the moment they did not display their usual flair for violence.

¹⁰ "Mayor Ole Hanson Who 'Sat Tight' at Seattle," *Literary Digest*, LX (March 8, 1919), 47–50.

¹¹ Hanson, *Americanism versus Bolshevism*, 24, 59; *Cong. Record*, 65 Cong., 3 Sess., 3637, quoting Hanson.

¹² Hanson, *Americanism versus Bolshevism*, 87.

¹³ Seattle *Times*, February 9, 1919, p. 6; Seattle *Star*, February 10, 1919, p. 1.

¹⁴ "More Lessons Than One in Seattle Strike," *American Federationist*, XXVI, pt. 1 (March 1919), 243.

¹⁵ *Christian Science Monitor*, February 11, 1919, p. 1, quoting Hanson; Seattle *Star*, February 11, 1919, p. 1; the cartoon is found in the Seattle *Post-Intelligencer*, February 11, 1919, p. 1.

¹⁶ Newspaper comment may be seen in Los Angeles *Times*, February 8, 1919, p. 6; *Rocky Mountain News*, February 8, 1919, p. 6; Washington *Post*,

February 10, 1919, p. 6; Cleveland *Plain Dealer*, February 8, 1919, p. 4; Chicago *Tribune*, February 7, 1919, p. 6.

[17] For various statements see "America Safe from Bolshevism," *Literary Digest*, LX (March 29, 1919), 17, and *Cong. Record*, 65 Cong., 3 Sess., 2915, 2943.

[18] For various opinions on Hanson see *Rocky Mountain News*, February 14, 1919, p. 6; Portland *Oregonian*, February 8, 1919, p. 8; Washington *Post*, February 11, 1919, p. 6; "The Fighting Mayor Who Would Banish Fear," *Current Opinion*, LXVI (April 1919), 226.

[19] *Literary Digest*, LX (March 8, 1919), 47, quoting Hanson.

[20] H. A. Simons, "Guilty: The General Strike," *Liberator*, III (August 1920), 12.

Chapter 5

[1] *Bolshevik Propaganda*, 1076, quoting an anarchist poster.

[2] Bomb plots are discussed in the Chicago *Tribune*, March 6, 1919, p. 13; "Current Event and Comment," *United Presbyterian*, LXXVII (April 10, 1919), 7.

[3] New York *Times*, April 29, 1919, p. 1.

[4] For details of the bombing see the Atlanta *Constitution*, April 30, 1919, p. 2; "Dreadful Bombs," *Liberator*, II (June 1919), 7–8.

[5] The New York *Times*, May 1, 1919, p. 3, presents Kaplan's own story; a diagram and description of bombs are found in the Pittsburgh *Post*, May 2, 1919, p. 7, and Salt Lake *Tribune*, May 2, 1919, p. 1.

[6] New York *Times*, May 1, 1919, p. 3; Chicago *Tribune*, May 1, 1919, p. 1. The numbers vary slightly, the total given by the Justice Department being only twenty-nine.

[7] *Attorney General A. Mitchell Palmer on Charges Made against Department of Justice by Louis F. Post and Others*, Hearings before the Committee on Rules, House of Representatives (Washington, D.C., 1920), 157–58, hereafter cited as *Attorney General A. Mitchell Palmer on Charges*.

[8] Sample newspaper comment may be found in the New York *Times*, May 1, 1919, p. 1; Atlanta *Constitution*, May 1, 1919, p. 1; San Francisco *Examiner*, May 1, 1919, p. 1; Chicago *Tribune*, issues May 1–6, 1919.

[9] For sample opinion see "Human Vermin," *American Law Review*, LIII (May 1919), 432; Washington *Post*, May 2, 1919, p. 6; Philadelphia *Inquirer*, May 3, 1919, p. 12; "Current Event and Comment," *United Presbyterian*, LXXVII (May 8, 1919), 7.

[10] New York *Times*, May 1, 1919, p. 3; Salt Lake *Tribune*, May 2, 1919, p. 1. Later Hanson denied having made such statements.

[11] Pittsburgh *Post*, May 3, 1919, p. 6; Seattle *Post-Intelligencer*, May 2, 1919, p. 6.

[12] "More Bombs," *Liberator*, II (July 1919), 6.

[13] New York *Times*, issues May 3–13, 1919.

[14] For details of the Boston rioting see 235 *Massachusetts Reports* 453; also Boston *Evening Transcript*, May 2, 1919, p. 1.

[15] 235 *Massachusetts Reports* 449.

[16] *Revolutionary Age*, May 10, 1919, p. 4.

[17] The New York *Times*, issues of May 2–3, 1919, describes the New York rioting. See also the *Christian Science Monitor*, May 2, 1919, pp. 2–3; "May

Day Rioting," *Nation*, CVIII (May 10, 1919), 726; New York *Call*, May 2, 1919, p. 1.

[18] The Cleveland *Plain Dealer*, May 2, 1919, pp. 1–3, gives a description of the Cleveland rioting.

[19] For radical opinion see the Cleveland *Socialist News*, June 14, 1919, p. 1, and *Revolutionary Age*, May 10, 1919, p. 4.

[20] For conservative opinion see the Cleveland *Plain Dealer*, May 2, 1919, p. 8; *Cong. Record*, 66 Cong., 1 Sess., 182.

[21] Salt Lake *Tribune*, May 3, 1919, p. 6; Washington *Post*, May 3, 1919, p. 6.

[22] Seattle *Post-Intelligencer*, May 3, 1919, p. 6; New Orleans *Times-Picayune*, May 2, 1919, p. 1.

[23] Detroit *News*, May 3, 1919, p. 4.

[24] Salt Lake *Tribune*, June 3, 1919, p. 1; San Francisco *Examiner*, June 3, 1919, p. 1; Atlanta *Constitution*, June 3, 1919, p. 1.

[25] *Charges of Illegal Practices*, 580; "What Is Back of the Bombs?" *Literary Digest*, LXI (June 14, 1919), 9.

[26] Milwaukee *Sentinel*, June 3, 1919, p. 1.

[27] Boston *Evening Transcript*, June 3, 1919, pp. 4–6. For pictures of the devastation see the Washington *Evening Star*, June 3, 1919, p. 1. For the claim there were two men involved instead of one see Blair Coan, *The Red Web* (Chicago, 1925), 48.

[28] *Attorney General A. Mitchell Palmer on Charges*, 165.

[29] *Literary Digest*, LXI (June 14, 1919), 9, quoting Palmer.

[30] *Ibid.*, 11; "More Bombs," *Liberator*, II (July 1919), 7; Robert Dunn, ed., *The Palmer Raids* (New York, 1948), 17.

[31] New York *Times*, June 4, 1919, p. 1.

[32] Examples of congressional opinion and action are found in *ibid.*, pp. 1–2; *Christian Science Monitor*, June 4, 1919, p. 1; A. Mitchell Palmer, "The Case against the 'Reds'," *Forum*, LXIII (February 1920), 179; Detroit *News*, June 12, 1919, p. 1.

[33] New York *Times*, June 14, 1919, p. 14; "The Bomb Conspiracy," *Liberator*, II (August 1919), 30.

Chapter 6

[1] Seattle *Post-Intelligencer*, May 3, 1919, p. 1, quoting Billy Sunday.

[2] Norman Hapgood, ed., *Professional Patriots* (New York, 1927), 154–60; this source should be used with some caution. See also American Defense Society, *What the American Defense Society Is Doing* (New York, n.d.); National Security League, *Before the War, During the War, After the War* (New York, 1918).

[3] See Hapgood, ed., *Professional Patriots*, 29, which quotes appeals.

[4] Much of the vital information on the patriotic societies and their chief supporters is found in *Investigation of the National Security League* (*House Reports*, A, No. 1173, 2 pts.).

[5] "League Wages War on Bolshevism and All Un-American Doctrine," *National Security League Bulletin*, II (May 1919), 5; National Security League, *Annual Report* (New York, 1920); "Flying Squadrons throughout the Country," *National Security League Bulletin*, II (May 1919), 8.

[6] American Defense Society, *Concerning Radical Literature* (in *Pamphlets*

on Socialism, Communism and Bolshevism, VII, Library of Congress, Washington); Hapgood, ed., *Professional Patriots*, 31, 55–56, 68–69; Sidney Howard, "Our Professional Patriots," *New Republic*, XL (September 3, 1924).

[7] For examples of the National Civic Federation's propaganda and Ralph Easley's writings see *National Civic Federation Review*, IV (April 25, 1919), 3ff; *ibid.*, IV (July 30, 1919), 1ff; *ibid.*, IV (August 20, 1919), 9ff.

[8] Hapgood, ed., *Professional Patriots*, 15, 140–45, gives examples.

[9] *Caucus of the American Legion, Proceedings and Committees at St. Louis, Missouri, 1919* (New York, 1919), 155.

[10] "Pershing's Warning to the Legion," *Literary Digest*, LXII (September 27, 1919), 10; the cartoon is from the San Francisco *Examiner*, September 26, 1919, p. 26.

[11] "First Commander of the American Legion," *Literary Digest*, LXIII (December 20, 1919), 58, quoting D'Olier.

[12] *American Legion Weekly*, issues June–July, 1919.

[13] Dixon Wecter, *When Johnny Comes Marching Home* (Boston, 1944), 432; *Charges of Illegal Practices*, 423.

[14] *Ku Klux Klan*, Hearings before the Committee on Rules, House of Representatives, 67 Cong., 1 Sess. (Washington, D.C., 1921), 68–77, 114–26, reprints the *Kloran*.

[15] See *ibid.*, 10–12 and index, for various statements of the Klan press; Emerson H. Loucks, *The Ku Klux Klan in Pennsylvania* (New York, 1936), 136–39; John M. Mecklin, *The Ku Klux Klan: A Study of the American Mind* (New York, 1924), 96–98.

[16] For an interesting, but biased, account see Hapgood, ed., *Professional Patriots*, 132–39.

[17] Sample sentiment is found in the *Open Shop Review*, XVI, issues January–August 1919.

[18] Washington *Post*, February 4, 1919, p. 1, quoting Williams. Opinion on the need for an investigation is seen in the Boston *Evening Transcript*, February 5, 1919, p. 3; *Cong. Record*, 65 Cong., 3 Sess., 2653–54.

[19] New York *Times*, February 6, 1919, p. 10; Cincinnati *Enquirer*, February 5, 1919, p. 1. The Fitzpatrick cartoon is from the St. Louis *Post-Dispatch*, February 6, 1919, p. 24.

[20] *Bolshevik Propaganda.*

[21] *Ibid., passim; Christian Science Monitor*, March 12, 1919, p. 1, quoting Senator Overman.

[22] Sample newspaper opinion is found in various issues of the Washington *Post*, New York *Sun*, New York *Herald*, and New York *Times* during February and March 1919; "Bolshevism's 'Heaven on Earth'," *Literary Digest*, LX (March 22, 1919), 15–18; headlines are quoted from the New York *Times*, March 11, 1919, p. 1, Boston *Evening Transcript*, March 11, 1919, p. 1, and Atlanta *Constitution*, March 11, 1919, p. 1.

[23] "New York State Probe of Bolshevism Asked," *National Civic Federation Review*, IV (March 25, 1919), 12–13.

[24] New York *Times*, issues March 21 and 27, and May 7, 1919.

[25] New York *Call*, June 13, 1919, p. 1; Cleveland *Socialist News*, June 21, 1919, p. 1; New York *Times*, June 13, 1919, p. 3, quoting Martens.

[26] New York *Tribune*, June 12–13, 1919, quoting Lusk and Newton; New York *Times*, June 19–20, 1919, for other remarks.

[27] New York *Tribune*, June 22, 1919, p. 1, quoting Lusk.

[28] For accounts of these raids see the New York *Sun*, June 22, 1919, p. 6, and New York *Times*, June 22, 1919, p. 3.

[29] Quoted in Zechariah Chafee, *Freedom of Speech* (New York, 1920), 308.

[30] New York *Call*, July 30, 1919, p. 8.

[31] "Lusk Committee," *Survey*, XLII (July 19, 1919), 602; "By Stevenson Out of Lusk," *New Republic*, XXVII (June 15, 1919), 64–66.

[32] New York *Tribune*, June 26, 1919, p. 8; New York *Times*, June 28, 1919, p. 3.

[33] New York *Times*, issues July 12, 19, 31, 1919; New York *Call*, July 31, 1919, p. 1.

[34] Actually the Lusk Committee pursued a spectacular course of unearthing conspiracies for almost a year, but wound up in general discredit because it persisted in overplaying the game. Later, in 1921, the results of its activities were published in four volumes, totaling 10,983 pages, which cost the state of New York more than $100,000 to prepare and print. Although the conclusions are erroneous and invalid, these four volumes represent one of the most complete published sources for radical literature, propaganda, manifestoes, documents, etc., that can be obtained.

Chapter 7

[1] John R. Commons, *Trade Unionism and Labor Problems* (Boston, 1921), 563–69.

[2] Lewis Lorwin, *American Federation of Labor: History, Policies, and Prospects* (Washington, D.C., 1933), 191.

[3] See David J. Saposs, *Left Wing Unionism* (New York, 1926), *passim*. This work is particularly good on radical labor unions.

[4] For labor opinion see the *American Federationist*, XXVI, pt. 1 (March 1919), 237, and XXVI, pt. 1 (April 1919), 316–18; see also "Advocates of Disorder," *United Mine Workers' Journal*, XXX (April 1, 1919), 7.

[5] Editorial, *American Federationist*, XXVI, pt. 1 (February 1919), 149; "This Thing Called Bolshevism," *ibid.* (March 1919), 237; Matthew Woll, "American Labor Is True to Democracy," *ibid.* (April 1919), 318–20; "Safety of Trade Unionism," *ibid.* (May 1919), 398–400.

[6] Stanley Frost, *Labor and Revolt* (New York, 1920), 181. This source must be used with caution.

[7] *Report of the Proceedings of the Thirty-Ninth Annual Convention of the American Federation of Labor, 1919* (Washington, D.C., 1919), 324, 333–39. Hereafter cited as *Report of the Proceedings, 1919*.

[8] *Ibid.*, 328, 361, 391, 396.

[9] Newspaper comment from "American Labor and Bolshevism," *Literary Digest*, LXI (June 21, 1919), 9–10; "The Convention of the Dead," *Liberator*, II (August 1919), 12.

[10] New York *Sun*, June 21, 1919, p. 7; New York *World*, June 22, 1919, editorial section, p. 2.

[11] Editorial, *American Federationist*, XXVI, pt. 1 (February 1919), 151; "American Labor and Bolshevism," *Literary Digest*, LXI (June 21, 1919), 11, quoting Gompers.

[12] For complete strike statistics see "Strikes and Lockouts," *Monthly Labor Review*, X (June 1920), 199–218.

[13] *Report of the Proceedings, 1919*, 43–45, table of gains and losses.

[14] "Canada's One Big Union," *Dial*, LXVII (September 20, 1919), 135; "The Winnipeg General Strike," *Independent*, XCVII (June 7, 1919), 344; Arthur E. Darby, "Winnipeg's Revolution," *New Republic*, XIX (July 9, 1919), 310.

[15] "The Causes of the Winnipeg General Strike," *New Statesman* (London), XIII (July 26, 1919), 413.

[16] Reports and opinion are found in the New York *Times*, issues May 22–23, 1919; "One Big Union," *Saturday Evening Post*, CXCII (July 26, 1919), 26; "The 'One Big Failure'," *United Mine Workers' Journal*, XXX (July 15, 1919), 7; editorial, *American Federationist*, XXVI, pt. 2 (October 1919), 961.

[17] "No Room for Destructionists in Our Movement," *American Federationist*, XXVI, pt. 1 (April 1919), 318.

[18] For anti-Mooney opinion see "Against Mooney Strike," *United Mine Workers' Journal*, XXX (June 1, 1919), 6; the example of exaggerated newspaper reporting is from the Chicago *Tribune*, June 8, 1919, p. 1; the headlines appeared in the San Francisco *Examiner*, July 4, 1919, p. 1, and Cincinnati *Enquirer*, July 4, 1919, p. 1.

[19] New York *Times*, July 4, 1919, p. 4; New York *Call*, July 4, 1919, p. 1.

[20] Chicago *Tribune*, July 4, 1919, p. 13; Boston *Evening Transcript*, July 3, 1919, p. 1; Philadelphia *Public Ledger*, July 5, 1919, p. 3; Los Angeles *Times*, July 4, 1919, p. 1; Portland *Oregonian*, July 4, 1919, p. 1.

[21] "News of the Week," *Christian Register*, XCVIII (July 10, 1919), 652.

[22] Glenn R. Plumb, "Plan of Organized Employees for Railroad Organization," *Public*, XXII (March 29, 1919), 427–29.

[23] Boston *Evening Transcript*, February 25, 1919, p. 10; Howard Brubaker, "May I Not," *Liberator*, II (October 1919), 25.

[24] New York *Wall Street Journal*, June 13, 1919, p. 1; for examples of labor support, see the April, May, and June issues of *Railway Carmen's Journal*. See also the editorial in *Railway Carmen's Journal*, XXIV (September 1919), 1315–20.

[25] See *Cong. Record*, 66 Cong., 1 Sess., 3765, 4089, for examples of congressional opinion.

[26] New York *Times*, August 6, 1919, p. 15; *ibid.*, August 9, 1919, p. 4; Salt Lake *Tribune*, August 4, 1919, pp. 1–2; New York *World*, August 8, 1919, p. 1.

[27] Dunn, *The Palmer Raids*, 23, quotes employer magazines; see also the issues of August 4–6, 1919, of the New York *Times*, Boston *Evening Transcript*, Atlanta *Constitution*, and Salt Lake *Tribune*.

[28] "Communist Party's Attitude toward Strikes," *Monthly Labor Review*, X (April 1920), 220, quoting the Manifesto.

Chapter 8

[1] For labor's position see *Report of the Fortieth Annual Convention of the American Federation of Labor* (Washington, D.C., 1920), 362ff. See also Claude M. Fuess, *Calvin Coolidge* (Boston, 1940), 205.

[2] "When the Police Strike," *Literary Digest*, LXII (September 20, 1919), 2–3.

[3] Fuess, *Calvin Coolidge*, 206–7.

⁴ *Ibid.*, 207; Perlman and Taft, eds., *Labor Movements*, 447; Boston *Evening Transcript*, August 2, 1919.

⁵ For discussions concerning Curtis's position see Gregory Mason, "No Bolshevism for Boston," *Outlook*, CXXIII (September 24, 1919), 124–25, and Boston *Evening Transcript*, September 8, 1919, p. 1.

⁶ Boston *Evening Transcript*, September 8, 1919, p. 1.

⁷ *Ibid.*, September 9, 1919, p. 12; Boston *Herald*, September 9, 1919, p. 1.

⁸ Boston *Evening Transcript*, September 9, 1919, p. 1; "Harvard Men in the Boston Police Strike," *School and Society*, X (October 11, 1919), 425–26.

⁹ See Fuess, *Calvin Coolidge*, 209–18, for discussions of incomplete precautions.

¹⁰ Boston *Evening Transcript*, September 10, 1919, p. 1.

¹¹ *Ibid.*, p. 4; Boston *Herald*, September 10, 1919, p. 1; Boston *Globe*, September 10, 1919, p. 1.

¹² Fuess, *Calvin Coolidge*, 217–25; Calvin Coolidge, *Autobiography* (New York, 1929), 130–32; "The Police Strike in Boston," *Current History*, XI (October 1919), 54–56.

¹³ *Ibid.*; see also Boston *Evening Transcript*, issues September 10–11, 1919.

¹⁴ Boston *Evening Transcript*, September 12, 1919; Perlman and Taft, eds., *Labor Movements*, 448.

¹⁵ San Francisco *Examiner*, issues September 10–11, 1919, p. 1; *Rocky Mountain News*, September 11, 1919, p. 1; Salt Lake *Tribune*, September 10, 1919, p. 1.

¹⁶ Such sentiment is found in the September 13, 1919, issue of the Milwaukee *Sentinel*, New Orleans *Times-Picayune*, and St. Louis *Post-Dispatch*. See also the New York *Wall Street Journal*, September 12, 1919, p. 1, and "The Policemen's Right to Strike," *Literary Digest*, LXII (September 27, 1919), 8, quoting the Philadelphia *Public-Ledger*. The cartoon is from the Los Angeles *Times*, September 12, 1919, pt. 2, p. 4.

¹⁷ New York *Times*, September 12, 1919, p. 1, quoting Senator Myers; headline from Los Angeles *Times*, September 12, 1919; Fuess, *Calvin Coolidge*, 223, quoting President Wilson.

¹⁸ Fuess, *Calvin Coolidge*, 223; "The Boston Police Strike," *Survey*, XLII (September 20, 1919), 882.

¹⁹ Such expression of opinion is found in the September 12–14, 1919, issues of the Kansas City *Star*, New York *Times*, New York *Evening World*, Baltimore *Sun*, and Pittsburgh *Post*; Columbus *Ohio State Journal*, September 14, 1919, p. 4.

²⁰ Coolidge, *Autobiography*, 134.

²¹ Gardiner, *Portraits and Portents*, 14.

²² Coolidge, *Autobiography*, 133–34; "Other Phases of Labor Unrest," *Current History*, XI (December 1919), 429.

²³ Newspaper comment is from "When the Police Strike," *Literary Digest*, LXII (September 20, 1919), and "The Policemen's Right to Strike," *ibid.* (September 27, 1919). Liberal and radical journals called Curtis an "autocrat" and claimed Big Business had maximized the strike in order to give labor a "black eye." For such sentiment see "The Police Strike," *New Republic*, XX (September 24, 1919), 217; Arthur Warner, "The End of the Boston Police Strike," *Nation*, CIX (December 20, 1919), 792; W. H. Crook, "The Boston Police Strike," *Socialist Review*, VIII December 1919, 38.

Chapter 9

[1] Perlman and Taft, eds., *Labor Movements*, 462; William Z. Foster, *The Great Steel Strike and Its Lessons* (New York, 1920), 41, 49; Samuel Yellen, *American Labor Struggles* (New York, 1936), 263, 265.

[2] For a complete picture of Foster's life see William Z. Foster, *From Bryan to Stalin* (New York, 1937), and William Z. Foster, *Pages from a Worker's Life* (New York, 1939). For the NAM's statement on Foster see National Association of Manufacturers, *Onward March of the Open Shop*, No. 47 (New York, n.d.), 7.

[3] Soule, *Prosperity Decade*, 192; Interchurch World Movement, *Report on the Steel Strike of 1919* (New York, 1920), 94.

[4] *Senate Reports*, A, No. 289 (Washington, D.C., 1919), 3–5; New York *Times*, August 21, 1919, p. 1.

[5] Cleveland *Plain Dealer*, September 1, 1919, p. 1. The idea of calling an industrial conference to alleviate existing labor unrest was suggested to the President by Tumulty as early as June 4, 1919; see James Kerney, *The Political Education of Woodrow Wilson* (New York, 1926), 446–47, letter from Tumulty to Wilson.

[6] Foster, *Great Steel Strike*, 94–95; New York *Times*, September 11, 1919, p. 1.

[7] Perlman and Taft, eds., *Labor Movements*, 464.

[8] *Senate Reports*, A, No. 289, pp. 5–7.

[9] See the New York *Times*, issues September 18–23, 1919; Washington *Post*, September 21, 1919, p. 4. Writing in 1925, Gompers declared that he knew from the beginning the steel strike would fail because of the radicalism involved. He asserted that Foster wanted to reconstruct the AFL "upon the Soviet revolutionary basis." See Samuel Gompers, *Seventy Years of Life and Labor; An Autobiography*, 2 vols. (New York, 1925), II, 517.

[10] "Is Gary Fighting Unionism?" *Literary Digest*, LXIII (October 18, 1919), 12, quoting the Chicago *Tribune* and the Springfield *Republican*. For liberal opinion see "Mr. Gary Moralizes," *Nation*, CIX (October 11, 1919), 488; "The Depth of Garyism," *New Republic*, XX (October 8, 1919), 280; "The Closed Shop," *Survey*, XLIII (November 8, 1919), 53–56.

[11] Foster, *Great Steel Strike*, 100, 103, 108; the Department of Labor subsequently set the official number at 367,000.

[12] Boston *Evening Transcript*, September 23, 1919, p. 12; Columbus *Ohio State Journal*, September 22, 1919, p. 4; "The Steel Strike," *Literary Digest*, LXIII (October 4, 1919), 12, quoting various newspapers. The cartoon entitled "Coming Out of the Smoke" is from the New York *World*, September 25, 1919, p. 12.

[13] Cleveland *Socialist News*, September 27, 1919, p. 1; Chicago *New Solidarity* and Chicago *Communist* quoted in *Lusk Reports*, II, 1149; *Senate Reports*, A, No. 289, p. 24, quoting the *One Big Union Monthly* (Chicago).

[14] Soule, *Prosperity Decade*, 194; Yellen, *American Labor Struggles*, 255.

[15] Interchurch World Movement, *Public Opinion and the Steel Strike* (New York, 1921), 95. Headlines from Los Angeles *Times*, September 23, 1919; Pittsburgh *Post*, September 25, 1919; *Christian Science Monitor*, September 30, 1919. For various back-to-work stories see issues of the Pittsburgh papers from September 24 to October 1, 1919, inclusive.

[16] Edward Levinson, *Labor on the March* (New York, 1938), 45–46.

[17] The examples are found in the Pittsburgh *Chronicle-Telegraph*, October 6, 1919, and Pittsburgh *Post*, October 3, 1919; see also the Baltimore *Sun*, October 31, 1919, Cincinnati *Enquirer*, October 30, 1919, and Los Angeles *Times*, October 24, 1919.

[18] William Z. Foster and Earl C. Ford, *Syndicalism* (n.p., 1911), 9.

[19] "The Labor Crisis and the People," *Outlook*, CXXIII (October 29, 1919), 225; New York *Times*, September 26–28, 1919; Baltimore *Sun*, September 26–28, 1919; Philadelphia *Inquirer*, September 26–28, 1919. Foster, in his *Great Steel Strike*, 154–55, declared such charges were wholly fictitious and were invented by the steel companies to kill the strike. However, seventeen years later, writing as America's Number 1 Communist, he declared in his *From Bryan to Stalin* (1937), 133, that he really was a "borer from within" and hoped success in the steel strike would supplant the AFL with a militant radical majority.

[20] *Cong. Record*, 66 Cong., 1 Sess., 5790, 5854–55.

[21] Washington *Post*, September 21, 1919, p. 1; New York *Times*, September 24, 1919, p. 1; Chicago *Tribune*, September 24, 1919, p. 1.

[22] New York *Times*, September 22, 1919, p. 1; Pittsburgh *Post*, September 21, 1919, sec. IV, p. 7; Louis Adamic, *Dynamite: The Story of Class Violence in America* (New York, 1931), 288.

[23] For an excellent survey of the steel strike and civil liberties see Interchurch World Movement, *Public Opinion and the Steel Strike*, 163–220.

[24] Interchurch World Movement, *Report on the Steel Strike*, 230, quoting a directive from steel officials to agents dated October 2, 1919. For a discussion of spies on the National Committee see Foster, *Pages from a Worker's Life*, 209–10.

[25] New York *Times*, October 10, 1919, p. 4, and October 22, 1919, p. 1.

[26] *Ibid.*, September 23, 1919, p. 16, quoting T. J. Vind, general organizer of the AFL in the Chicago district.

[27] Chicago *Tribune*, October 5, 1919, p. 1.

[28] *Ibid.*, October 6, 1010, p. 1, and October 7, 1919, p. 1.

[29] New York *Times*, issues October 14, 16, 25, 1919.

[30] Portland *Oregonian*, October 6, 1919, p. 8; Atlanta *Constitution*, October 25, 1919, p. 1; Boston *Evening Transcript*, October 28, 1919, p. 12.

[31] New York *Times*, October 14, 1919, p. 1, quoting radical pamphlets; Chicago *Tribune*, October 24, 1919, p. 6, quoting Mother Jones; Chicago *Communist*, October 25, 1919, p. 1.

[32] For the official transcript of the conference see *Proceedings of the First Industrial Conference, October 6 to 23, 1919* (Washington, D.C., 1920). Hereafter cited as *Proceedings of the First Industrial Conference*.

[33] *Reports of the Department of Labor, 1919* (Washington, D.C., 1920), 23.

[34] Boston *Christian Science Monitor*, October 23, 1919, p. 1, quoting Samuel Gompers. A slightly different wording of Gompers's speech appears in *Proceedings of the First Industrial Conference*, 274–75. It is interesting to notice that of the twenty-two men who represented the public, eighteen had corporation affiliations, among them John D. Rockefeller and Judge Elbert H. Gary! That these two, in particular, should have represented the public was an absurdity.

[35] Chicago *Tribune*, October 23, 1919, p. 1; Washington *Evening Star*, Oc-

tober 23, 1919, p. 6; Baltimore *Sun*, October 23, 1919, p. 8; Denver *Rocky Mountain News*, October 23, 1919, p. 1; New York *Wall Street Journal*, October 23, 1919, p. 1.

[36] "Has Foster Changed?" *Open Shop Review*, XVI (October 1919), 419; *Cong. Record*, 66 Cong., 1 Sess., 6869, quoting Senator Poindexter.

[37] "Red Threats of Revolution Here," *Literary Digest*, LXIII (November 8, 1919), 15–16, quoting various newspapers; "Red Forces Disrupting American Labor," *ibid.*, LXIII (October 25, 1919), 11–14, quoting various labor publications and leaders.

[38] "Pittsburgh or Petrograd?" *Liberator*, II (December 1919), 10.

[39] *Senate Reports*, A, No. 289. This investigation was the result of a resolution introduced by Senator William S. Kenyon of Iowa and passed on September 23, 1919.

[40] Interchurch World Movement, *Report on the Steel Strike*. The commission was created on October 1, 1919, with Bishop Francis J. McConnell (Methodist) as its head.

[41] *Senate Reports*, A, No. 289, pp. 14–17.

[42] Interchurch World Movement, *Report on the Steel Strike*, 4, 15, 33, 38–39, 247.

[43] New York *Times*, January 9, 1920, p. 1; Foster, *Great Steel Strike*, 192; Yellen, *American Labor Struggles*, 286–87.

Chapter 10

[1] New York *Times*, September 14, 1919, p. 8.

[2] United Mine Workers of America, *Proceedings of the Twenty-Seventh Annual Convention*, 2 vols. (Indianapolis, 1919), I, 78; *ibid.*, II, 950–51.

[3] United Mine Workers of America, *The Case of the Bituminous Coal Mine Workers* (Indianapolis, 1920), 27, 33, 44–45, 47; Bruce Minton and John Stuart, *Men Who Lead Labor* (New York, 1937), 91–92.

[4] "The Great Enterprise," *United Mine Workers' Journal*, XXX (November 1, 1919), 6.

[5] Radical pamphlets are quoted in *Lusk Reports*, I, 853, and *Attorney General A. Mitchell Palmer on Charges*, 303.

[6] Examples of pressure on Congress are seen in *Cong. Record*, 66 Cong., 1 Sess., 7407, 7619, 7665, 7912; Minton and Stuart, *Men Who Lead Labor*, 92.

[7] The samples of government opinion are taken from *Cong. Record*, 66 Cong., 1 Sess., 7709, 8186; Albert Shaw, ed., *The Messages and Papers of Woodrow Wilson* (New York, 1924), II, 1134–35.

[8] The headlines are quoted from the Chicago *Tribune*, October 26, 1919, and Pittsburgh *Post*, October 30, 1919; "The Irrepressible Conflict in Industry," *Literary Digest*, LXIII (November 8, 1919), 13, quoting New York *Tribune*.

[9] Josephus Daniels, *The Wilson Era; Years of War and After, 1917–1923* (Chapel Hill, North Carolina, 1946), 547.

[10] *Ibid.*, 545, on Wilson's reticence to discuss or handle any new domestic matter; for Tumulty's remarks see Joseph P. Tumulty, *Woodrow Wilson as I Know Him* (New York, 1921), 446.

[11] For the Cabinet's role in all this see Desk Diaries in Robert Lansing

Papers (Library of Congress, Washington, D.C.) and also Private Memoranda in Robert Lansing Papers (Library of Congress, Washington, D.C.). Hereafter these are cited as Lansing Desk Diaries and Lansing Private Memoranda. Actually, Tumulty called Lansing on October 22 to ask what Cabinet action, if any, ought to be taken on the impending strike. Lansing told Tumulty to call a Cabinet meeting for November 1, which somehow got pushed up to October 30. In any event, when the Cabinet met on October 30 it was faced with a *fait accompli*. Palmer had already seen the President and had secured the injunction. See the entries for October 22, 25, 1919, Lansing Desk Diaries.

[12] New York *Times*, October 31–November 1, 1919, p. 1.

[13] "The Coal Miners' Strike," *Current History*, XI (December 1, 1919), 4211; Samuel Gompers, "The Broken Pledge," *American Federationist*, XXVII, pt. 1 (January 1920), 41; New York *Times*, November 1, 1919, p. 10, quoting John L. Lewis.

[14] Examples of press opinion are found in the Atlanta *Constitution*, October 31, 1919, p. 12; St. Louis *Post-Dispatch*, November 1, 1919, p. 12; New York *Times*, November 1, 1919, p. 1; Portland *Oregonian*, October 31, 1919, p. 10.

[15] New York *Times*, November 2, 1919, p. 1; Pittsburgh *Post*, November 1, 1919, p. 1; Atlanta *Constitution*, November 1, 1919, p. 1, Seattle *Post-Intelligencer*, November 1, 1919, cartoon.

[16] Los Angeles *Times*, November 4, 1919, p. 1.

[17] For examples of press opinion and headlines see *ibid.*, November 9, 1919, p 4; Boston *Evening Transcript*, November 5, 1919, sec. 2, p. 6, Atlanta *Constitution*, November 5, 1919, p. 1; "The Victory in Massachusetts," *Congregationalist and Advance*, CIV (November 13, 1919), 672.

[18] Josephus Daniels, *The Wilson Era; Years of War and After, 1917–1923*, 315, quoting the Wilson telegram of November 5, 1919. Daniels suggests Wilson may have made Coolidge president by his support in this gubernatorial election.

[19] The cartoon is from the Philadelphia *Inquirer*, November 9, 1919, p. 1.

[20] "The Coal Strike and the Mandatory Injunction," *American Federationist*, XXVI, pt. 2 (December 1919), 1125–28.

[21] Cincinnati *Enquirer*, November 12, 1919, p. 6, quoting Lewis.

[22] Gitlow, *The Whole of Their Lives*, 57, quoting Howatt. Howatt was expelled from the UMW by John L. Lewis the following year. Shortly thereafter Howatt joined the Communist party.

[23] New York *Times*, issues December 5–7, 1919.

[24] "Moscow's Campaign of Poison," *Review*, CII (January 24, 1920), 77–80; A Mitchell Palmer, "Three Strikes and Out," *Review*, CII (May 22, 1920), 243; New York *Times*, January 4, 1920.

[25] James A. Wechsler, *Labor Baron* (New York, 1944), 24; Ray S. Baker and William E. Dodd, eds., *War and Peace*, 2 vols. (New York, 1927), II, 445, quoting Wilson.

[26] "Public Opinion Defeating the Strikes," *Literary Digest*, LXIII (November 22, 1919), 11, quoting the New York *Evening Post*.

[27] Interchurch World Movement, *Public Opinion and the Steel Strike* (New York, 1921), 89.

[28] Examples seen in "Fallacy of the One Big Union," *American Federationist*, XXVI, pt. 2 (November 1919), 1050–55, and Samuel Gompers,

"Trade Unions and Bolshevism," *American Federationist*, XXVI, pt. 2 (December 1919), 1131.

²⁹ Jerome L. Toner, *The Closed Shop in the American Labor Movement* (Washington, 1941), 128; Savel Zimand, "Who Is behind the Open Shop Campaign?" *New Republic*, XXV (January 26, 1921), 255–57.

³⁰ National Association of Manufacturers, *Open Shop Encyclopedia* (New York, 1921), 206–11, quoting various clergymen. Nevertheless, the Catholic Church, the Federal Council of Churches of Christ in America, and the Methodist Church all denounced the open-shop crusade, along with such liberal journals as the *Nation*, *New Republic*, *Public*, and *Dial*.

³¹ Sample opinion is found in *Cong. Record*, 66 Cong., 1 Sess., 5849–51.

Chapter 11

¹ Graham Wallas, "The Price of Intolerance," *Atlantic Monthly*, CXXV (January 1920), 116.

² "What Is Back of the Bombs?" *Literary Digest*, LXI (June 14, 1919), 9–11, quoting Rogers's observations.

³ The example is from the New York *Sun*, May 4, 1919, p. 12.

⁴ The poem entitled "Bol-she-veek!" by Edmund Vance Cooke appears in *Public*, XXII (July 19, 1919), 772.

⁵ "Bolshevistic School Teachers," *Literary Digest*, LX (April 5, 1919), 31–32; New York *World*, June 2, 1919, p. 9, example.

⁶ Sidney Howard, "Our Professional Patriots," *New Republic*, XL (October 1, 1924), 119–23; Hapgood, *Professional Patriots*, 48, 196–204; *Lusk Reports*, I, 1112–32; Richard M. Whitney, *Reds in America* (New York, 1924), 59–62.

⁷ "Bolshevistic School Teachers," *Literary Digest*, LX (April 5, 1919), 31.

⁸ "Americanism in New York," *Journal of Education*, LXXXIX (April 23, 1919), 382–83.

⁹ New York *Times*, May 10, 1919, p. 8; New York *Call*, May 29, 1919, p. 1, quoting Glassberg; "Freedom of Speech in the New York City Schools," *School and Society*, IX (May 18, 1919), 178, quoting the *New Republic*.

¹⁰ New York *Times*, May 15, 1919, p. 9, *Literary Digest* advertisement; *Christian Science Monitor*, May 4, 1919, p. 18.

¹¹ Portland *Oregonian*, October 1, 1919, p. 10; Toledo *Blade*, November 14, 1919, p. 6.

¹² New York *Times*, November 20, 1919, p. 7; "The Dismissal of Communist Teachers in New York City Schools," *School and Society*, X (November 22, 1919), 605–6; Whitney, *Reds in America*, 10, quoting a Boston elementary teacher; Woodsworth Clum, *Making Socialists Out of College Students* (Better America Federation Pamphlet, n.d.), photostatic copy of Calhoun's statement contained in a letter written to a colleague at Minnesota.

¹³ Whitney, *Reds in America*, 10; New York *Times*, November 20, 1919, p. 7, quoting Ettinger.

¹⁴ Ralph Easley, "Radicals Mislead Churches about Labor," *National Civic Federation Review*, IV (March 25, 1919), 3–4.

¹⁵ "The Churches vs. the Open Shop," *Literary Digest*, LXVIII (February 19, 1921), 32, describing the attitude of the church; Interchurch World Movement, *Report on the Steel Strike*, 7.

[16] *Lusk Reports*, I, 1112–39; Hapgood, *Professional Patriots*, 196–204.

[17] "Bolshevism and the Methodist Church," *Current Opinion*, LXVI (June 1919), 380–81, quoting Dr. Ward; Graham Taylor, "The 'Bolshevism' of Professor Ward," *Survey*, XLI (March 29, 1919), 920–21.

[18] Sidney Howard, "Our Professional Patriots," *New Republic*, XL (October 8, 1924), 143–45; Hapgood, *Professional Patriots*, 196–204.

[19] New York *Wall Street Journal*, December 23, 1919.

[20] Portland *Oregonian*, January 3, 1920, p. 8; "Misleading the Bolsheviki," *World's Work*, XXXIX (February 1920), 326–27; Coan, *The Red Web*, 25, 29.

[21] Elizabeth Dilling, *The Red Network* (Chicago, 1934), 111–12, 119. Except as an indication of the extent to which hysterical sentiment will go in dubbing all opponents "Communists," Miss Dilling's work is worthless.

[22] Toledo *Blade*, November 14, 1919, p. 6; Lillian Symes and Travers Clement, *Rebel America* (New York, 1934), 332; Oswald G. Villard, *Fighting Years* (New York, 1939), 461.

[23] New York *Times*, June 28, 1919, p. 3, and June 30, 1919, p. 10.

[24] *Ibid.*, July 28, 1919, p. 10; Chicago *Tribune*, July 28, 1919, p. 6; Cincinnati *Enquirer*, October 6, 1919, p. 6. See also "Significance of Negro Riots," *National Civic Federation Review*, IV (August 30, 1919), 11; "What Negroes Think of the Race Riots," *Public*, XXII (August 9, 1919), 848; *Investigation Activities of the Department of Justice*, 187.

[25] *Investigation Activities of the Department of Justice*, 163–81, quoting various Negro journals.

[26] "A Plea for Publicity," *Nation*, CVIII (April 26, 1919), 649.

[27] *World Almanac, 1920*, pp. 722, 729, 747.

[28] For three stirring accounts of the Centralia affair see 115 *Washington Reports* 409–28; Ralph Chaplin, *The Centralia Conspiracy* (Chicago, 1924); Arthur G. Hays, *Trial by Prejudice* (New York, 1933), 254–60.

[29] 115 *Washington Reports* 408–11.

[30] *Ibid.*, 412. George Seldes in his *Witch Hunt* (New York, 1940), 34, claims the marchers first attacked the IWW; Louis Adamic in his *Dynamite*, 304, quotes labor radicals as claiming that someone in the parade started the firing, not the IWW's. This latter is definitely not true according to the trial testimony.

[31] Haywood, *Bill Haywood's Book*, 355–56. Most newspapers erroneously referred to Everest as Brick Smith, secretary of the IWW local.

[32] For a description see Chaplin, *The Centralia Conspiracy*, 73–79; also see Haywood, *Bill Haywood's Book*, 356, and Hays, *Trial by Prejudice*, 260. For the most recent account see Robert L. Tyler, "Rebels of the Woods," *Oregon Historical Quarterly*, LV, No. 1 (March 1954), 29–30.

[33] Hays, *Trial by Prejudice*, 260, quoting the coroner.

[34] New York *Times*, issues November 13–15, 1919. For the *Union-Record* squabble see the Seattle *Post-Intelligencer*, November 13, 1919, p. 1. About a week later, the courts held that the *Union-Record* had been suspended and suppressed unlawfully. Meanwhile, labor in the city raised a fund for a "bigger, better *Union-Record*."

[35] *Cong. Record*, 66 Cong., 1 Sess., 8374, quoting Representative Johnson; *ibid.*, 66 Con., 2 Sess., 448, quoting Senator Jones; Portland *Oregonian*, November 13, 1919, p. 1, quoting Senator Poindexter.

[36] The headlines are from Salt Lake *Tribune*, November 12, 1919, Seattle

Post-Intelligencer, November 12, 1919, and Cincinnati *Enquirer,* November 13, 1919.

[37] Chaplin is quoted in the Los Angeles *Times,* November 13, 1919, p. 3; Haywood is quoted in the Detroit *News,* November 12, 1919, p. 4; Chicago *New Solidarity,* November 22, 1919, p. 1.

[38] Newspaper comment is found in the Pittsburgh *Post,* November 13, 1919, p. 6; Columbus *Citizen,* November 14, 1919, p. 10; and Chicago *Tribune,* November 13, 1919, p. 8. See also "Current Event and Comment," *United Presbyterian,* LXXVII (November 20, 1919), 8. The cartoon is from the Washington *Evening Star,* November 13, 1919, p. 1.

[39] 115 *Washington Reports* 428. By 1933 only one of those convicted remained in jail. The rest were paroled during 1930–33.

[40] The juror is quoted in Hays, *Trial by Prejudice,* 265.

[41] "Centralia: An Unfinished Story," *Nation,* CX (April 17, 1920), 509.

[42] "Cutting Down the Corpse," *Review,* I (November 22, 1919), 596.

Chapter 12

[1] Palmer's support is seen in his various letters to Wilson, the most notable example being his letter to Wilson dated May 11, 1912, in Papers of A. Mitchell Palmer, box 47, Woodrow Wilson Collection (Library of Congress, Washington, D.C.). Hereafter this is cited as Palmer Papers.

[2] For the full text of letters between Palmer and Wilson see James Kerney, *The Political Education of Woodrow Wilson* (New York, 1926), 301–2. Wilson's gratitude for Palmer's various services is seen in letters to Palmer dated April 11 and May 13, 1912, Palmer Papers; Palmer's letter to Wilson declining the secretary of war post is dated February 24, 1913, Palmer Papers.

[3] "A. Mitchell Palmer, 'Fighting Quaker'," *Literary Digest,* LXIV (March 27, 1920), 51–52. Palmer was appointed attorney general mainly upon Joseph Tumulty's insistence; see Kerney, *The Political Education of Woodrow Wilson,* 303.

[4] Louis F. Post, *The Deportations Delirium of Nineteen-Twenty* (Chicago, 1923), 49, quoting the Baltimore *Sun.*

[5] For a detailed although somewhat biased account of the FBI's role during the Red Scare period see Max Lowenthal, *The Federal Bureau of Investigation* (New York, 1950), *passim.*

[6] *Annual Report of the Attorney General, 1920,* pp. 13, 172–73.

[7] National Popular Government League, *Report upon the Illegal Practices of the United States Department of Justice* (Washington, D.C., 1920), 64–66, hereafter cited as *Report upon Illegal Practices;* for a facsimile of the advertisement given to the newspapers by the Justice Department, see *Nation,* CX (March 6, 1920), 299.

[8] "The Deportations," *Survey,* XLI (February 22, 1919), 722–24; "Skimming the Melting Pot," *Literary Digest,* LX (March 1, 1919), 16.

[9] "Skimming the Melting Pot," *Literary Digest,* LX (March 1, 1919), 16, quoting Duluth *Herald;* New York *Call,* February 14, 1919, p. 1; "Exile Made to Order," *Nation,* CVIII (February 22, 1919), 270.

[10] New York *Times,* March 29, 1919, p. 12.

[11] *Cong. Record,* 66 Cong., 1 Sess., 6871–72.

[12] *Ibid.,* 7063.

[10] *Investigation Activities of the Department of Justice*, 30–34, examples of orders.

[14] *Attorney General A. Mitchell Palmer on Charges*, 166–68; Winthrop D. Lane, "The Buford Widows," *Survey*, XLIII (January 10, 1920), 392.

[15] New York *Times*, November 8, 1919, p. 1.

[16] *Charges of Illegal Practices*, 656; *Report upon Illegal Practices*, 11–12; Constantine M. Panunzio, *The Deportation Cases of 1919–1920* (New York, 1921), 25. Panunzio has backed up each assertion with sworn statements of the aliens involved.

[17] *Annual Report of the Commissioner General of Immigration, 1920* (Washington, D.C., 1920), 32.

[18] The quotations are taken from such newspapers as the Boston *Evening Transcript*, November 10, 1919, p. 12; Salt Lake *Tribune*, November 9, 1919; Cincinnati *Enquirer*, November 10, 1919, p. 6; Columbus *Ohio State Journal*, November 12, 1919, p. 4; Atlanta *Constitution*, November 10, 1919, p. 6. The cartoon is from the New Orleans *Times-Picayune*, November 12, 1919, p. 8.

[19] The Senate ordered Palmer's report printed as Senate Document 153, *Investigation Activities of the Department of Justice*.

[20] *Cong. Record*, 66 Cong., 2 Sess., 2206, quoting the anarchist pamphlet; *Lusk Reports*, II, 1188, reprint of Chicago *New Solidarity* dated November 15, 1919; *ibid.*, 1154, reprint of Chicago *Communist* dated November 15, 1919.

[21] For comment on the one-track quality of Wilson's mind see David F. Houston, *Eight Years with Wilson's Cabinet, 1913–1920* (New York, 1926), II, 169; on orders not to bother the President see *ibid.*, II, 38; on Cabinet meetings see *ibid.*, II, 64, 69–70, and various date entries October 1919 to February 1920 in Lansing Desk Diaries. For discussions at some of these meetings see Lansing Private Memoranda.

[22] Fall's remark is found in Josephus Daniels, *The Wilson Era; Years of War and After, 1917–1923* (Chapel Hill, North Carolina, 1946), 513.

[23] Wilson's many speeches on his western tour reflect this sentiment. See Ray S. Baker and William E. Dodd, eds., *War and Peace, 1917–1924*, II. *passim.*

[24] Daniels, *The Wilson Era; Years of War and After, 1917–1923*, 365, quoting Wilson. For a further discussion of Wilson's attitude see the entry dated November 7, 1919, Lansing Desk Diaries; also letter from Wilson to Palmer, dated August 1, 1919, Palmer Papers.

[25] For annual message statement see Albert Shaw, ed., *The Messages and Papers of Woodrow Wilson* (New York, 1924), II, 1144–45.

[26] For examples see Baker and Dodd, eds., *War and Peace, 1917–1924*, II, *passim.* See especially *ibid.*, 10, speech delivered at Kansas City, Missouri, September 6, 1919.

[27] Saul K. Padover, ed., *Wilson's Ideals* (Washington, D.C., 1942), 47.

[28] Daniels, *The Wilson Era; Years of War and After, 1917–1923*, 546, quoting the President.

[29] Anne W. Lane and Louise H. Wall, eds., *The Letters of Franklin K. Lane, Personal and Political* (Boston, 1922), 317, 326.

[30] For Lansing's attitudes see Lansing Desk Diaries, entry May 2, 1919, and Lansing Private Memoranda, entries July 26, September 1, November 7, and November 13, 1919.

[31] Burleson's sentiments are revealed in a letter, Wilson to Burleson, dated

February 28, 1919, and a letter, Wilson to Tumulty, June 28, 1919, in Burleson Collection (Papers of Albert S. Burleson and Scrapbook Materials in Library of Congress, Washington, D.C.). Hereafter this is cited as Burleson Collection.

³² For Tumulty's relationship with Palmer and his connection with the Red Scare see John M. Blum, *Joe Tumulty and the Wilson Era* (Boston, 1951), 187, 191, 197, 217–21.

³³ New York *Times*, November 23, 1919, p. 1; "Ellis Island Gates Ajar," *Literary Digest*, LXIII (December 13, 1919), 17–18. For Howe's sentiments toward aliens and his own account of Ellis Island see Frederic C. Howe, *The Confessions of a Reformer* (New York, 1926), 274–77, 326–28.

³⁴ New York *Times*, November 27, 1919, p. 3, quoting Inspector Fagan.

³⁵ *Cong. Record*, 66 Cong., 2 Sess., 60, 315. For a sample cartoon on the status of deportations see the Brooklyn *Eagle*, November 24, 1919, p. 6.

³⁶ *Cong. Record*, 66 Cong., 2 Sess., 37, 990, 1334, quoting Senator McKellar.

³⁷ *Annual Report of the Commissioner General of Immigration, 1920*, p. 32. Louis Post in his *Deportations Delirium*, 27, gives the figures as 184 members of the URW, 51 anarchists, and 14 others.

³⁸ "The Buford Widows," *Survey*, XLIII (January 10, 1920), 391; Toledo *Blade*, December 22, 1919, p. 1. The official number is 12 although some claim 13, others 20, and still others as high as 39.

³⁹ Washington *Post*, December 22, 1919, p. 1; Toledo *Blade*, December 23, 1919, p. 6.

⁴⁰ "Shipping Lenin's Friends to Him," *Literary Digest*, LXIV (January 3, 1920), 15, quoting Goldman.

⁴¹ *Ibid.*, 14, quoting New York *Evening Mail* and Boston *Evening Transcript*; "Sanctuary," *Saturday Evening Post*, CXCII (February 7, 1920), 28; "Topics in Brief," *Literary Digest*, LXIII (November 29, 1919), 20, quoting New York *Tribune*.

⁴² "Shipping Lenin's Friends to Him," *Literary Digest*, LXIV (January 3, 1920), 15, quoting various newspapers.

⁴³ *Lusk Reports*, II, 1254, quoting Eastman. For the cartoon see the *Liberator*, III (February, 1920), 4.

⁴⁴ Philadelphia *Inquirer*, December 23, 1919, p. 10; Portland *Oregonian*, December 23, 1919, p. 10; Cleveland *Plain Dealer*, December 23, 1919, p. 10.

Chapter 13

¹ *Annual Report of the Attorney General, 1919* (Washington, D.C., 1919), 15; Zechariah Chafee, Jr., *Free Speech in the United States* (Cambridge, Massachusetts, 1941), 209.

² *Annual Report of the Attorney General, 1920*, 175–76; Post, *The Deportations Delirium of Nineteen-Twenty*, 79; the direct quotation of the rule is is taken from *Charges of Illegal Practices*, 764.

³ *Charges of Illegal Practices*, 767. This rule as changed by Abercrombie had actually been in effect until March 1919, when Secretary Wilson had reworded it in order to give the alien more protection. See *ibid.*, 398–99.

⁴ Chafee, *Free Speech in the United States*, 202; Edith Abbott, *Immigration Select Documents and Case Records* (Chicago, 1924), 288; Chafee, *Freedom of Speech*, 238–39.

⁵ *Report upon Illegal Practices*, 41–42; *Attorney General A. Mitchell Palmer on Charges*, 213–15, copy of orders.

⁶ *Charges of Illegal Practices*, 381, 494; 265 *Federal Reporter* 20, 38–39, 45.

⁷ *Charges of Illegal Practices*, 353, 499; *Boston Evening Transcript*, January 3, 1920, p. 1; *Report upon Illegal Practices*, 55.

⁸ *Ibid.*, 18–19; quoting various prisoners; Panunzio, *The Deportation Cases of 1919–1920*, 78.

⁹ *Report upon Illegal Practices*, 19.

¹⁰ Post, *The Deportations Delirium of Nineteen-Twenty*, 115–17.

¹¹ Panunzio, *The Deportation Cases of 1919–1920*, 27.

¹² Post, *The Deportations Delirium of Nineteen-Twenty*, 108.

¹³ *Report upon Illegal Practices*, 22; *Charges of Illegal Practices*, 706–9; Frederick R. Barkley, "Jailing Radicals in Detroit," *Nation*, CX (January 31, 1920), 136–37.

¹⁴ Barkley, "Jailing Radicals in Detroit," *Nation*, CX (January 31, 1920), 137.

¹⁵ *Ibid.*; *Report Upon Illegal Practices*, 22; *Charges of Illegal Practices*, 733.

¹⁶ Chicago *Tribune*, January 2, 1920, p. 1. Newspapers erroneously claimed that John Reed was taken in these raids. Reed was in Russia at the time.

¹⁷ Seattle *Times*, January 9, 1920, p. 6.

¹⁸ Post, *The Deportations Delirium of Nineteen-Twenty*, 124; Kansas City *Star*, January 3, 1920, p. 1.

¹⁹ Washington *Evening Star*, January 3, 1920, sec. 1, p. 6.

²⁰ Washington *Post*, January 4, 1920, p. 4.

²¹ "Extent of the Bolshevik Infection Here," *Literary Digest*, LXIV (January 17, 1920), 14–15; Chicago *Tribune*, January 3, 1920, p. 1; Philadelphia *Inquirer*, January 5, 1920, p. 10.

²² For this minority opinion see Baltimore *Sun*, January 6, 1920, quoting labor resolutions; "Extent of the Bolshevik Infection Here," *Literary Digest*, LXIV (January 17, 1920), 14, quoting Charles Schwab; *Charges of Illegal Practices*, 346, quoting Francis Kane.

²³ For newspaper comment see "Extent of the Bolshevik Infection Here," *Literary Digest*, LXIV (January 17, 1920), 13–15; "Deporting the Communist Party," *Literary Digest*, LXIV (February 14, 1920), 18; Baltimore *Sun*, January 4, 1920.

²⁴ For sample opinion see the New York *Call*, January 3, 1920, p. 1; "Deporting a Political Party," *New Republic*, XXI (January 14, 1920), 186; "Sowing the Wind to Reap the Whirlwind," *Nation*, CX (January 17, 1920), 94; "Improving on the Czar," *Nation*, CX (April 10, 1920), 459; *Attorney General A. Mitchell Palmer on Charges*, 404, quoting the Chicago *New Solidarity*; Howard Brubaker, "Leap-Yearlings," *Liberator*, III (February 1920), 20.

²⁵ Palmer is quoted in "Extent of the Bolshevik Infection Here," *Literary Digest*, LXIV (January 17, 1920), 13, and *Attorney General A. Mitchell Palmer on Charges*, 27.

²⁶ *Charges of Illegal Practices*, 624; Flynn is quoted in the Kansas City *Star*, January 3, 1920, p. 1.

²⁷ James P. Cannon, *The History of American Trotskyism* (New York, 1944), 9; Gitlow, *I Confess*, 65.

²⁸ *Annual Report of the Attorney General, 1920*, p. 176, quoting report made to the Third International.

[29] The original cartoon is from the New York *Tribune*, January 7, 1920, p. 14. For a sample recopy see the *Nation*, CX (March 6, 1920), 299.

[30] New York *Times*, February 29, 1920, sec. 2, p. 1.

Chapter 14

[1] 250 *U.S.* 617–21.

[2] 250 *U.S.* 630.

[3] "Topics in Brief," *Literary Digest*, LXIII (November 29, 1919), 20, quoting the Brooklyn *Eagle*.

[4] *Berger Hearings*, I, 3, 9, 48, 144, 148. See also *Cong. Record*, 66 Cong., 1 Sess., 8–9.

[5] *Berger Hearings*, I, 192; *House Reports*, B, No. 413 (Washington, D.C., 1919), 16.

[6] *Cong. Record*, 66 Cong., 1 Sess., 8261.

[7] Washington *Post*, November 12, 1919, p. 6; Toledo *Blade*, November 12, 1919, p. 6; Baltimore *Sun*, November 12, 1919, p. 8.

[8] Salt Lake *Tribune*, November 12, 1919, p. 6; New York *Times*, December 20, 1919, p. 1, quoting Berger's opponent.

[9] "Milwaukee's Secession," *Outlook*, CXXIV (January 14, 1920), 62; "Why Milwaukee Insists on Berger," *Literary Digest*, LXIV (January 3, 1920), 20, quoting Buffalo *Evening News*; Boston *Evening Transcript*, December 30, 1919, p. 10; Howard Brubaker, "Leap-Yearlings," *Liberator*, III (February 1920), 20.

[10] New York *Times*, December 20, 1919, p. 1, quoting Dallinger; *Cong. Record*, 66 Cong., 2 Sess., 1339.

[11] *Cong. Record*, 66 Cong., 2 Sess., 1340–41, 1343.

[12] "News of the Week," *Christian Register*, XCIX (January 15, 1920), 52.

[13] *Cong. Record.*, 66 Cong., 2 Sess., 2207.

[14] *Ibid.*, 1338.

[15] *Ibid.*, 2207; St. Louis *Post-Dispatch*, January 7, 1920, p. 24, quoting Palmer.

[16] F. G. Franklin, "Anti-Syndicalist Legislation," *American Political Science Review*, XIV (May 1920), 291–98; Chafee, *Free Speech in the United States*, 163; *The Consolidated Laws of New York*, XXXIX, pt. 1 (New York, 1944), pars. 161–63.

[17] Elbridge F. Dowell, *A History of Criminal Syndicalist Legislation in the United States* (in *John Hopkins University Studies in Historical and Political Science*, Series LVII, No. 1, Baltimore, 1939), 77, 87–88, 110. This is the most definitive account of criminal syndicalist legislation for the period covered.

[18] *Ibid.*, 87–88.

[19] *Throckmorton's Annotated Code of Ohio* (Cleveland, 1934), pars. 13421–26.

[20] See Chafee, *Free Speech in the United States*, 326, 575 *et seq.*; for a summary of such legislation see *Investigation Activities of the Department of Justice*, 22–30; *Cong. Record*, 66 Cong., 2 Sess., 2577–78.

[21] Boston *Evening Transcript*, January 12, 1919, sec. 3, p. 2.

[22] Franklin, "Anti-Syndicalist Legislation," *American Political Science Review*, XIV (May 1920), 291–92; Chafee, *Free Speech in the United States*,

159, 575 *et seq.*; for New York laws see *The Consolidated Laws of New York*, XXXIX, pt. 2, index.

[23] These figures are not too reliable, but are the only ones available. See Alexander Trachtenberg and Benjamin Glassberg, eds., *American Labor Yearbook*, IV (New York, 1922), 26.

[24] "Dealing with Red Agitators," *Current History*, XII (July 1920), 698–99.

[25] *Ibid.*; *Annual Report of the Attorney General, 1920*, 178; Gitlow, *The Whole of Their Lives*, xi. Gitlow was pardoned three years later by Governor Alfred E. Smith.

[26] 274 *U.S.* 363–66. Mrs. Whitney was later pardoned by the governor of California. See also Clare Shipman, "The Conviction of Anita Whitney," *Nation*, CX (March 20, 1920), 365–67.

[27] New York *Times*, January 8, 1920, p. 1.

[28] Hillquit, *Socialism on Trial*, 44, quoting an assemblyman.

[29] Frederick L. Allen, *Only Yesterday* (New York, 1931), 69.

[30] *New International Yearbook, 1920* (New York, 1920), 638.

[31] *World Almanac, 1921*, pp. 829–30.

[32] New York *Times*, April 26, 1920, p. 3.

[33] Chafee, *Free Speech in the United States*, 309, quoting Governor Smith. With Smith's return to office in 1923, the Lusk legislation was repealed.

Chapter 15

[1] Forrest Crissley, "Our Soviet Sleeping Sickness," *Saturday Evening Post*, CXCII (May 15, 1920), 10.

[2] "Albany's Ousted Socialists," *Literary Digest*, LXIV (January 24, 1920), 19.

[3] *Ibid.*, 19–20, quoting various newspapers. The cartoon is found in the New Orleans *Times-Picayune*, April 12, 1920, p. 8.

[4] "Mock Hysteria," *Review*, II (January 17, 1920), 43, quoting Harding and Pound; *Christian Science Monitor*, January 26, 1920, p. 1, quoting Palmer; Helen O. Mahin, *The Editor and His People* (New York, 1924), 338, reprint of editorial by White dated February 25, 1920; Claude G. Bowers, *Beveridge and the Progressive Era* (Boston, 1932), 511, quoting Beveridge; *Christian Science Monitor*, January 9, 1920, p. 1, quoting LaGuardia; "News of the Week," *Christian Register*, XCIX (January 15, 1920), 52, quoting Governor Smith.

[5] New York *Times*, January 11, 1920, p. 1.

[6] Newspaper comment in "The Socialists' Hour at Albany," *Literary Digest*, LXVII (October 2, 1920), 11; New York *Times*, September 23, 1920, p. 2, quoting Hughes.

[7] Newspaper comment in "Drastic Sedition Laws," *Literary Digest*, LXIV (January 24, 1920), 18; New York *Times*, January 7, 1920, p. 20; San Francisco *Examiner*, January 8, 1920, p. 17.

[8] Holmes's opinion in "The Red Hysteria," *New Republic*, XXI (January 28 1920), 250; Samuel Gompers, "The Graham-Rice 'Sedition Bill' Would Manufacture Law-Breakers," *American Federationist*, XXVII, pt. 1 (February 1920), 138; "Freedom of Opinion and the Clergy," *New Republic*, XXI (February 11, 1920), 304.

[9] "The Dead-Line of Sedition," *Literary Digest*, LXIV (March 6, 1920), 18, quoting Kansas City *Star*.

[10] *Communist and Anarchist Deportation Cases*, Hearings before a Subcommittee of the House Committee on Immigration and Naturalization (Washington, D.C., 1920), 1–3.

[11] Washington *Post*, January 25, 1920, p. 6.

[12] *Report upon Illegal Practices*, 57.

[13] *Charges of Illegal Practices*, 11.

[14] *Ibid.*, 176–77.

[15] *Investigation of the Administration of Louis F. Post, Assistant Secretary of Labor, in the Matter of Deportation of Aliens*, Hearings before the House Committee on Rules (Washington, D.C., 1920), 84–121, hereafter cited as *Investigation of Louis F. Post*.

[16] Post, *The Deportations Delirium of Nineteen-Twenty*, 79, 209.

[17] *Investigation of Louis F. Post*, 27; *Cong. Record*, 66 Cong., 2 Sess., 164.

[18] See Post, *The Deportations Delirium of Nineteen-Twenty*, 226, 233; "Justice for Alien 'Reds'," *Literary Digest*, LXV (May 22, 1920), 25.

[19] *Investigation of Louis F. Post*, 3, 6, 12, 35.

[20] *Ibid.*, 53, 58, 71, 74, 147.

[21] *Ibid.*, 152–55, the Miller decision.

[22] *Statutes at Large*, XLI, 1008.

[23] 265 *Federal Reporter* 79; *Charges of Illegal Practices*, 483–538, court record.

[24] *Christian Science Monitor*, June 25, 1920, p. 16.

[25] The numbers vary slightly from one report to another. See *Annual Report of the Commissioner General of Immigration, 1920*, p. 33; Post, *The Deportations Delirium of Nineteen-Twenty*, 167.

[26] Josephus Daniels claimed that Palmer was so badly stung by the presidential bee in the summer of 1920 that he never quite recovered. See Daniels, *The Wilson Era; Years of War and After, 1917–1923*, 559.

[27] See April 20–30 issues of the New York *Times*, Cleveland *Plain Dealer*, Chicago *Tribune*, and Washington *Post* for examples of Justice Department warnings.

[28] New York *Times*, May 1, 1920, p. 1; Boston *Evening Transcript*, May 1, 1920, p. 1; Pittsburgh *Post*, May 1, 1920, p. 1.

[29] The cartoon is found in the New Orleans *Times-Picayune*, May 1, 1920, p. 8.

[30] Newspaper comment is from New York *Times*, May 2, 1920, pp. 1–2, and *Rocky Mountain News*, May 2, 1920, p. 6.

[31] *Attorney General A. Mitchell Palmer on Charges*, 266–67.

[32] *Report upon Illegal Practices*, 3, 4–8.

[33] *Attorney General A. Mitchell Palmer on Charges, passim*.

[34] *Charges of Illegal Practices*, 582.

[35] *Cong. Record*, 67 Cong., 4 Sess., 3005–27, Walsh's report.

[36] New York *Times*, September 17, 1920, p. 1; "The Wall Street Massacre," *Independent*, CIV (October 2, 1920), 16, sets the damage figure at $3,000,000.

[37] Edmund Gilligan, "The Wall Street Explosion Mystery," *American Mercury*, XLV (September 1938), 63–67; see also the New York *Times*, issues September 18–19, 1920.

[38] New York *Times*, September 18, 1920, p. 1.

[39] *Rocky Mountain News*, September 18, 1920, p. 6; "Wall Street's Bomb Mystery," *Literary Digest*, LXVII (October 2, 1920), 13, quoting various newspapers; Cleveland *Plain Dealer*, September 18, 1920, p. 6.

[40] See A. Mitchell Palmer, "If He Were President," *Independent*, CII (April 10, 1920), 46–47; Schriftgiesser, *This Was Normalcy*, 41; Blum, *Joe Tumulty and the Wilson Era*, 245.

[41] Mark Sullivan, *Our Times*, VI (New York, 1935), 179; Chauncey M. Depew, *My Memories of Eighty Years* (New York, 1924), 342.

[42] Quotations by Harding from Sullivan, *Our Times*, VI, 179, and Sherman Rogers, "Senator Harding on Labor," *Outlook*, CXXV (August 18, 1920), 670.

[43] Editorial, *Review*, III (November 10, 1920), 432.

Chapter 16

[1] Examples are found in *Pamphlets on Socialism, Communism, and Bolshevism*, VII; Sidney Howard, "Our Professional Patriots," *New Republic*, XL (September 13, 1924), 12–16.

[2] For examples see the *American Legion Weekly*, issues June 1920 to May 1921. For Klan attitudes see Loucks, *The Ku Klux Klan in Pennsylvania*, *passim*, and various pamphlets of the KKK (see Note on Sources).

[3] Evan J. David, comp., *Leonard Wood on National Issues* (New York, 1920), 77–78.

[4] *Cong. Record*, 67 Cong., 1 Sess., 152, index of debates.

[5] *Statutes at Large*, XLII, pt. 1, 540; XLIII, pt. 1, 153 *et seq.*; XLIV, pt. 1, 1455; XLV, pt. 1, 400.

[6] For accounts on the Sacco-Vanzetti case from various points of view see John Dos Passos, *Facing the Chair* (Boston, 1927); Eugene Lyons, *The Life and Death of Sacco and Vanzetti* (New York, 1927); Felix Frankfurter, *The Case of Sacco and Vanzetti* (Boston, 1927); G. L. Joughlin and E. M. Morgan, *The Legacy of Sacco and Vanzetti* (New York, 1948).

[7] For pertinent facts on the open-shop crusade see Perlman and Taft, eds., *Labor Movements*, 493–94; National Association of Manufacturers, *The Open Shop "Conspiracy,"* pamphlet No. 52 (New York, 1922); *American Labor Yearbook*, IV, 1920–22; Zimand, "Who Is behind the Open Shop Campaign?" *New Republic*, XXV (January 26, 1921).

[8] For examples of the AFL's fight against the open shop campaign see Samuel Gompers, "The Union Shop and Its Antithesis," *American Federationist*, XXVII, pt. 2 (August 1920), 746–51; Samuel Gompers, "'Open Shop' Hypocrisy Exposed," *ibid.*, XXVIII, pt. 1 (February 1921), 109–13.

[9] Examples are seen in *American Federationist*, XXVII, pts. 1 and 2; *ibid.*, XXVIII, pt. 1. Consult also the index in *Report of the Proceedings of the Annual Convention of the American Federation of Labor*, for the years 1920, 1921, and 1922.

[10] Dulles, *Road to Teheran*, 181, quoting AFL resolution.

[11] Examples seen in Duplex Printing Co. v. Deering, 254 *U.S.* 443 (1921); Truax v. Corrigan, 257 *U.S.* 312 (1921); Adkins v. Children's Hospital, 261 *U.S.* 525 (1923).

[12] Figures for union membership vary slightly. AFL membership, alone, was only 2,926,000 in 1923. Of course, there were other factors besides the Red Scare causing this decline.

[13] See Bessie L. Pierce, *Public Opinion and the Teaching of History in the United States* (New York, 1926), 74–92.

[14] *Ibid.*, 100–1. For a detailed description of all the factors playing a part in the revision of textbooks see *ibid.*, 206–301.

[15] Pierce *et al.* v. U.S., 252 *U.S.* 239 (1920); Schaefer v. U.S., 251 *U.S.* 266 (1920); Gilbert v. Minnesota, 254 *U.S.* 325 (1920); Milwaukee Social Democratic Publishing Co. v. Burleson, 255 *U.S.* 407 (1921).

[16] 268 *U.S.* 652–73.

[17] 274 *U.S.* 357

[18] 274 *U.S.* 328.

[19] The earliest indication of the changing trend was Fiske v. Kansas, 274 *U.S.* 380 (1927), in which the Kansas syndicalist law was declared invalid. Other examples are DeLonge v. Oregon, 299 *U.S.* 353 (1937), which invalidated the Oregon syndicalist law; Stromberg v. California, 283 *U.S.* 359 (1931), which invalidated the California Red flag law.

[20] See Chaplin, *Wobbly*, 310–27, 332.

[21] *Ibid.*; Chafee, *Free Speech in the United States*, 354.

[22] For the Martens affair see *Senate Reports*, B, No. 526 (Washington, D.C., 1920); for an account of the hearings see *Russian Propaganda, Hearings before a Subcommittee of the Senate Committee on Foreign Relations* (pursuant to S. Res. 263 Directing Foreign Relations Committee to Investigate Status and Activities of One Ludwig C. A. K. Martens) (Washington, D.C., 1920). See also "Decision of the Secretary of Labor in the Case of Ludwig C. A. K. Martens," *Monthly Labor Review*, XII (January 1921), 194.

[23] Dulles, *Road to Teheran*, 166, quoting Secretary of State Colby.

[24] Chicago *Communist* (UCP), June 12, 1920, p. 3. William Foster in his surprisingly accurate *History of the Communist Party of the United States*, p. 176, gives the figure as 10,000.

[25] For Socialist and IWW sentiment on the Communists see "Labor's Retreat from Moscow," *Literary Digest*, LXVII (October 16, 1920), 14; Chicago *Communist* (UCP), August 1, 1920, p. 2; *American Labor Yearbook*, IV, 153; Gambs, *Decline of the IWW*, 206.

[26] Foster, *From Bryan to Stalin*, 291–95; Symes and Clement, *Rebel America*, 346.

[27] Irwin, *How Red Is America*, 133, quoting Zinoviev.

[28] Oneal and Werner, *American Communism*, 11. Foster in his *History of the Communist Party of the United States*, p. 261, gives the figure as 9642 in 1929. There were of course other factors involved besides the Red Scare in the decline of the domestic Communist movement. Even so, the Red Scare remained the most important single factor.

INDEX

Index